Morris Phillips

Abroad and at Home

Vol. 1

Morris Phillips

Abroad and at Home
Vol. 1

ISBN/EAN: 9783337419813

Printed in Europe, USA, Canada, Australia, Japan

Cover: Foto ©Andreas Hilbeck / pixelio.de

More available books at **www.hansebooks.com**

ANNOUNCEMENTS.

ESTABLISHED 1850.

INMAN LINE.

UNITED STATES AND ROYAL MAIL STEAMERS

CITY OF PARIS, . . 10,500 Tons.   CITY OF BERLIN, . . 5,491 Tons.
CITY OF NEW YORK, 10,500   "   CITY OF CHICAGO, . 6,000 "
CITY OF CHESTER, 4,770 Tons.

New York, Queenstown and Liverpool.

FIRST CABIN PASSAGE from $60 to $650,

ACCORDING TO STEAMER AND LOCATION OF ACCOMMODATIONS.

NOTE.—Round Trip Tickets issued at reduced rates, and the return portion can, if desired, be used by **RED STAR LINE** from Antwerp to New York or Philadelphia.

INTERNATIONAL NAVIGATION CO.,
General Agents.

6 BOWLING GREEN   NEW YORK.

ANNOUNCEMENTS.

SIMPSON'S
(LIMITED)
DIVAN TAVERN,
103 STRAND,
Opposite Exeter Hall, - - - LONDON.

THE premier Restaurant in the Strand, established upwards of fifty years, which still retains its supremacy for being the house to get the best English Dinner in London at a moderate price. There is also a magnificent Ladies' Dining Room where ladies can dine in the same style and cost as gentlemen do in the room down stairs. Private rooms for large or small parties.

Noted for Soups, Fish, Entrees and Joints. Saddles of Mutton specially cooked to perfection from 12.30 to 8.30 p.m. Originator of professed Carvers to attend on each customer at separate tables. Matured wines and spirits. The largest stock of any tavern in the kingdom.

E. W. CATHIE, MANAGING DIRECTOR.

ANNOUNCEMENTS.

LONDON & NORTH WESTERN RAILWAY
THE OLD ROUTE IN THE OLD COUNTRY.   THE TOURISTS' FAVORITE.

IRISH AND SCOTCH ROYAL MAIL ROUTE.
SHORTEST AND QUICKEST FROM

LIVERPOOL (Lime Street Station) to **LONDON** (Euston Station), under FOUR AND A-HALF HOURS to **GLASGOW** (Central Station), in FIVE AND THREE-QUARTER HOURS.

QUEENSTOWN to LONDON via Dublin and Holyhead, in SIXTEEN HOURS AND TEN MINUTES.

Baggage Checked Through from New York to London.

At **LIVERPOOL, Family Omnibuses** from Landing Stage, and **Special Trains** from Alexandra Dock to Lime Street Station and Hotel.

NORTH WESTERN HOTEL, Lime Street Station, Liverpool, the best and largest—the hotel for Americans.

SPECIAL TRAINS from Liverpool to London when requisite to make close connection with steamers arriving from America.

Elegant Vestibule Drawing-Room Cars without extra charge. Compartments with lavatories, and private saloon and family carriages for parties without extra charge.

Sleeping Cars with Compartments and brass Beds, 5s. per berth in addition to first-class fares.

DINING CARS on principal trains and "American Specials."

Luncheon Baskets at the principal Stations.

In **LONDON, Family Omnibuses** can be obtained, at the **Euston Hotel** (at the Station), noted for its **Cellar** and its French **Cuisine**, will be found most comfortable.

THE LONDON AND NORTH WESTERN RAILWAY has **NOT** abolished Second Class Carriages; passengers to whom economy is an object, but who do not wish to travel Third Class, can combine comfort with economy by traveling Second Class by this line. First and Second Class on all trains. Third Class Carriages on all trains except the **Irish Mails** to and from Dublin.

The Company's Agents, **Mr. W. STIRLING, at Queenstown**, and **Mr. FRED. W. THOMPSON, at Liverpool**, meet the American Steamers on arrival, and secure omnibuses, seats, saloon carriages, rooms at hotel, and give general information.

THROUGH TICKETS to London, Glasgow, **Paris**, and principal stations in **England, Scotland, Ireland, Wales**, and Continent of Europe.

TICKETS, Time Tables and information as to travel and hotels can be obtained from the Company's Agent, **Mr. D. BATTERSBY, 184 St. James St., Montreal**, and

Mr. C. A. BARATTONI, Gen'l Agent for the U. S. and Canada, **852 Broadway**, near Union Square, **New York**.

G. P. NEELE,	**E. MICHEL,**
Superintendent of the Line.	Foreign Traffic Superintendent.

London, Euston Station.   **G. FINDLAY, Gen'l Manager,**

HOTEL WINDSOR,

VICTORIA STREET,

Westminster,   LONDON, S.W.

Convenient and central location; European or American system; the only hotel in London with Turkish and other baths; elevators; electrically lighted throughout, day and night.

     J. R. CLEAVE & CO., PROPRIETORS.

ABROAD AND AT HOME

PRACTICAL HINTS FOR TOURISTS

MORRIS PHILLIPS

EDITOR OF

THE HOME JOURNAL

NEW YORK

NEW YORK
BRENTANO'S
PARIS   WASHINGTON   CHICAGO   LONDON

TO THE MEMORY OF

GEORGE W. HOWS,

MY FAITHFUL FELLOW-WORKER AND DEAR FRIEND OF MANY YEARS, THIS VOLUME OF SKETCHES IS AFFECTIONATELY INSCRIBED.

"Travel is the great source of true wisdom."
—BEACONSFIELD.

CONTENTS.

	PAGE
Preface, by the Hon. A. OAKEY HALL,	5

GREAT BRITAIN.

London on Wheels,	9
London Hotels,	24
A Few Boarding Houses,	47
Where to Lunch in London, and Where Not to Lunch,	49
Railway Travelling in England,	59
An Hour with Spurgeon,	67
The Crypt of St. Paul's,	71
The Queen's Mews,	74
A Question of Hats,	77
London Oddities,	79
Poverty and Charity in England,	85
Where is Charing Cross?	88
Margate,	89
Two Brighton Hotels,	97
A Visit to Bleak House,	100
Takin' Notes in Edinboro' Town,	105
The Burns Monument,	112
Rt. Rev. the Moderator, James MacGregor, D.D.,	116
Crossing the Channel,	123

PARIS.

Paris Hotels,	124
Pensions of the First Class,	134
The Restaurants of Paris,	137

CONTENTS—Continued.

	PAGE
The Anglo-American Banking Co.,	146
Au Bon Marché,	147

THE UNITED STATES.

GEORGIA—

The De Soto, Savannah,	149
Thomasville,	155
A New Southern Resort,	165

FLORIDA—

A Cuban City (Key West),	171
St. Augustine,	180
About Tampa,	185

CALIFORNIA—

Monterey,	190
San Diego and Coronado,	199
Santa Cruz,	213
Redondo Beach,	221
Pasadena,	225
Los Angeles,	231
The California Hotel, San Francisco,	235
Salt Lake City,	239
The Auditorium Hotel, Chicago,	243
Max O'Rell on American Hotels,	249

PREFACE.

A continuous residence in London of eight years has satisfied me that precisely such a book, so far as it relates to that city, which my friend and once junior legal associate now presents is popularly needed.

That in such respect it will be vitally interesting, even to readers who have never been tourists thither, "goes without saying." Moreover, there are in these pages views, comments and sights of the "abroad" and "at home" additionally valuable; therefore I gladly accept his invitation to prepare a short preface to this volume of an American M. P. in the Parliament of Letters.

He first broached his idea of papers about London at a capital luncheon, when meeting together there we discussed with palates, forks and wine glasses a tempting *menu* during the summer of 1890, as guests of Host Vogel, of the new Albermarle Hotel in Piccadilly, at the top of the historic St. James's street.

We then and there drank success to the M. P. idea, and I doubt not, that every reader of this volume will be disposed to heartily duplicate that toast at his first dinner which shall follow its perusal.

When a tourist first arrives in London, beneath the inviting shadow of the Northwestern Railway station hotel, that is flanked by two smaller inns and its centre pierced by several taverns, or direct from Southampton at the Waterloo station, within rifle shot of which a score of hotels invite his luggage and his wearied frame, that tourist's earliest question will be, which hospitable *caravanserai* shall I patronize?

His second question will concern his vehicular desires for transportation by cab, 'bus or railway. Other queries will suggest themselves regarding the "How," the "Where," the "Which" and the "Why" of his new London surroundings.

With this volume on shipboard *en route:* or in railway carriage *in transitu*, the tourist will already possess answers in his mind to those queries or similar ones respecting Edinburgh or Glasgow; and will not be at the mercy of chance or of confusing porters, or of contestant "cabbies," or of the shady sharpers who throng railway platforms.

Once well housed in any of the places herein mentioned, and once understanding, by the aid of the ensuing pages, how to get about in the vast metropolis—wherein one may ride sixteen miles from extreme north to a suburban south, and fourteen miles from west to east without quitting paved and lighted streets, or the continuity of habitations—a traveler's eyes and ears will be all the Mentors he will require.

Of so-called guide books (of which class this is not), there are in London and elsewhere abroad confusing scores, but the average tourist ought to shun guide-books as he would a Bradshaw, unless he loves charades, puzzles and conundrums.

Every mother knows that when her infant obtains his footing, the child will walk confidently. This volume serves to give the person who arrives in London or Edinburgh and kindred cities an instant footing. In the parlance of the race course, it is the "starter."

On arrival, the first thing to do is to demand and learn the points of compass; because all enquiries about the "Where" in London hinge on those.

The papers by M. P. about cabs and omnibuses will be found as valuable as they are piquant. He tells of certain trips (and tips) on top of a 'bus; he vividly describes how the best way for exploring London is to ride in its every direction on the tops of omnibuses—devoting days to the task, or rather pleasure—and when, as street after street is passed, reading their names, which are always sign-affixed to the turn—a convenience even for residents which, in late years, is strangely unknown in New York City. Thereby locality and prominent buildings and often-referred-to neighborhoods become fixed in an observer's mind for future uses of memory.

I learned to know London "like a book"—as common phrase goes: and, I therefore fully appreciate how much this book will serve to teach new tourists how to begin to learn London; how much it will revive pleasant memories in former tourists; how greatly it will instruct intending tourists; how pleasantly it will amuse those who may not expect to practically patronize the hotels; how well it will instruct as to London's vehicles and the wonders of the English city, which is practically seventeen centuries older than New York.

But there are other sides and hues to this prismatic volume. Not only is it inviting to Americans who wish to know about the "across-the-ocean-ferry," but it will be attractive to the countrymen of the M. P. who may travel or who would like to travel Westward, "where the star of Empire takes its way." And also to the foreign tourist who may for only one week reside, *in transitu* to the States, upon the floating greyhoundish hotels which we call steamships.

Marvelous as London is to the American tourist, the wonders, the hotels, the coasts, and the traveling—especially toward the Pacific ocean—are equally marvelous to English M. P.'s and foreign ladies and gentlemen of fortune or leisure who seek transcontinental scenes and comforts.

Merely "turning the leaves," a phrase happily used as a heading for book notices by the author of "Kissing the Rod" in his *World* newspaper of London, will at once show any buyer of this volume what I have implied.

A. OAKEY HALL.

LOTOS CLUB, January 21, 1892.

LONDON ON WHEELS.

ABOVE GROUND, ON THE GROUND, AND UNDER GROUND.

THE UNDER-GROUND LINES.

How the five millions of people in London "get about" to their daily avocations and homes is a mystery to those who have not made the subject a study. So I have gathered some information which will throw a little light on it.

Let me start out with the statement that besides the ten large terminal stations, like the Euston Square and the Midland, both in Euston Road, there are four hundred and thirty railway stations within the metropolis, and the under-ground lines alone carry annually one hundred and twenty-five millions of passengers. The under-ground roads have been in existence for more than a quarter of a century, and are found to answer the purpose admirably of relieving the over-ground traffic. They are convenient, cheap and comparatively quick; but decidedly unpleasant, if not positively unhealthy.

They now form a network of rails under the surface, and they have been a success from the first. They are a great engineering triumph, and may be said to have marked a new epoch in the history of London. The act permitting the tunneling was passed in 1853. Mr. John Fowler conducted the herculean labor, and underneath the streets of the busiest of cities, down where the soil was honeycombed with other works—gas pipes, water mains, drains and sewers—a railway line, costing upwards of one hundred and fifty thousand pounds per mile, was constructed almost without the knowledge of those above. For three years—from the spring of 1860 to the beginning of 1863—two thousand men, two hundred horses and fifty-eight engines were employed. When completed another difficulty presented itself, but was overcome by Mr. Fowler, who invented a locomotive which could be worked in the open air like an ordinary engine, but which, while in the tunnel, emits neither steam nor smoke, being so constructed as to be able to condense the one and consume the other.

And yet, after a long ride in the under-ground, you always emerge with a headache.

Of course the cars have to be lighted artificially, and they had not learned to use the electric light in them when I last was in London in October, 1891. Gas is a poor substitute in such a place. You are forced to read your newspaper in a dim light, and the gas consumes much of the oxygen which gets into the tunnel from the stations, and from openings en route, which are made for the purpose.

Yet you do not get about as quickly in the underground as you would imagine. To avoid obstructions, and for mechanical reasons, the road takes a circuitous route and you frequently must ride a long way around to go a comparatively short distance.

Millions of Londoners, who go direct from home to business, seldom get into an under-ground train. There are many over-ground lines built on brick arches which go to the suburbs, where rents are low; for every Englishman must have his own house, no matter how small, which he regards as his "castle." These trains are quick and cheap, and you are blessed with ample light and good air—at least as good as you can get in foggy, smoky London.

On all roads, whether on trunk lines, on local, overground or underground lines, there are first, second and third-class cars, or "carriages," as they call them. Even some omnibuses that ply from the trunk line stations also have compartments for different classes; your Englishman is very particular with whom he rides.

Occasionally you meet with unpleasant companions in third-class carriages of local or suburban lines, but on through trains, say between Liverpool and London, the third-class carriages are comfortable, and the travelers of a respectable class.

There is a great difference in the rates, and on a long journey it is worth consideration. First-class fare is almost double that of third-class. Second-class is neither one thing nor the other, and on some lines it has been abolished.

It is an old saying that only princes, Americans and fools travel first-class. I don't care under which head they place me, so long as they place me in a first-class "carriage." That it is more comfortable is incontrovertible, if you'll pardon such a big word. I say this in the face of what John Stuart Mill said, that the only reason he rode third-class was because there was no fourth.

ELECTRIC LINES UNDER GROUND.

The *Forum* last summer printed a very good description from the pen of Simon Sterne, of the new electric under-ground railway in London, and the Sunday *Sun* last autumn had an elaborate article on the subject, which, with illustrations, occupied nearly a whole page.

It is a quick and convenient means of locomotion, and to accomplish it was a work of wonderful engineering skill for which the inventor, Mr. Peter Greathead, cannot be praised too highly; but the riding is by no means pleasant.

In a lift large enough to accommodate fifty passengers, you descend a distance of eighty feet below the surface—part of the road running beneath the bed of the river Thames. The cars are small and fairly well lighted, but they have an unpleasant vibration, and although the air is not noticeably impure, there is an uncanny feeling with the knowledge that you are burrowing, as it were, in the bowels of the earth.

The road, probably an experimental one, is only three miles long, extending south from "the monument" in the city. It has not, thus far, proved a success pecuniarily, the cost of construction being so great, although no land was purchased except for the stations.

HANSOMS AND FOUR-WHEELERS.

Street cars are not needed in the city. Nearly all London streets are in as good condition for driving as our Central Park roads. There are eight thousand hansoms, four thousand four-wheelers, and two thousand omnibuses, so that you are not obliged to walk on account of the absence of cars. The four-wheeled cabs, or "growlers," as they term them, are dilapidated, uncomfortable vehicles, which lack new springs, and are dirty both inside and out. The horses and the drivers are old and superannuated; they have all seen better days in private carriages or hansom cabs. You never take a four-wheeler if you are alone, or if the party consists of only two persons. You must engage one if you have a trunk, but if you are going to catch a train or boat you had better allow a half hour's margin.

The London cab service is the best and cheapest in the world. I say this, notwithstanding that I remember hiring a cab in Key West, in the Gulf of Mexico, for a dime. But such cabs and such horses! The rate in a hansom is sixpence per mile for one or two persons, no fare less than one shilling (twenty-five cents); by the hour, two-and-six (sixty-two cents).

HOW THEY DRIVE.

England is the only place I know of where they drive to the left. English drivers say that by sitting on the right and driving to the left, they can better watch the hubs of approaching wheels, and thus prevent collisions. A cabbie's attention is given entirely to the roadway; pedestrians must look out for themselves or be run over. That is why so many of the London police are engaged solely in attending to street traffic. Yet with all their vigilance, more accidents occur in London, proportionately, than elsewhere. London drivers are polite and very civil to each other. If an obstruction appears in front of a horse, or if for any reason he is obliged suddenly to slow up, the driver will immediately notify the driver in the rear by holding out horizontally his left arm; and this sign is passed down from one driver to another, until the very end of the line of blocked vehicles is reached.

People who have not visited London for several years, will find cabs greatly improved. There is a new, patent hansom. In these you are saved the trouble of opening and closing the doors; this is done by the driver by touching a lever on the top of the vehicle. The new style of cab has thick rubber tires, which add considerably to ease and comfort in riding. So little noise does the vehicle make in going over London's smooth-paved streets, that these cabs are provided with bells to warn pedestrians of their approach. The interior fittings include a holder for lighted cigars, a box of matches, a small, bevelled mirror on either side of the cab, and a swinging rubber bulb attached to a rubber tube with a whistle at the end. You lightly press the bulb, and in this way whistle to Cabbie on top, who hears the summons above the roar of the streets, and responds by opening his trap door in the roof to receive instructions.

The law does not permit the drivers of these well-appointed and rather luxurious vehicles to charge more than do the drivers of the ordinary cabs; but as the new hansoms cost the drivers more to hire, and as they are so much superior to the old style, you do not begrudge paying a trifle extra. The drivers pay for these improved hansoms sixteen shillings (four dollars) per day, except during "the season," when the owners exact a guinea per day, about five dollars.

The speed with which the London cabs are driven is something alarming—alarming to a stranger. In New York a cab driver has some little regard for the lives and limbs of pedestrians; in Paris the horses are so poor and skeleton-like, and go so slow, that pedestrians have no fear whatever; but in London you must look out wholly for yourself; Cabbie will certainly not look out for you. If he is engaged by the course, he only has his destination in mind. London cab horses are the best horses in the world used for such a purpose. With rubber tires to the wheels, and the wheels going over clean and perfectly smooth roadways, there is nothing to obstruct their speed, and the animals go like the wind. They and their drivers seem to stand in fear of nothing but a policeman, and as London has good laws for regulating vehicles, and as these laws are strictly obeyed, the mere warning look of a policeman is respected and obeyed.

London drivers are not so brutal nor so ill-tempered as New York drivers. They do not, as a rule, curse or swear at each other as ours do, who are always ready with a foul oath. If a "block" occurs they take it good-naturedly and get out of it with the aid of the police as quickly as possible. Our drivers are only satisfied when they can take a mean advantage of their fellows, get in their way and put them to inconvenience. It may be Yankee "goaheadativeness," or the spirit of freedom and independence which prompts this show of ill-temper, but for my part I prefer the laughing, jocular, good-tempered London driver.

On my last visit to London, where I stayed one month, I saw a great many "blocks," but heard only one quarrel between drivers, and that was not at all serious. They will, however, chaff each other, saying something like this :—"Oh, come, pull yourself together there ;" or "I say, country, why don't you learn to drive before you come up to London?" The term "up to London," by the way, is put to singular use there. Although London is in the south of England, you always go "up to London," if you even go from Carlisle, which is in the extreme north, on the Scotch border.

STREET CARS.

There are no street cars run by the trolley, storage or any other electric system ; no cable cars, no horse cars ; not a track is laid for a surface road in "the city" proper. Many Americans leave London without ever seeing a street car of any kind, and yet in the metropolis one thousand street cars run daily over one hundred and twenty miles of track, but they are not permitted in crowded thoroughfares ; they are confined to the outlying districts. I have only seen them in the east end, in the district known as "The Boro'" and near the Victoria Station. The street cars are "double deckers," and, like the 'buses, they carry more outside than inside passengers, but the number of passengers is limited. When the car has reached its limit it will take up no more passengers. Every passenger has the right to a seat, and, to use a paradoxical phrase, every Englishman stands up for his right to a seat.

OMNIBUSES.

The two thousand omnibuses keep employed eight or nine thousand horses. The number of miles run annually by the omnibuses is five and a half millions, and the number of passengers carried not less than forty-eight millions.

Such a heavy, slow-going, cumbersome vehicle as the London omnibus could not be used on our rough-and-tumble roads. It is poorly ventilated, if you can call it ventilated, for the windows are closed and are immovable. The only means of ventilation is by the door, in the rear, near which everybody tries to get. As fast as the choice seats near the door are vacated, they are occupied by the less fortunate passengers, and the last comer is always obliged to take the worst place, which is nearest the front. But in fine weather a man never gets inside while there is a vacant seat on top, and it is no strange sight to see women occupying outside seats to escape the stifling air inside.

Nor does wet weather deter an Englishman from taking an open air seat. Most Englishmen wear a "mackintosh" in threatening weather and there's a great deal of such weather in London. To every seat on the top of a 'bus there is attached a woolen-lined leather apron to protect the knees, and with an umbrella, which is always part of an Englishman's costume, they manage to keep perfectly dry.

The omnibuses are so freely used for advertising purposes, the outside is so nearly covered with attractive and gaudy signs of business houses that it is exceedingly difficult to read or discover the route or destination of the vehicle. You may be looking for Blackwall or Putney, but you will read "Hyams' thirteen-shilling trousers" or "Day & Martin's blacking is the best."

The 'buses do not confine themselves to the middle of the roadway and allow passengers to pick and fight their way through a crowd of vehicles, New York-like; they pull up to the curb to allow passengers to enter or leave without the least possibility of danger or trouble. Conductors will also leave their perch, approach the sidewalk (Anglice, pavement) to consult or advise with a prospective passenger who is in doubt as to which 'bus he should take. Time seems of no importance: they are not in such a rush or whirl of excitement as we are. Whether from the excessive competition or from some other cause I know not: I do know that public servants in England are much more civil and polite than they are in this "free" country.

There are rules which control London omnibuses, and these it is the duty of the police to strictly enforce. A 'bus is licensed and allowed to carry only so many passengers, and this license or limit must be posted on a conspicuous part of the vehicle. The majority are "licensed to carry twenty-six passengers; twelve inside and fourteen outside."

In 1890 the London police force numbered thirteen thousand eight hundred and fifty-five men, not counting the nine hundred and two officers who form a special organization in what is termed "the city." A considerable part of the time and attention of the police is devoted to governing street traffic. Policemen will watch and follow a 'bus for several blocks if they think it contains more passengers than the law allows. When they are assured that this is the case they go to a magistrate and lay a complaint, and then woe betide the poor driver or conductor who disregarded the law.

The 'buses make special stops at certain points of their route and these seem very long and prove tedious to one who is in a hurry; but if your time is valuable you would never take a 'bus. They are not allowed to stop when near or nearing these special stopping-places, not even if a passenger expresses a desire to alight. I remember once, simply for information, asking the driver to stop in the middle of Trafalgar square, just as we were passing Nelson's monument, on the way to the Strand, cityward. "Well," said the polite but uneducated Jehu, "you carn't expect me to get a four-shilling summons for a penny fare, can you?" meaning that if he pulled up where I indicated he would be summoned the next day on the complaint of a vigilant "bobby" and be obliged to pay four shillings for accommodating me.

In American street cars or omnibuses—excepting, as I remember in San José, California, a passenger who rides only a few blocks helps to pay the fare of the man who rides the full length of the road, for the charge to both is the same. It is not so (mis) managed in England. The charge there is by distance, about one penny (two cents) a mile and you pay according to the distance you ride. There are two or three lines of omnibuses whose only fare is a half-penny (one cent). One line runs between Westminster bridge and Trafalgar square. They pick up no passengers between the two points. They each carry only twelve passengers; there are no outside seats.

There is a great deal of pilfering going on among omnibus conductors, and drivers also, for they divide the spoils; and the company winks at it, knowing that the pay of these men is too small. The company is satisfied if it receives a fair average return, but in this way it puts a premium on dishonesty. There is no check against the conductors—no mechanical contrivance to record fares. They are supposed to enter every fare and the exact amount they receive from each passenger on a paper slip placed in a frame, the frame being fastened to the inside of the omnibus door, but it is only a supposition. Passengers are requested to see that the amount paid is properly entered, but the request is wholly unheeded. It is, to say the least, a very careless way of keeping accounts, and invites dishonesty. On some lines they use tickets showing the amount each passenger pays, but a conductor sometimes *forgets* to hand you a ticket. An Inspector will occasionally mount a 'bus to see that all the passengers are supplied with tickets, and then the conductor with a treacherous memory has reason to be sorry. Keep out of a "pirate 'bus." The rate in these 'buses is not uniform, and overcharges are not uncommon.

ON THE TOP OF A 'BUS.

The driver is generally a jolly, red-faced fellow and very smartly dressed, especially on Sunday. He then always wears a "top hat:" in winter it is of black silk, in summer a pearl gray felt with a wide mourning band to set it off. His coat is often a double-breasted drab cassimere, and in the top buttonhole of the left lapel is a large and loud nose-gay. A showy scarf and a pair of heavy, tan-colored driving gloves complete his costume. He makes quite a picture as he sits on the box, with a leather strap across his waist which holds him securely in his seat, and a black leather apron to protect the lower part of his body from wind and rain. He carries a showy whip with a very long and loose thong, with the end of which he can pick off a fly from the ear of his leader.

The 'bus driver is permitted to smoke while on duty. He comforts himself with a briarwood pipe unless a generous passenger treats him to a cigar, for he is not above accepting a small present.

Leopold Rothschild, who lives on a street through which omnibuses pass, has taken a great fancy to these men and in the autumn he presents a pair of pheasants to every omnibus driver and conductor who passes his door.

Everybody who has visited London knows that the best way of seeing the city is from the top of a 'bus. Get a front seat, next to the driver, hand him a tip in the shape of a sixpence and ask him a few questions. You will find that he is intelligent, well-informed on every-day subjects, quick-witted and a judge of human nature.

I had a very interesting ride last summer on the top of a "Kilburn" 'bus. These 'buses start from Victoria station, and run northwest to Kilburn, through some very beautiful thoroughfares, in which reside many titled people and some prominent members of London society.

In Grosvenor place, soon after starting from the station, the driver will point out, for instance, the residences of the Dukes of Northumberland, Grafton and Portland; that of the Earl of Scarborough, at No. 1 Grosvenor place; the Dowager Lady de Rothschild; Sir Edward Cecil Guinness; that of the late Right Hon. William H. Smith; also the homes of a number of members of parliament, more or less well-known.

The 'bus goes a short distance through Piccadilly and passes the residences of Baron Ferdinand Rothschild, Lord Rothschild, the Duke of Wellington and the Duke of Hamilton, in Hamilton place.

Then it turns into one of London's most aristocratic streets, Park Lane (alongside Hyde Park), where reside the Duchess of Somerset, the Marquis of Londonderry,

Lord Brassey, Alfred Rothschild, Lord Dudley, the Countess of Dudley, Lord Grosvenor, cousin to the Duke of Westminster, and the Duke of Westminster himself. The Duke's wealth is untold, and he owns miles of valuable land in this and the adjacent districts.

A 'bus marked "Hammersmith" will take you westward, through Piccadilly, past the clubs, the parks, some stylish shops, and fashionable residences. You will see St. James's Palace and historic Addison Road, *en route*, and you can ride across Hammersmith Bridge. You can also go to Kew Gardens and to the famous "Star and Garter," at Richmond, by 'bus.

Here's another very interesting ride. If you are at Oxford Circus you will see omnibuses with the horses' heads turned eastward, and you will hear the Cockney conductor calling out "Benk, benk, Charing Cross, benk." Take a ride with him. The vehicle goes through Regent street, Trafalgar Square, the Strand, Fleet street, then down Cheapside (which is anything but cheap), and Cornhill, where there is neither corn nor hill. At the end of Cornhill you see the most crowded and bustling crush of vehicles you ever saw in your life. To the right is the Mansion House (corresponding with our City Hall); a little further on "The Monument," with its gold torch at top, looms up; immediately in front is The Royal Exchange, with its Peabody statue, while to the left stands the demure Bank of England, as solid from a financial point of view as it is architecturally. On this route you pass and have in view The National Gallery, Landseer's lions, several famous hotels and theatres, the Law Courts, Temple Bar, the principal newspaper establishments, and St. Paul's Church. The same 'bus, if you wish to pursue your journey eastward, will take you through Leadenhall street and into the very heart of Whitechapel—even to Blackwall and the docks, if your taste lies in that direction.

There is no better way of seeing London than from the top of a 'bus if you get a seat next to an old and wide-awake driver, and the cost is but a few pennies. There are one hundred and forty different routes in the whole city to choose from.

THE CITY TRAFFIC.

One of the busiest thoroughfares is that narrow street called "the Strand," where it is crossed by Wellington street. You drive north, through Wellington street, past the Lyceum Theatre to get to Holborn, Covent Garden Market and elsewhere; southward there is great traffic over Waterloo Bridge, leading to the Surrey side of London, while from the east and west come continuous streams of omnibuses, cabs, carriages and heavy wagons and freight trucks. Policemen stand in the middle of the roadway and regulate this enormous traffic by merely raising a white-cotton-gloved hand. They are calm and immovable, and seem to pay not the slightest heed to their own safety amid the crowded crush of vehicles about them. All come to a standstill before the stiff and fearless "bobby." When by waving his hand he directs that a certain stream of vehicles may proceed this way or that, it proceeds, but not until he gives permission.

London Bridge is said to be the greatest thoroughfare in the world. More vehicles and foot passengers cross it than pass through any other street, and special provision is made for vehicular traffic. In New York, for instance, a heavily laden four-house truck or wagon may block Broadway for a great distance. If you are behind it in a phaeton or light carriage, you must wait till the driver in front of you, who may be sullen and obstinate, leisurely moves out of the way. No matter in how much haste you are—you may be trying to catch a train or an ocean steamer—you must wait. Not so in London's most crowded streets. On London Bridge, for instance, slow-going and heavily-laden vehicles must keep to the side near the curb and pavement, while carriages, cabs and light vehicles are allowed the middle of the roadway for quick movement. That part of the roadway directly next to the curb has a smooth surface, and there is also a smooth surface about a foot wide for the outer wheel of heavy wagons—this only on London Bridge and in a few other very busy thoroughfares. It is a capital plan, and gives satisfaction to all concerned.

ADVICE FROM CHARLES DICKENS.

But in such a vast city, with such enormous traffic, nothing can prevent great loss of life and accidents innumerable from crossing the streets. The point mentioned above is only one of the busy parts of one street—the Strand—from another point, down by the Law Courts and Temple Bar, it is said that two hundred more or less mangled bodies are sent to the Charing Cross Hospital every year.

The present Charles Dickens, in his "Dictionary of London," thinks it worth while to suggest that the only way to go from curb to curb is to make up your mind what course you will take, and then stick to it. London cabbies will thus divine your intentions. To change your mind while crossing is to confuse the cabmen, and cause you (so Dickens suggests) to make your return journey to America in the form of freight.

As all vehicles in London are driven to the left, keep to the left curb. I found this suggestion of Oakey Hall's valuable: "As you leave a curb, look to the right; as you approach a curb, look to the left."

LONDON HOTELS.

Until the year 1880 there was only one hotel in London that came up to the expectations of American travelers, which compared in size and appointments with American hotels of the first-class. This was the Langham Hotel in Portland place. When the Langham was built, nearly thirty years ago, and for several subsequent years, as the writer can attest, for he was a guest there in 1871, and has been a frequent visitor there since, the Langham was large enough to accommodate all American tourists in London.

This, however, has been greatly changed. Americans at that time merely passed through London; they took it as a sort of stepping-stone *en route* for Paris. In the days of the Second Empire, when Louis Napoleon wielded the sceptre, and Eugenie set the fashions for the civilized world, Americans flocked to Paris like so many sheep. Then it was said: "See Paris and die." With the downfall of the empire and its accompanying glories our compatriots found Paris less attractive, and they discovered what everybody knows—that London is, in many respects, the most interesting city in the world. A presentation to Her Majesty, and hob-nobbing with the Prince of Wales, are the things now most desired, and to be in the very height of fashion, one must hire a London house for "the season,"—May, June and July.

THE LANGHAM HOTEL.

But this is a digression. The ground, the structure and the furnishing of the Langham Hotel, which was formally opened by the Prince of Wales in June, 1865, cost a million and a half dollars, and it was a wonder and a revelation to the English people. Its noble granite front of two hundred and twelve feet, its dining hall, forty-seven by one hundred and twenty feet; its music room, drawing-room, and its public rooms generally, were on such a grand scale that Londoners opened wide their eyes in astonishment and admiration. The Langham, by liberal outlay of money and constant improvement, keeps up with the times, and notwithstanding that many splendid establishments have been erected within the last decade, it retains its place in the very front rank. People who have not seen the interior of the Langham Hotel, London, since 1890, will notice some changes and marked improvements. Heretofore the dining-room was only entered by a comparatively dark and roundabout way, near the drawing-room; now it is approached from "the office" direct, through a wide and handsome "vestibule," which is flooded with light and richly furnished, making an appropriate entrance to the beautiful dining-room. The drawing-room, which, for its size, its pleasing shape and rich furniture is yet one of the most attractive salons in England, has also been greatly improved.

Colonel Sanderson, its first manager, an American, died many years ago. He was brother to Harry Sanderson, famous in his day in New York as a pianist. But English capitalists and business men are not given to making changes, and so we find that Mr. Walter Gosden, who was in the service of the Langham under Mr. Sanderson's management, has been for many years and is now the manager of the hotel. You can get a nice room with bèautiful outlook, and a very good breakfast here for less than two dollars a day. This estimate includes the charge for attendance. Address, Walter Gosden, Portland place, Regent street, W.

THE GRAND.

During the past twelve years, however, many superb buildings for hotel purposes have been erected in the English metropolis. Among the largest and most popular are the three grouped together, as it were, in one short street, Northumberland avenue, which, only two blocks long, extends in a southerly direction from Trafalgar square to the banks of the Thames. These are the Grand, the Métropole and the Victoria, to name them in the order they were erected. So popular has this cluster of hotels become, and so many well-to-do Americans do they attract, that property in the neighborhood has largely increased in value, and the tradespeople blame the "Yankees" for the increased rents they have to pay, never speaking of the increased patronage which they enjoy from these same "Yankees."

The features of the Grand Hotel, the longest established of these three, are well-known, but former patrons will scarcely recognize the reception-room, which, with its new, solid-looking furniture and rich, dark decorations, is now one of the most attractive apartments of its kind to be seen, even in these days of the upholsterer and decorator. While artistic and costly, it has an air of utility and comfort which you will not find very often repeated. The drawing-room of the Grand was to be "done up" during last winter, so the secretary informed me, and "it will be just as handsome as the reception-room." Cable, Granotel, London.

HÔTEL MÉTROPOLE.

To American visitors in London the Métropole is one of the most attractive of the more recently built hotels. Situated as it is, and being replete with all the latest conveniences and features, no hotel in the metropolis approaches nearer to the ideal which was first evolved in the United States of the model modern caravansary. To dwell upon the subject of the general characteristics of the Hôtel Métropole would be superfluous; they and it are too well known to Americans who have visited London, but a short description of the celebrated "grand salon" of the Métropole, as it has lately been refitted and decorated (Sept. 1891), will be read with interest.

The scheme of adornment is most tasteful, and perfectly and harmoniously carried out in all details. Two shades of maroon in contrast with white and gold are the leading features of the *ensemble*, and the general effect of this combination is extremely felicitous and pleasing. The wall space between the lofty windows and the immense mirrors is covered with stamped Utrecht velvet of a soft, natural tint and richness of design. The pillars are painted in maroon, with gilt capitals, an arrangement of color which is at once novel and agreeable to the eye. The patterns on the flutings of the beams which support the roof are picked out in gold on a white ground.

The roof panels are covered with dull gold of a peculiarly restful tint, and the design introduced in various portions of the general decoration have an unusually æsthetic character. The electric lights, of which there are a considerable number, are surrounded by cut crystal pendants and greatly enhance the brilliancy of the illumination. In the center of the room is a palm, the leaves of which shadow a space thirty feet in circumference. It towers toward the ceiling, and for grace and beauty is not easily equalled in Florida, nor greatly excelled even in California. Tree palms are placed at intervals throughout the spacious room, producing a pleasing effect of verdure, and each of the separate tables is adorned with flowers ; while the rich candelabra, with handsome shades placed upon each table, afford the subdued light which is preferable to the cruder glare of the former style of lighting. The general *coup d'œil* in the grand salon is singularly graceful and attractive.

A large number of public and private banquets take place at the Hôtel Métropole, this being one of the recognized resorts for ceremonies of that description.

At the Métropole the "show" apartments are known as the Eugenie and Marie Antoinette suites, and they have afforded many a descriptive writer material for an article. Probably no hotel sleeping chambers equal these for rich and costly decoration—for the laces, the frescoes and luxurious furniture. The reader will know that ample means were at command when told that in the selection of site, in constructing and furnishing the Métropole, half a million sterling (two and a half million dollars) were expended. And such a success has the Métropole proved that the company were encouraged to invest further in hotel property with the result that they now own and control three hotels of the first class in London, also five other hotels in different parts of Europe. Among these are the Métropole at Monte Carlo, the Métropole at Cannes, and the Métropole at Brighton, the last named being the latest hotel erected by this company, and one which will compare in many respects with the most renowned hotels of the world. Rooms at the London Métropole from five shillings to one pound per day ; breakfast from two-and-six-pence to four shillings ; table d'hôte dinner, six shillings—one dollar and a half. Manager, Wm. T. Hollands.

HOTEL VICTORIA.

The latest constructed of these three hotels is the Hotel Victoria. Printed words cannot easily convey to the mind an adequate idea of the magnificence of this structure. The public rooms of the Victoria are palatial in their proportions and appointments, the grand staircase is a marvel of beauty, and the sleeping rooms contain all the conveniences and contrivances found in modern hotels of the highest class. Besides the comforts characteristic of an English house, and the luxurious cuisine of a continental hotel, the attention and the discipline which rule at the Victoria remind one of an American hotel.

You need have no fear at the Victoria that the cards of friends calling will not be promptly sent to you : nor is there any delay or trouble at this house, as there is at certain hotels in the Strand, about the delivery of telegrams, letters and packages. Each guest is known to the officials and servants, not by name, but by number—the number of the room he occupies. Letters are placed in your box up to a certain hour of the evening, after that hour they are sent to your room. There is a package-room, also a "package clerk," who receives all bundles, signs therefor, and enters the same in a book, so that it may be known immediately if a package has been received for a guest.

If a telegram or a card from a caller is received and the key to your room is not in its box, thus indicating that you are in your room, or at least in the house, a servant is immediately dispatched to your room, while a little page in livery is started off through all the halls and public rooms calling out in a loud voice your room number in this fashion, "Number 630, please." If you are anywhere under the roof you are sure to be found by this excellent method.

A feature of the Hotel Victoria is a corps of valets. There are seven floors in the building, each accommodating about sixty or seventy guests, and to each floor a valet is assigned who performs all the ordinary duties of such a servant. Shoes are not carried down below to be mixed and confused with hundreds of others, but are polished by the valet on your floor. The valet also enters your room during your absence, removes all the clothes he finds hanging or lying about, brushes and folds the same and puts them back neatly. It is a convenience, returning to your hotel late in the evening and in haste to dress for dinner or the theatre, to find your evening suit nicely folded and brushed, ready to put on. These and other provisions for the comfort of guests indicate the general care in management and the close attention to detail which obtain at the Victoria, and which have given it its wide reputation. The appointments include a billiard room with five full-sized tables. Good rooms on fifth floor, a dollar and a half a day. This includes attendance and lights. Breakfast from two shillings to three-and-six; table d'hôte luncheon about the same; table d'hôte dinner, one dollar and a quarter. Manager, Henry Logan.

LONG'S HOTEL.

There is another trio of London hotels that may be grouped together, on account of their proximity—the Hotel Albemarle (Albemarle street and Piccadilly), Long's hotel (Bond street), and the Hotel Bristol (Burlington Gardens, between Bond and Regent streets). The last two are but a few yards apart. They are all entirely new buildings, and new also in name and history, except Long's, which was erected on the ground where the first Long's stood for *two hundred years*. Long's, though not of great capacity, has a larger number of richly furnished bedrooms than the Ponce de Leon, in St. Augustine, Fla. For the beauty of the exterior and the magnificent surroundings of the Ponce de Leon, as well as for the Oriental splendor of its public rooms, no words of praise can be too lavish. But the two hotels, "the Ponce" and Long's, cannot be compared; their characteristics are so different. One is like a royal palace in the country, the other resembles a gentleman's quiet, city home. Long's differs from every other hotel I have seen in this respect, that all of its bedrooms have rich hangings, and the walls of each are decorated with works of art. The apartments are not cold and bare, as are the bedrooms of most hotels; they suggest home-like comforts, and are furnished in the best taste. The walls of the dining-room at Long's are hung with Gobelin tapestry, and on the whole it may be called a beautifully appointed hotel. H. J. Herbert, manager.

THE BRISTOL.

They have some very attractive hotels in Boston; the Brunswick, for example, and everybody has heard of the beautiful Spanish hotels in St. Augustine, and the great Auditorium in Chicago. I have lived at all these houses, also at the Hotel del Coronado, Coronado Beach, and at California's other famous house, the Hotel del Monte, at Monterey, with its 126 acres for a garden. There are few or none that are more gorgeous than these, and they always come to one's memory when discussing the best hotels, but certainly New York City cannot boast of a hotel interior that equals in tasteful decorations those of the Bristol in London. It is a gem in its way.

A veritable bijou of a room is the reception room of the Bristol. It is minus the onyx tables and costly paintings you see at the Ponce de Leon in St. Augustine, and the "gold" chairs that dazzle your eyes in so many American hotels : everything in this room at the Bristol, from the soft carpet on the floor to the decoration on the ceiling, is rich, but also quiet in tone—soothing and harmonious. The Royal Academy, the Burlington Arcade (a fashionable shopping street) and Piccadilly are all within a few hundred feet of the Bristol. The Bristol is patronized by such well-known New Yorkers as the Vanderbilts, the Twomblys and the owner of the New York *World*. Telegraph or write to the Bristol Hotel, Burlington Gardens, London, W.

THE HOTEL ALBEMARLE.

Although rebuilt and opened as recently as the beginning of 1890, the Hotel Albemarle has already gained a position and reputation as one of the most select and fashionable hotels in London. Its situation, to begin with, has undoubtedly had much to do with its immediate success. It conspicuously fronts the north end of the celebrated thoroughfare, St. James's street, in the centre of the court quarter of London, and stands at the corner of Albemarle street and Piccadilly. No better location for a hotel destined to be at once aristocratic and accessible to the traveling public could have been selected. Towering high above the surrounding buildings, the Albemarle, with its double façade, seventy-five feet on Piccadilly and seventy-five feet on the street from which it takes its name, cannot fail to attract observation. It is built of terra cotta in the Francis I. style of architecture, and the general effect is both graceful and imposing.

The main entrance is in Albemarle street. The interior of the hotel is furnished and decorated in a variety of styles of the Renaissance period. The furniture and decoration of the dining-room, ladies' drawing-room on the ground floor, the fitting and decoration of the hall and staircase, are treated in the style of Francis I. The style of Henri II. has been adopted for the first and second floors; the third floor is in the style of Louis XV., and the fourth in that of Louis XIV. Special mention must be made of the "Rubens Room," furnished and decorated effectively in the Louis XV. style. This apartment derives its name from a fine painting which adorns the ceiling, and which is believed to be from the brush, either of Rubens himself or of one of his pupils.

The furnishing, fitting and decorating of the Hotel Albemarle were effected by the well-known London firm of Shoolbred, after designs from a famous French artist. The building being of such recent erection, it is scarcely necessary to state that none of the modern improvements has been neglected in its construction. The most careful attention has been paid to sanitary arrangements, and the hotel is lighted throughout by electricity. In the two years which have elapsed since it was opened, it has quickly become renowned for the excellence of its cuisine and service. Its wine cellar is one of the choicest in London.

Royalty, the nobility, and visitors of the highest fashion patronize the Hotel Albemarle. During the London season, in particular, its rooms are crowded with distinguished guests. To Americans, especially, it should prove a most attractive resort, if only on account of the brilliant and aristocratic neighborhood in which it is situated. St. James's Park, St. James's Palace and Marlborough House are near at hand. Hyde Park, with its "Drive" and "Row," is within five minutes' walk. The Art Galleries, the theatres, the Opera House, the Houses of Parliament, the clubs, Westminster Abbey, and several of the principal museums are within the compass of a shilling cab fare. The best and most fashionable shops in London are situated in the near vicinity, in Piccadilly and in Bond and Regent streets, while Oxford street, where many of the cheaper shops are to be found, is but a short distance off—in short, it may be said that the Hotel Albemarle stands almost in the centre of the fashionable life and business of London.

Interest attaches to Albemarle street itself as an historical thoroughfare. During the last century it enjoyed peculiar reputation as a place of residence at the west end of the metropolis, and not a little of this old-time prestige clings to it still. The Prince of Wales, afterwards George the Second, once lived in Albemarle street, and when Louis the Eighteenth of France was in England in 1814 he made it his place of stay, and held, at the now defunct "Grillon's Hotel," his receptions of the leaders of the English nobility. The famous publishing house, Murray's, through whose doors have passed such celebrities in the world of letters as Byron, Scott, Southey, Crabbe, Hallam, Tom Moore, Gifford, Lockhart, Washington Irving and many others, is situated immediately opposite the entrance to the Hotel. You would never imagine that it was a publishing house or business house of any kind. It looks like an ordinary private dwelling, and the only sign on the building is one small, dull brass plate on the front wall upon which is engraved "Mr. Murray."

The proprietor of the Hotel Albemarle is Mr. A. L. Vogel. He is to be congratulated on the rapid success he has met with in his efforts to establish one of the best of London hotels. Mr. Vogel has purchased the freehold of property adjoining the Albemarle Hotel, and a large addition to the hotel will be erected presently, thus affording room for a new *salle a manger* and some thirty more bedrooms,

LONDON HOTELS.

Mr. Vogel issues as a "Guide to London" a comprehensive and, in its way, a complete little book of fifty pages. illustrated and prettily bound in cloth. It is sent free to any address in the world on application. Address The Albemarle, Albemarle street, Piccadilly, London.

THE BURLINGTON HOTEL.

The Burlington is in Cork street, a select, and fashionable business thoroughfare between Bond street and Regent street. In this immediate locality are also to be found Long's Hotel, the Bristol, Almond's Hotel, patronized by Chauncey Depew and his family, and Brown's Hotel in Dover street. The last-named house affects not to desire American patronage. The Burlington has enjoyed for over a century a truly unique reputation and position in London. The hotel, as seen from the Burlington street side, has a dignified exterior. It was erected in the year 1723, after designs by Kent, by Richard, third earl of Burlington, but the Cork street side was added to the old hotel in 1828.

It contains about one hundred and fifty rooms, and among these are as fine apartments as may be met with in any hotel in the world. The hotel entrance and the staircase are strikingly attractive, and the galleries, opening from the staircase to the first floor, have a most charming effect. Pretty alcoves occupy the ends of the gallery, and on the side opposite to the colonnade, which looks on to the staircase, is a richly ornamented doorway leading to the drawing-rooms. The latter possess curiously decorated ceilings, painted in oil, with vases, birds, foliage, etc., the work of an Italian artist of the eighteenth century.

The bedrooms are also interesting, as they retain their original carved wood mantelpieces and doorways.

There are several noble old rooms on the ground floor with tastefully designed mantelpieces, panelling, cornices, doorways and richly painted ceilings, which might have served for the background of one of Hogarth's pictures.

In the halls are fine, delicately carved benches by Grinling Gibbons. In their time the old frescoes have been admired by many famous celebrities who have sojourned at the Burlington. "Kitty," the celebrated Countess of Queensberry, friend of Gay, dispensed her well-known hospitality at this hostelry, and Florence Nightingale occupied a suite of apartments there for some months after the Crimean war. Here, too, Macaulay wrote a portion of his famous history.

Coming to more recent times, there is scarcely a well-known face in London that does not know this aristocratic hotel. Lord Beaconsfield, when he was plain "Mr. Disraeli," was president of a committee which met there weekly for the purpose of erecting a statue to the memory of the late Earl of Derby. The ex-premier, Mr. Gladstone, and his family have patronized the Burlington for the past fifty years. The Marquis of Salisbury may be occasionally passed in the corridors on his way to the royal apartments of King Leopold, and the Prince of Wales arrives unattended to visit august relatives, who patronize the Burlington. Henry Irving gives his delightful dinner parties there, and the Royal College of Physicians have dined there monthly since 1830. Among distinguished Americans whose names are on the books, may be found George Peabody, the philanthropist, who resided there for eight months, also Jefferson Davis, John Jacob Astor, Mr. Bancroft, General Schenck and General Sandford. Henry M. Stanley also is on the cosmopolitan list of celebrated guests of the Burlington.

The Burlington, as well as the Buckingham Palace Hotel, opposite Buckingham Palace, has for many years been managed by Mr. George Cooke, who is one of the proprietors, and under whose administration both hotels have acquired a reputation second to none in Europe. Electric light, new sanitation and every other modern improvement have been introduced, and both the British public, as well as American visitors to London, have been quick to appreciate Mr. Cooke's effort to make his hotels real London homes for people of taste and refinement.

THE SAVOY.

A London hotel that has, so to speak, jumped into popularity is the Savoy Hotel. It is a new house, on the Victoria embankment, with the Strand at its back, the public gardens in front and the Thames at its feet. It lies between Charing Cross and Waterloo Bridge, and for a "finger post" it has Cleopatra's needle. There is an entrance for foot passengers from the Strand and a carriage drive from the embankment directly into the courtyard, like that of the Palace Hotel in San Francisco, the Grand Hotel in Paris, and the Grand in Brussels. In fact, the Savoy is more like a continental than an English house, and the owners call it "the Hotel de Luxe of the world." Luxurious in site, size and appointments, the Savoy certainly is. It is not continental, however, in its system of charges. Nor for that matter is it like any other London hotel, its system being American. In all Parisian hotels candles are a separate charge: in nearly all European hotels attendance is a separate item, and in most hotels in the civilized world you must pay extra for baths. Not so at the Savoy. When you are told the rate for an apartment everything is included—everything of course but meals—bedroom, lights, attendance and baths. There are sixty-seven bath rooms in the house, and beneath it there is an artesian well four hundred and twenty feet deep. The boiling water, as well as the cold, like Jacobs's bottle, is inexhaustible, and you can bathe to your heart's content. You can hire a room for two persons for two dollars a day, or you may engage a suite at twenty dollars a day.

As to table, you may live economically at the Savoy, or you may live like a prince—a rich prince. Here are the definite and fixed rates at the Savoy :—bedrooms for one person, from seven and sixpence (nearly two dollars) per day ; for two persons, ten-and-six ; suites of apartments containing sitting-room, bed-room, dressing-room and private bath-room, from thirty shillings per day. Breakfast from two shillings to three-and-six ; luncheon, four shillings ; dinner, seven-and-six ; dinner served in private rooms ten-and-six. Guests' servants are boarded at six shillings per day ; price of room according to location. If you want to live in style and enjoy, at its best, life in London, engage a suite at the Savoy, including parlor and bath-room, with private lobby and private balcony overlooking the Thames. It makes no difference what floor you select : there are "lifts " in the house, so large and luxurious as to be justly called "ascending rooms :" they run day and night. The rooms on the top floor are equal in height of ceiling to those on the lower floors, and the furniture is of the same quality throughout the house. General manager, C. Ritz ; acting manager, L. Echenard.

HOTEL WINDSOR.

The Hotel Windsor is in Victoria street, only five minutes' walk from Victoria Station, two minutes' walk from the American Legation, a few steps from Westminster Abbey, Westminster Bridge, the Houses of Parliament, St. James's Park and the Home Office. The dining-room of the Windsor is an especially cheerful apartment and it overlooks the pretty garden of a church. The great plate glass windows in this dining-room are larger than the windows in any other hotel, so large that they are only moved up or down by ropes to which handles are attached. They let in plenty of daylight, almost as much as streams freely into the dining-room of the Hotel Pasaje, Havana, which opens on the street, and which is not encumbered with windows at all.

The Hotel Windsor is not only kept by a "proprietor" in the accepted American use of that term, but the furniture, the building and the ground on which it stands are owned in fee ("freehold," as English people call it), by two men, J. R. Cleave and V. D. B. Cooper, the first named being the actual and active manager of the house, who makes it his home, the title of the firm being J. R. Cleave & Co. The premises include fifteen thousand square feet of ground, which, without the imposing ten-story stone structure upon it, is valued at forty-five thousand pounds sterling—not far short of a quarter million dollars.

The Windsor is fortunate in its location. A shilling cab takes you to any theatre or to the shopping centre, and 'buses pass the door every minute for Charing Cross, Trafalgar square and the Strand. Time, ten minutes; fare, two cents, inside or out.

There is a lift at the Windsor of modern style; the house is lighted by electricity; there are Turkish and swimming baths on the lower floor; to avoid disagreeable odors the kitchen is at the top of the house; the bedrooms are scrupulously clean, the *cuisine* and wines are of the best quality, and the charges moderate. You can live at the Windsor, if you prefer it, on the American plan—rate, about four dollars a day. The European plan is also moderate in price for rooms and meals—a delicious lunch for sixty cents: choice service.

If this is the description of a model hotel, worthy in every respect of the best patronage, "that," as humorist Gilbert says, "is the idea I intended to convey." The Windsor was built about twelve years ago. Address, J. R. Cleave, manager, Victoria street, Westminster, S. W.

BAILEY'S HOTELS.

Americans going to London for business, intent upon shopping, theatre-going and a round of sight-seeing, find hotels in the Strand, or hotels near Trafalgar square, very convenient. Reference is made to the Grand, the Métropole, the Savoy, and the Victoria, in their alphabetical order. The Langham, in Portland place, and those select houses near Burlington Gardens and Piccadilly—Long's, the Bristol, the Burlington and the Albermarle, are also central, convenient, and in a fashionable district.

If, however, a family is going to London for a protracted stay and the desire of their hearts is to be in an ultra-fashionable locality, where the aristocracy reside, and where quiet and selectness reign and salubrity is assured, then Bailey's Hotel, on the corner of Gloucester and Cromwell roads, is recommended and recommends itself. If you are in haste and do not care for a cab, the "underground" will take you from "the city" or from Charing Cross to Bailey's Hotel in fifteen minutes, fare five cents, third class; fifteen cents in a first-class carriage.

When you reach Gloucester Road Station you are at Bailey's Hotel, and within a few minutes walk of Hyde Park, Kensington Gardens, Cromwell Gardens, Stanhope Gardens, Queen's Gate Gardens, etc., etc. Near at hand are the Albert Memorial, Albert Hall, and South Kensington Museum. Not only is Bailey's Hotel in the heart of this fashionable locality, surrounded by the residences of members of the nobility and others, but the hotel itself is under royal patronage, and has entertained the Prince of Wales, the Duke of Edinburgh, the Duke of Connaught, the Princess Marie, the Princess Louise, and other members of the royal household.

The hotel, which stands on the property of Lord Harrington, who owns all the land hereabouts, was built in 1875. It is a brick building, six stories high—a modern hotel with modern improvements, and all possible safeguards against annoyances and dangers. There are accommodations for two hundred and fifty guests. In the rear of the house is a beautiful garden.

The decorations and furnishings of the apartments are in admirable taste, and display an individual and artistic sense of fitness. The style is especially English, but also especially beautiful—there is no gaudiness, but neither is there dinginess. Unlike American hotels, little space is given to halls, bar-room, etc., but there is a cosey, homelike atmosphere, which is enhanced by the rich and substantial surroundings. Because the bar, with its glitter of glass and brass does not obtrude itself, let it not be supposed that wine is eschewed. On the contrary, the wine cellar is a feature of the house, and the stock of wines is valued at ten thousand pounds. As to the quality of the wines, and, by the way, that of the cuisine, they are unsurpassed in London. The sanitary arrangements bear the closest inspection. Some of the very old and small London hotels are not to be trusted in case of fire. Bailey's Hotel is American-like in the particulars of fire-escapes and preparations for extinguishing a fire.

There is no attempt to lead people to believe that very low prices prevail or that Bailey's is a "cheap house" in any sense of the term. On the contrary, you pay for the best, and you get it. You can live at Bailey's Hotel on the European plan at about the same rate as at an American hotel of the first-class. Single rooms rent at about one dollar per day; double rooms from a dollar and a half; suites from four dollars and a half upward. These are the winter rates. They are a trifle higher during "the season."

As at all English hotels, breakfast varies in price from fifty cents to seventy-five cents; luncheon from sixty cents; table d'hôte dinner, one dollar and twenty-five cents. Of course it is English, and there are some extras. It is a rule at every English hotel, except the Savoy in London, to make a separate charge for "attendance," about thirty-five cents per day for each person, and Bailey's conforms to the rule. No American likes it and it seems odd, but it is the custom in England, and when in Rome——. Four dollars per week is the charge for each member of the canine race.

So much for Bailey's Hotel proper, but the same proprietor, Mr. James Bailey, is also proprietor of the South Kensington Hotel, and, strange to say, the two hotels are distant from each other only five minutes' walk, the South Kensington being in Queen's Gate Terrace.

Being in the same locality, and having the same proprietor, the above remarks and particulars will apply, almost word for word, to both houses. Americans who prefer a quiet, aristocratic quarter, and especially those who have children, will make no mistake in applying for rooms at either hotel, each with its surrounding parks and gardens being particularly adapted to families. For the South Kensington, address Queen's Gate Terrace, London, S. W.

IN JERMYN STREET.

A couple of small, quiet hotels in Jermyn street—a street which runs parallel with Piccadilly—may be found pleasant by families or by ladies without escort. They lack that bustle and noise to which some people object, and they are not "company hotels," that is to say the head and front of each is always visible and approachable. Mr. Rawlings is proprietor of the Rawlings Hotel, and Mr. Morle with his family keeps and manages the house which bears his name.

While Jermyn street is narrow and its two hotels are quiet, plenty of life and gayety are to be had near at hand. Bond street and Regent street, two of the most fashionable shopping streets of London, are hard by, and the parks and palaces are within walking distance. Rawlings' Hotel is famous for its cuisine, and a feature at Morle's is that you can arrange to live on the American plan if you prefer, the charges being "inclusive," as they call this plan there, and very moderate withal. Both these houses are homelike and comfortable, but they are not strictly fashionable.

Do not confuse Morle's in Jermyn street with Morley's in Trafalgar square. Morley's has a magnificent outlook, with the noble Nelson Monument, Landseer's lions and the playing fountains in front, and the dinner served at Morley's is of the best quality, but the house is very old and rather worn, notwithstanding its white and attractive exterior.

THE NORFOLK'S MODERATE CHARGES.

If you want to get away from the Strand, Regent street and Piccadilly; if you are tired of the glare and blare of showy "American hotels," and you prefer a very quiet, but healthy locality, jot down in your memorandum book, "Norfolk Hotel, Harrington Road, South Kensington, S.W." The Norfolk was built in the year 1889, not by a company, but by Mr. A. Fatman, who himself keeps the house. It is not large, there is room only for eighty guests, but these eighty can be made very comfortable.

It is not like a hotel in certain respects. The rooms are not all of one size nor of one shape. The furniture does not look as if it were turned out by machinery in Grand Rapids and bought by the car-load. It has character and distinction, no suites of furniture being alike. There is nothing at the Norfolk to remind you, for instance, of a Salt Lake hotel, with its great halls and corridors, and its cold, bare walls. Good taste, as well as money, was used in building and furnishing the Norfolk, and the result is an attractive, cosy, home-like house.

After entering the Norfolk and admiring its pleasant surroundings, the tariff of charges will surprise you. Rooms are let as low as two-and-six (about sixty cents) a night, and, wonderful to relate for a London hotel, there is no charge for attendance. Fish breakfast, one-and-six (thirty-five cents); afternoon tea, sixpence; the same price for hot or cold bath.

THE FIRST AVENUE.

Don't be prejudiced at the sound of "First Avenue Hotel." It is in Holborn, a bustling, busy thoroughfare, but which has nothing in common with our First avenue in New York. The Gordon's Hotel Company made a mistake in naming the house; they meant to say Fifth Avenue Hotel, for the First Avenue Hotel ranks probably with our Fifth Avenue Hotel in New

York, only the First Avenue is not an old house. Holborn is one of London's main arteries, a continuation, east, of Oxford street. The First Avenue is not very far from St. Paul's and Newgate. The former being a noble cathedral, you will wish to get into; the latter being a prison, you will wish to keep out of, unless for a temporary visit.

OTHER HOTELS.

Another hotel in Holborn which may be commended is the Holborn Viaduct Hotel, near the city station of the London, Chatham and Dover Railway.

A pleasant house in High Holborn is the Inns of Court; neither fashionable nor grand, but select and comfortable; largely patronized by English people. Terms moderate. The main entrance is in Lincoln's Inn Fields.

There are some famous old houses farther east, in the city, in such a bustling, busy quarter as St. Martin's le Grand, near the General Post Office. The Queen's Hotel in this neighborhood is best known.

Not far from this locality is the Manchester Hotel, in Aldersgate street. The proprietor of the Manchester Hotel especially solicits American patronage.

Those who desire to make frequent visits to the Houses of Parliament and that grand old pile, Westminster Abbey, will find the Westminster Palace Hotel convenient. It has an imposing front, in Victoria street, Westminster, almost opposite to the Abbey. Within five minutes' walk of this hotel are the Home Office, St. James's Park, the Horse Guards, Westminster Bridge, leading to the Surrey side of London, the United States Legation, and the Victoria Station of the London, Chatham and Dover Railway, The favorite and well kept

Hotel Windsor, referred to elsewhere, is also in Victoria street, and still nearer to the Station and the Legation before mentioned.

Convenient to Hyde Park are the Alexandra Hotel, 16 to 21 St. George's Place, Hyde Park Corner, and the Hyde Park Hotel. The latter is at the west end of Oxford street, in Hyde Park Place, near the Marble Arch.

Claridge's Hotel used to be considered "the crack" house of London, and it is still patronized by the nobility, members of the diplomatic corps and by royalty. Nos. 49 to 55 Brook street, Grosvenor Square.

The Hotels connected with the railway stations are large structures, solidly built, fire-proof, as a general rule, and fitted up with every modern contrivance. They are desirable stopping places if you arrive late at night or if you intend to make an early start by rail, from the station, in the morning. They were erected for that purpose and they serve it admirably.

There are very many reputable hotels in London which are worthy of the best patronage, detailed reference to which, in this limited space, it would not be possible to make.

If none of the hotels described or alluded to in the foregoing list suits your plans and purposes, consult friends who have had experience in such matters. But don't go, hap-hazard, into the smallest and oldest London hotels of whose very existence you never heard. Some of them are unpleasant, as residences; others are unhealthy. If your stay in London is short there is every reason why you should put up at the best houses. If you make a protracted visit and desire to economize, go to a boarding house or take lodgings. You will see signs in windows all over London : hire rooms and eat where your fancy or purse directs. London housekeepers are glad to "eke out" by letting rooms in the summer, and with a small tip now and then to the maid, life can be made very comfortable in London lodgings.

A FEW BOARDING HOUSES.

There are plenty of first-class boarding houses where Americans are welcome. Five or six come to mind—Mrs. Pool's, No. 20 Bedford place ; Mrs. Goodman's, No. 13 Montague place ; Mrs. Philp's, No. 6 Montague place ; Mrs. Wright's, No. 15 Upper Woburn place, and Mr. Cooper's, No. 1 Bedford place, Russell square. Mrs. Philp is an American whose husband keeps the Cockburn Hotel in Glasgow; and there is a Philp's Cockburn Hotel in Edinburgh. Mrs. Philp's drawing-room is beautiful, the dining-room cheerful, and there is a pretty garden which is backed by the walls of the British Museum, so Mrs. Philp is easily found.

Those who want to live economically but comfortably are recommended to the handsome private hotel or *pension* of Mrs. Marcus Pool, 20 Bedford place, Russell square. This is a pleasant and convenient quarter of the city—quite handy for the British Museum, not far from Charing Cross, and a shilling cab fare to railway stations and places of amusement. The house is furnished and appointed on a liberal scale ; the drawing-room is large and cheerful ; the bedrooms are luxuriously fitted up in the best taste, and they have a pleasant outlook. There is a Broadwood piano, also a new billiard room, with a table from the famous firm of Bennett. The house has a refined, home-like air, well representing the character of Mrs. Pool and her charming daughter. French and German are spoken. The terms at the Pool pension are from two dollars a day, which include breakfast, table d'hôte dinner and attendance—"everything inclusive." Those are the terms "in the season ;" the winter rates are lower. The cuisine is of the substantial English quality, but not heavy. At Pool's pension you are sure to meet cultivated and select people. Those who have been Mrs.

Pool's guests appear perfectly satisfied; for they return again and again. Mr. Cooper keeps a good house and he caters to people accustomed to refined surroundings. He is a typical Londoner of the middle class—honest, blunt and out-spoken. Mrs. Lucy H. Hooper, wife of the American Vice-Consul in Paris, recommends No. 1 Bedford place. Mrs. Hooper makes it her stopping place when she is in London.

"American Family Home."—An establishment which meets with especial favor among fastidious tourists is Demeter House, 13 Montague place, Russell square, W. C. The location is select, within easy access of the centres of shopping and amusement. The house is kept by Mrs. A. Goodman, who aims to maintain a house replete with the comforts and freedom of a refined home and the advantages of a hotel, but with less expense. The house is spacious and well furnished, the table excellent and carefully provided. Many leading American families make this their home during their annual visits to London.

Put down "No. 15 Upper Woburn place, Tavistock square," and note that it is not far from Euston station. It is a quiet street. The house is kept by an English woman of refinement, Mrs. Wright and her maiden daughters, and it may be commended as a pleasant Christian home, where grace is said before meals.

Of these boarding houses, like all the hotels mentioned in this article, the writer speaks from his own knowledge and experience. But don't count on getting accommodation in London hotels in the season, without making previous arragements or giving notice in advance of your arrival, or you may be disappointed.

WHERE TO LUNCH IN LONDON,
AND WHERE NOT TO LUNCH.

It may be set down at the outset that there are no restaurants in London equal to Delmonico's in Fifth avenue, or the Café Savarin in the Equitable Building, New York, and no London restaurant serves a table d'hôte dinner at any price equal in quality and style of service to that furnished at the select and elegant "Cambridge," Fifth avenue and 33d street, New York.

Neither is there a restaurant of the third class that will compare with Mouquin's, in Ann street, where everything is cooked to a turn, and where even a fastidious *gourmet* need not find fault. There are two or three Italian places in Regent street where they serve a "Chateaubriand," enough for two persons, for one dollar, but nowhere do you get a dish of maccaroni that is more palatable than at Mouquin's, and neither in London nor Paris do you get as good Burgundy for the price as Mouquin's beaujolais—half bottle, forty cents.

The foreign halls are more richly gilded, and the furniture is of finer texture, but if you are looking for as good food and as well served at that at Mouquin's, at Mouquin's prices, you will look in vain.

In the price of wines, however, no first-class hotel or restaurant anywhere that I know of sells wines as low as the manager of the Hotel del Monte, Monterey, Cal. In France, on the Swiss border, I found *vin ordinaire* almost as cheap as water, in the small inns. The Hotel del Monte, please bear in mind, is a superbly appointed and grand establishment, and they serve you a half bottle of good California Zinfandel for fifteen cents. But then this hotel company own their own vineyards, and make no profit on wine served at table. It is a sort of "sample" or advertisement for their wines.

"The Aerated Bread Shops," which are as "thick as flies" in London, are probably good enough places to drop into if you are in a great hurry, for a cup of coffee or cocoa and a roll or piece of dry, digestible seed cake. If you abhor marble tables, if you must have a *serviette* and you would avoid a crowd and mixed company, keep out of the "aerated bread shops," and by the same token and by all means keep out of the Lockhart lunch shops. The "aerated bread shops" are tolerable; the others are not.

Much more worthy of patronage than aerated bread shops or Lockhart's lunch shops is the confectionery and cake counter of William Buszard, 197 and 199 Oxford street, where everything is clean and inviting. A similar place of the first-class is that in "the city" of Alfred Purssell & Co., No. 80 Cornhill, E. C. The proprietor of this establishment is related to the late William Purssell, founder of the famous restaurant in Broadway which still bears his name. There are several pleasant places in and near Piccadilly where you may obtain a cup of tea or cocoa and a dainty sandwich, just enough to "stay the appetite." One of the best of these is Callard's, 146 New Bond street, but even in this neat and clean little shop they don't know what a *serviette* is.

Romano's, called "The Vaudeville," 399 Strand, is recommended for its moderate charges, but this is a place I have never tried. So much for the confectioners and the cheap restaurants.

The Tivoli restaurant, up stairs, connected with the Tivoli Music Hall, is in the Strand, just East of Charing Cross. "La Haute Cuisine Française," as they term it, is in charge of a famous *chef*, M. Gerard. A Table d'Hôte

Luncheon, at 2s. 6d., from 12 to 3; Parisian dinner, at 5s., from 6 to 9, served in the Flemish Room.

Londoners are proud of their Holborn Restaurant, 218 High Holborn, where the glass and the brass and the marble columns are resplendent and imposing, and where you are regaled with vocal music (English glees) during the dinner hour, but the meals are not daintily served: the butter is not cold, and the plates are not warm, and unless you order a costly meal at the Holborn Restaurant, the waiter may wait on you with condescension. Dinner, three-and-six.

If you are in "the city," in the neighborhood of the Bank (the Bank of England), and you have a desire to see how and where some of the brokers and commission merchants lunch, step into the Winchester House in Bishopgate street—a well-lighted, well-furnished restaurant, where no charge is made to customers, strange to say, for use of water and soap.

Ladies who are in the neighborhood of Westminster Abbey or who have business at the American Legation, are recommended to the Army and Navy stores, in Victoria street, opposite the Windsor Hotel, where a dainty lunch is served at a very moderate sum. You can do your shopping in the same large establishment. They sell everything, from a poached egg to an Axminster carpet or a wedding outfit. The Army and Navy stores is on the coöperative plan. To gain entrance you must either use a member's ticket number or use good judgment.

Gatti is a well-known name in the Strand, where the Gattis have two large, gaudily furnished restaurants, one of which extends to King William street. The Gattis are also owners of the Adelphi Theatre, where you may always enjoy a drama — if you enjoy melodrama. The Gattis are Swiss, and one of the brothers is a legislator in one of the Swiss Cantons. They commenced in a small way, in the east end of London, many years ago and made a reputation for their ices. They long since moved to the west end, where they increased their business and they now conduct a thriving trade. All Gatti's waiters are foreigners. They are a talkative set and some people might prefer that their linen be nearer the color of snow.

IN REGENT STREET.

If you are in the neighborhood of Piccadilly Circus, a fair place to get luncheon at a fair price is "the Florence" in Rupert stree., Regent street. It is an Italian restaurant; the lunch is served table d'hôte and the price is one shilling and sixpence. But there is no profit to the restaurateur in the mere lunch : you are expected to order wine — indeed that is the expectation in all English restaurants and hotels—all hotels that are not temperance houses. At the Florence you can get dinner from six to nine, for half-a-crown—sixty-two cents—and you order wine of course.

If you are fond of high living, and you don't mind paying for it, take a meal in the middle of the day or *early* in the evening at the Hotel Continental. It is in the lower part of Regent street, on the corner of Waterloo place, within the shadow of the Duke of York column. It was one of the first houses in London to adopt the French style in name—Hotel Continental in lieu of Continental Hotel—and it was one of the first to serve a first class dinner in the French style. The reputation for its *cuisine* is second to none, and the hotel prides itself upon the accuracy of the names and vintages of the wines supplied. It has the monopoly in London of that famous brand of champagne, "*Medaille d' Or*," which received the grand prize in the French Exhibition of 1878 over sixty other competing wines. Cigarettes made of the finest tobacco are manufactured expressly for the hotel in Constantinople and Salonica.

There is always a very gay scene in the Hotel Continental supper room after the theatres close; it might become too lively in the early hours of the morning, but the police regulations oblige such places as the Continental to close their doors at one A.M. Dinner from seven-and-six to twelve-and-six, without wine, of course; for although you are in the Continental you are not on the Continent. A. Y. Wilson, who has been connected with the house since its opening, is the manager.

More attention is given to "the inner man" in London than in any other place I wot of. They seem to live to eat there, not eat to live, and yet some one has noted this difference—you eat dinner in London, while in Paris you dine. Mention the subject of restaurants in London and the majority will ask you, "Have you dined at Verrey's in Regent street?" Yes, I've been to Verrey's and I found it very gloomy, and very expensive not to say oppressive. You are in the middle of the house and the room is lighted from a skylight. It is not at all cheerful.

Blanchard's, "The Burlington," 169 Regent street, is patronized by the higher classes. Dinner from five shillings to twelve-and-six. No higher priced dinner in London.

For a healthful, nicely-served meal, whether it consist of a mutton chop and a boiled potato or a dinner of several courses, much better than the aforesaid establishments in Regent street is the Café Royal, at No. 68 Regent street. In the "Grand Café Restaurant Royal," where dinner is served, prices rule high. For luncheon go into the "Grill Room" of the Café Royal. You will find the rates reasonable, the food of the best, the appointments on a grand scale, and the service satisfactory. These remarks will also apply to "The Monico," at Piccadilly Circus and Shaftesbury avenue.

The St. James Restaurant, which extends from Piccadilly to Regent street, with entrances on both streets, is a large, showy place, with plenty of glitter about it, and wearing the big-sounding title of St. James Hall. The rates are not low, the food is not of the choicest quality, the service is not of the best, and the waiters may overcharge you unless you watch them closely. The charge for washing your hands at the St. James, be you a patron or not, is two-pence. This is a regular charge made by the proprietors, but if you don't also fee the man who hands you a towel or fills your basin, you might get a cold reception down-stairs the next time you call, and you may fill your own basin.

At the Criterion, in Piccadilly Circus, you can take your choice ; go up stairs, and the charges are higher ; down in the basement the same dishes are served at a lower price. To quote their bill, "table d'hôte three-and-six, *le diner Parisien*, five shillings."

English people when they are thirsty drink beer, wine, or something stronger ; Americans who live in cities, American women at least, prefer something weaker, soda water, for instance, which, charged with gas, looks cool and inviting as it comes bubbling from a highly polished, silver-plated fountain. Not until recently could American taste in this matter be gratified in London. Now there are two "American confectioneries" kept by Fuller, one, the principle establishment, at 206 Regent street ; the other, at 358 Strand, both central locations. The first is close to Oxford Circus and not far from the Langham Hotel. At Fuller's you can get ice-cream soda and "caramels fresh ever hour." In fact, on a pleasant summer day Fuller's, in Regent street, will remind you of Huyler's on Broadway, and if you are a New Yorker, you will meet many familiar faces there. If you retain a juvenile *penchant* for peanuts, that taste can also be gratified at Fuller's.

THE GRILL ROOM OF THE GRAND.

So many of the transient guests at hotels in London are out shopping and sight-seeing, that they generally take only breakfast, or, at most, breakfast and dinner, at their hotels, always lunching wherever convenience may permit. The meals at European hotels being usually a separate charge, the hotel is a sufferer by this custom, so that at some, if not most houses, it is understood that, if you take your meals out, a higher charge will be made for your apartment. The manager of the Grand Hotel, however, has opened a restaurant of his own, in his own house, which is so attractive that it not only keeps together his regular guests, but allures "the outside world," and thus the "Grill Room," as it is called, of the Grand has become famous in London.

While within and a part of the Grand Hotel, it is not reached by the main entrance in Northumberland avenue. It is at the eastern end of the building, around the corner, in the Strand, and is in what we would call in New York a basement, but no ordinary "basement" is this, and the staircase leading to it is anything but ordinary. The Grill Room of the Grand is a well-lighted, cheerful apartment, richly carpeted and finely furnished. The chairs are comfortably upholstered, the walls are gorgeous with polished tiles, the table furniture is dainty, the food is of prime quality, and the tariff of charges moderate.

Don't be surprised at the charge, two-pence, for washing your hands in the Grill Room lavatory, and unless you occupy a room, the charge for use of lavatory in the hotel proper is three-pence; but it it worth half a crown merely to see the lavatory, or rather the staircase and landing leading to it, so beautiful are the colored marble fountain, the eastern rugs, the fernery and the Oriental lamps, with which this lower part of the house is decorated. The view of this lower part from the marble staircase on the main floor has been called fairy-like; it is certainly very pleasing.

Strangers are not allowed the run and freedom of the hotels in Europe as they are in "the States." They can't use the smoking-room, read the newspapers, loiter about the halls, make a general rendezvous of the house and help themselves to stationery in European hotels as they do on this side. Their hotels lack some of our popular features and the excellent service and discipline of the American hotels, but, on the other hand, they are not so noisy, and are more private. American hotels suit Americans, and the hotels in England satisfy the wants and desires of English people.

SIMPSON'S DIVAN.

A Characteristic English Restaurant.—A good, plain, thoroughly wholesome English dinner is served in an appetizing way by English waiters at Simpson's, in the Strand, next door to Terry's Theatre, opposite Exeter Hall. You get a bowl of good soup, a course of fish, a cut from the joint, a salad, two kinds of vegetables, with bread and butter, a biscuit and a bit of rich Gorgonzola or dry Wiltshire cheese to wind up with, and your whole bill will be four shillings, to which add threepence for "attendance," which is charged in the bill, and about threepence more which you will hand to the waiter. A feature of the place is that the hot joint, over a chafing dish and on a small table, is wheeled round to you, and it is there cut before your eyes and transferred to your plate. You can get a lower-priced dinner in London, and higher-priced dinners where you please, but none of a better quality and none that is more satisfactory unless you demand fancy fol de rols, indigestible entrées and French dishes made of little or nothing.

Simpson's is justly celebrated for its "fish" dinners. Both these and the meal above described are served in the middle of the day and in the evening also. On Sunday the evening dinner only is served; the place is closed until 6 P.M.

Simpson's enjoys the patronage of Henry Irving and of other people famous in the theatrical world, just as it did in the last century. Henry Irving's Lyceum Theatre, by the way, is in the Strand, near Simpson's, but on the opposite side of the street. In the summer of 1890 I saw D'Oyly Carte enjoying his dinner at Simpson's. This is a special compliment to the place, because that magnificent hotel, the Savoy, in which this theatrical manager is interested, is just around the corner from Simpson's, on the Thames Embankment. During the summer of '91 I met at Simpson's another theatrical manager, our own Augustin Daly, with his wife. Mr. and Mrs. Daly occasionally left the Hotel Métropole, where they had aparments, to partake of one of Simpson's substantial, well-cooked and appetizing meals. There's no Simpson now, the founder died long ago, but "Simpson's" is there yet, as it was a hundred years ago, although it is now a limited company. Howard Paul eulogizes this place, and Stephen Fiske recommends it. Besides being a brilliant writer on dramatic matters, Mr. Fiske has made a study of the gastronomic art, and he lived in London continuously during nine years. The reading public put faith in Stephen Fiske's dramatic criticism; his intimates also trust to his good taste and judgment in ordering a dinner.

It is a well-known fact that changes in the employees at this establishment are seldom made. Some of the waiters have stood at the tables for nearly two decades, and the head waiter has been there (probably not always as head waiter) for more than thirty years. The name of this head water is Charles Flowerdew, so he informed me, and I can impart this piece of information—that this same Flowerdew is a character worth studying. There is nothing of the "Yellowplush" type about him, but he is such a character, courteous and civil (yes, seemingly servile to an American's eye), such as Dickens delighted to draw.

Mr. Flowerdew knows all the old customers at Simpson's, and, what is of more consequence to a hungry man, he knows all the choice cuts. He will suggest the best dishes, the rare bits, and he will serve you from the joint, *ad libitum*, as he proudly remarks. When next you go to London, go to Simpson's, 103 Strand. You will be sure to meet a few London notabilities, you will be sure of a good dinner, and last, but by no means least, you will see the polite and dignified Mr. Charles Flowerdew. Managing director, E. W. Cathie.

RAILWAY TRAVELLING IN ENGLAND.

While our facilities in railway travelling have wonderfully improved in the past ten years, it must not be supposed that in conservative England they have stood still entirely. But the improvements in carriage accommodation there have been so steady and gradual that passengers hardly recognize how much more they get for their money now than they did a generation back. For instance, the old first-class carriage of forty years ago was fifteen feet long, six and a half feet broad, and less than five feet high, and this was constructed to seat eighteen passengers; in other words, each person had about twenty-six cubic feet of space. In the carriages built to-day to accommodate ten first-class passengers, each one has ninety cubic feet.

Nor because we in America have such luxurious Pullman and vestibuled cars must it be imagined that the English railway carriages have not comforts and luxuries of their own. Some of them, for example, are built to seat only two or three persons, thus securing complete privacy to a party of that number.

I have never occupied a more comfortable railway carriage than in going, as I did, last September, from Edinburgh to London over the lines of the Caledonian and London and Northwestern railways, on the world-famous train called the "Flying Scotchman"—and a flyer it is. The distance is four hundred miles, and it is run in eight and one-half hours. You leave Edinburgh at 10.15 A.M. and reach Euston square before 7 P.M. As there are several important stations between the two cities at which long stops are made, the train must make between many of the stations much more than fifty miles an hour. The speed was so great at times that it caused unusual vibration, and at times it gave me a slight reminder of sea-sickness.

The carriage was built to seat two persons only. In it there were two large, softly-upholstered, sleep-inviting arm-chairs, one on each side of the car. Between the two chairs at the back was a door leading to a lavatory for the sole use of the two passengers. It was supplied with iced water, washing water, towels, mirror and all the etceteras and conveniences that are desirable in travelling. The car had in all six windows—two at each side and two in front. Between the two front windows was a handsomely-framed bevelled mirror. The floor was richly carpeted and the carriage was supplied with a number of brass brackets and hooks for the travellers' impedimenta. But more than this—across the front, breast high, was a shelf about six inches wide to hold books and papers, and below this another shelf about the same width for a foot-rest.

The carriage was seven feet square and seven feet high. Here a man and wife or two friends can make themselves about as comfortable as if they were at home in their own drawing-room. You exchange your shoes for slippers, don your smoking jacket and if your companion does not object, you can enjoy a fragrant Havana. To be sure this is against the rules of the company and your indulgence in the weed would cost you forty shillings if you were found out, but the distances are great and the stops few on this "flying Scotchman," so there is ample time to enjoy a smoke undisturbed. No extra fare is demanded for this most luxurious vehicle; it is simply ranked as a first-class carriage, but you had better write to the station master and engage such a carriage a day or two in advance of your intended journey, for not more than one of these small private cars is by chance attached even to a "flying Scotchman." No extra charge is made for this engagement in advance.

The complaint years ago that passengers were locked in the cars can seldom now be made. The custom is almost entirely abolished; it caused so many accidents. The aim of each and every passenger on a British railway is to secure a seat with his back to the engine. In this way he avoids draughts of air: draughts from a bottle they never object to. In fact both men and women drink often and deeply during a journey, but it does not seem to affect them.

Time tables are not given away as with us: the charge is a penny, two cents. You never hear "all aboard" at railway stations, but the much pleasanter sounding words, "take your seats, please."

LUGGAGE AND BAGGAGE.

You do occasionally get a paper check or receipt for baggage on a continental railway, but in England seldom or never. Still a piece of baggage is seldom lost on an English railway. It gets to its proper destination at last, but it seems to be more by good luck than by good management. Baggage, or "luggage," as they term it, goes astray sometimes, but on the other hand, the system for tracing and finding it is excellent. They have a "lost luggage" department in the principal stations.

They are very particular as to the quantity of baggage. Each passenger is allowed so many pounds. At every station there is an official who keeps a sharp eye on the porters who handle trunks, and at the slightest suspicion of overweight the official will order a trunk on the scales with which all stations are supplied.

There are strong racks in every car for light luggage, but a great deal of what we should term heavy baggage finds its way on the racks and under the seats. Englishmen travel with an extraordinary quantity of impedimenta. They carry large satchels, also portmanteaus resembling a good-sized trunk—all because no checks are given. Everybody wants to keep his luggage in hand or in sight.

There is a prominent sign posted in some of the large stations to this effect: "Any porter who is discovered accepting a fee will be instantly dismissed." And yet you can't get your trunk moved an inch without dropping a few coppers into a porter's hand. The fee system prevails everywhere, from the station master who furnishes information to the uniformed porter who whistles for a "four-wheeler" or hansom. In many cases the door of the toilet room is only unlocked by dropping a penny in a slot. But this is a better arrangement than exists at stations on the continent, where an old woman stands guard, whom you must fee before you are allowed to leave.

A ROYAL RAILWAY TRIP.

When the Queen of England makes a railway journey it is an event of no ordinary importance. With her it is not, as with the President of the United States for example, so simple a matter as climbing up the steps of a Pullman or getting into a Pennsylvania Florida special or Chicago limited, and proceeding without fuss. No, when Queen Victoria is about to travel preparations are made long beforehand and all the regular arrangements of the road are subservient to the accommodation of the royal train.

When Her Majesty journeyed by the Caledonian Railway from Carlisle to Aberdeen, en route to Gosport and Ballater, many days previous there was issued the table of instructions for working the trains over the line on that day. They were intended for the use of the company's employees only, who were forbidden to make known their contents. A pilot engine was sent over the road twenty minutes before the royal train, in charge of the foreman of the locomotive department. This engine maintained throughout the journey the uniform interval of twenty minutes. No other train, engine or vehicle, except passenger trains, was permitted to travel on the other track between the passing of the pilot and the royal train, and even passenger trains had to slow down to ten miles per hour.

One of the orders issued was this: "Drivers of such trains as are standing on sidings or adjoining lines, waiting for the passing of the royal train, must prevent their engines from emitting smoke or making a noise by blowing off steam when the royal train is passing."

Brakesmen were enjoined to see that nothing projected from their trains. Each foreman plate-layer, or "section-boss," as we would say, after examining his length of line, stationed himself at the south end and an assistant at the north; after the pilot had passed they walked till they met, seeing that all was right. The stations were kept clear and the public admitted at one station only, the last. Even here, cheering or other demonstration was forbidden, "the object being that Her Majesty should be perfectly undisturbed during the journey." These instructions, signed by James Thompson, general manager, and Irvine Kempt, general superintendent, were obeyed in their minuest detail.

It must not be supposed that the company has to pocket the loss when the Queen travels. The royal lady not only does not travel on "passes," but she pays all expenses incurred. A copy of the instructions printed in gold are presented to the Queen and she cannot fail to be gratified by the care and thought exhibited by the company.

The entire mileage of the Caledonian Railway is one thousand miles; the main line from Carlisle to Aberdeen, over which the queen travelled, is about two hundred and forty miles. It traverses a beautiful country. From this great trunk run out branches and connections by steamer in all directions—reaching to all big towns of the country, most of the small ones, and all the districts famed in Scottish song or history, the highlands, the lochs, the seaboard, etc. The road is a model road and one of the best appointed in Great Britain. The tourist, the student and the sportsman are offered strong inducements to avail themselves of the tours arranged by the Caledonian company.

THE NORTHWESTERN RAILWAY.

One of the largest English railway systems is that of the London & Northwestern. The territory covered by this railway extends from London in the south to Carlisle in the north, and from Cambridge in the east to Holyhead in the west—an area of three hundred miles in breadth. The main office of the government is in London, but the capital, so to speak, is Crewe, a town of thirty-five thousand inhabitants consisting entirely of the employees of the railway and their families. The total number in the railway's service does not fall far short of sixty thousand. The annual budget amounts to ten million pounds, while the funded debt has reached a total of one hundred million pounds sterling.

The London and Northwestern shops at Crewe have to keep in repair a stock of engines that is worth five million pounds sterling, and while they do not indeed put a girdle round the earth every forty minutes, they do literally every four hours, and in doing so the engines consume a million tons of coal per annum. On an average, it is reckoned that every five days an old engine is withdrawn and replaced by a new one.

Of late years the company has been experimenting on an extensive scale with a system of metallic permanent way. Steel "keys" fasten the rails into steel "chairs," which in their turn are riveted down to steel sleepers. About thirty miles of line has been laid on this system, with about sixty thousand sleepers. So far the results are understood to be satisfactory. The question involved in the conflict between steel and wooden sleepers is gigantic. A rough calculation shows that to replace the wooden sleepers on existing lines in Great Britain only would require about four million tons of steel, without reckoning the weight of the chairs and keys. And great Britain has only one-fifteenth of the railway mileage of the world.

In some ways the goods traffic arrangements of the road at Liverpool are even more remarkable than those in London. At Liverpool the Northwestern has six goods stations, two of them reached by tunnels each a mile and a quarter in length, constructed for their use alone. One of these stations, Edgehill, is called a goods "yard," but this yard contains fifty-seven and a half miles of land, covers two hundred acres of ground, and has cost about two million pounds sterling—nearly ten millions of dollars.

The conductors on the New York street cars, like the New York policemen, are sullen and sour; they seem ill-tempered, if not ill-natured. You seldom or never see a smile on their lips, and as for giving utterance to the common and easy phrase, "thank you," when they receive a fare, they wouldn't be guilty of such a piece of politeness; not they.

It is different in England, on the Continent, everywhere in Europe. Whether on a steam road, a steamboat, a tram or an omnibus, no officer nor conductor would think of receiving a fare without thanking a passenger audibly, and even when an officer opens the door or looks into the window of a carriage for the purpose of examining tickets, you will not hear the short, sharp, curt demand, "tickets," as in the States, but "all tickets, please," in a pleasant and agreeable tone.

AN HOUR WITH SPURGEON.

LONDON, October 1, 1890.

The Rev. C. H. Spurgeon still draws crowds to his tabernacle, which is situated in a part of London called Newington Butts. It is by no means a fashionable district, being in the Southeast end of the city. You tell any "cabby" to drive you to Spurgeon's church and he will put you down at the door. But it is only a twenty minutes' ride on a 'bus from Charing Cross; fare four cents.

That Mr. Spurgeon attracts great throngs of hearers, every one knows, but here are a few figures: His tabernacle accommodates between six and seven thousand people, and on Sunday morning, September 28, when the writer was present, five thousand four hundred people listened to him. This was in September, be it remembered, when everybody is out of town and "London is empty."

The regular members and attendants ascend the stone steps and enter the church through the front door; strangers and visitors get in by a side entrance, through an alleyway, and as they pass in, a tiny paper envelope is handed to each person. You drop into the envelope as much or as little coin as you please (for no human eye is watching you) and this envelope you in turn drop into an open box on your left, this method probably taking the place of a collection, which would be so difficult to manage where five or six thousand people have to be approached.

People sometimes ask what is the secret of this preacher's distinguished success? The foundation of his success is his earnestness and evident sincerity.

He impresses his hearers with the belief that he believes what he is preaching. He does not seem to be making a profession or business of religion. There is nothing perfunctory in his manner; he rejoices in his calling.

Then again Spurgeon is a good and effective speaker. He talks in a slow, deliberate way, his enunciation being clear and his pronunciation perfect. Each word is distinct and clean cut. His accent is cosmopolitan; there is nothing local in it. Except for the pronunciation of a few words, such for instance, as the word "after," to which Mr. Spurgeon gives the broad sound heard in England, you might be puzzled to know whether the great divine was born "within the sound of Bow Bells" or graduated from Columbia College.

His language hypercritical people might not call choice, but I beg to differ with them; it is exceedingly choice, being directly to the point, and like the man himself, simple and strong. There is no searching for fine phrases and well-rounded periods. His ideas flow freely and they quickly find expression : there is no effect aimed at. The man trusts to the matter of his discourse, never troubling himself about his manner.

His gesticulations are few, natural and not at all dramatic. He will raise his right hand or occasionally take a step towards a small table hard by : nothing more. His voice is not musical, nor is it especially pleasing to a stranger's ear ; but it is firm, clear and penetrating, possessing those qualities most demanded in a public speaker.

On the morning of which I write Mr. Spurgeon took his text from Psalm 63, 7th verse, and held his hearers spell-bound for about forty minutes by his brilliant illustrations, his convincing arguments and his earnestness, for above and beyond all he is deeply in earnest. His prayer is beautiful ; he touches a responsive chord in every heart in his fervent appeals to God for mercy and help.

Before the sermon there was singing of psalms and hymns. Mr. Spurgeon gave out hymn No. 916, "Going to Worship." It was congregational singing, without instrumental music, one man near the pulpit acting as a sort of leader. The singing was too slow for the preacher. After the second verse he called aloud to the congregation to sing faster, himself beating time with his right hand. Psalm 34 was next given out, but when the first verse had been sung Mr. Spurgeon stopped the singing abruptly and said in a tone which was meant to be commanding : "I must beg that if you sing at all, you sing faster : there's more heart in it if you sing quicker. Praise God as if you meant it ; put your soul in the words : it will be more welcome if there's spirit in it."

Mr. Spurgeon's deacons, about twelve in all, are seated on two rows of seats behind him, he and they occupying a high platform and prominent place—probably fifteen feet above the floor of the church, where all can get a good view of the man's features—all except the deacons.

The great preacher is now in his fifty-sixth year. Like his character and his language, physically he looks strong and rugged, but his health is not good.

Mr. Spurgeon belongs to a family of gospel ministers. His grandfather was an English divine ; his father, Rev. James Archer Spurgeon, still living, now occupies, or did occupy until very recently, a pulpit in London ; and he has two sons who follow his profession—one at Greenwich, near London, and one at Auckland, New Zealand.

P. S.—Mr. Spurgeon died at Mentone, France, on Sunday, January 21, 1892, deeply regretted by all who had ever heard him or heard of him.

THE CRYPT OF ST. PAUL'S.

All Americans who go to London visit Westminster Abbey, and some of them make more than one visit. There is a rare charm about the grand old pile. I never go to London without visiting the Abbey, and this was also the custom of the late Aaron J. Vanderpoel, with whom I had the honor of crossing once or twice. On one voyage westward, a fellow passenger was James R. Cuming, of the famous law firm of Vanderpoel, Cuming and Goodwin. Mr. Cuming and I were fellow students in the old law firm of Brown, Hall and Vanderpoel in the days of District Attorney Blunt, never-mind-how-many years ago. Mr. Cuming's hair is now tinged with gray, but he has the same genial, agreeable qualities, and he is just as modest, eminent and successful lawyer though he now is, as he was when he and I were boys together in the Broadway Bank building on the corner of Broadway and Park place. But none of this personal matter has aught to do with the subject in hand.

I was about to say that while all Americans go to Westminster Abbey to see the monuments and other interesting things, all of them do not know that two of England's greatest men, their most renowned heroes of modern times, are buried in St. Paul's Cathedral—Lord Nelson and the Duke of Wellington,

One reason why American and other tourists who visit St. Paul's seldom see the tombs of these great men is because they do not know that the cathedral contains them. The tombs are in the crypt, and unless you knock on the great iron gates leading to the crypt and pay a sixpence, you cannot obtain admission.

But besides the tombs of these two celebrities, a number of other eminent Englishmen lie buried in the cathedral. Among the monuments (over their tombs) may be read the names of General Gordon, Admiral Napier, Sir Christopher Wren, the architect, and the famous artists, Sir Joshua Reynolds and J. W. M. Turner—in fact, as there is a Poet's corner in Westminster Abbey, so there is a Painter's Corner in St. Paul's Cathedral.

Nelson's remains are covered by a great sarcophagus of black marble, which was intended for the tomb of Cardinal Wolsey. The Duke of Wellington is buried in a sarcophagus of porphyry, of which the upper part, forming the lid, alone weighs seventeen tons.

A visit to St. Paul's discovers many other interesting things, and it is the opinion of the writer that it is one of the three grandest public buildings of modern times, the other two being the Capitol in Washington and the Palais de Justice in Brussels.

The cathedral itself has an interesting history. The first St. Paul's Cathedral was built by Ethelbert of Kent, in the year 610. It is said to have been destroyed by fire in 961, rebuilt and again destroyed by fire in 1086, rebuilt again and for the third time destroyed by fire in 1666. The present structure was built by Sir Christopher Wren and took thirty-five years to complete, being finished in 1710, at a cost of something like £747,954 sterling—nearly four millions of dollars. It covers more than two acres of ground. The height from the pavement to the top of the cross is three hundred and sixty-four feet three inches. You get a good view of the building from the Thames. The best view of the building, however, is from the top of an omnibus going east down Fleet street, but this view is now somewhat marred or obstructed by the railway arch which crosses Ludgate Circus.

A few figures about the bell and the clock may not be without interest. The former, called Great Paul, weighs sixteen tons, fourteen hundredweight, two quarters, nineteen pounds; height, eight feet ten inches; diameter at base, nine feet six and a half inches; thickness where the clapper strikes, eighteen and three-quarter inches. The clapper is seven feet nine inches long and weighs four hundredweight. The note is E flat. The clock has two faces, each nearly twenty feet in diameter. The minute hand is nine feet eight inches long and weighs seventy-five pounds; the hour hand is five feet nine inches long and weighs forty-four pounds. The hour figures are two feet, two and a half inches long. The pendulum is sixteen feet long and to it is attached a weight of one hundred and eight pounds. It beats once in two seconds.

THE QUEEN'S MEWS.

Windsor, the royal residence, twenty-five miles from London, attracts of course many American visitors, its features of interest including, besides the castle and park, the celebrated stables. But as for stables, the Queen's Mews, near the centre of London, offer a much more brilliant show. Admission is gained with little difficulty or formality—by Americans. You simply call at the American Legation in Victoria street, two or three blocks (as we'd say in New York), from the Victoria railway station—a "penny 'bus" from Charing Cross passes the door. It is not necessary to ask for Minister Lincoln; your card sent to Mr. White, the secretary of the legation, or, in his absence, to Mr. McCormick, the courteous assistant secretary, will secure you in return the necessary pasteboard for yourself and party to visit the Queen's Mews in Buckingham Palace road—a very short walk from the legation and a stone's throw, so to speak, from Victoria station.

The stables cover a few acres of ground. They contain the royal harness, the carriage of state and other carriages, and have stalls for about one hundred horses, in the care of all of which about thirty or forty men are employed, those longest in the service being privileged to live on the premises. There is nothing very remarkable about the horses' quarters; the stalls are not more luxurious nor are they kept in better condition than many private gentlemen's stables in New York and Newport, nor are the horses particularly worthy of note, excepting the ten large black stallions and eight cream-colored stallions, used in drawing the state carriage on state occasions, as, for instance, when the Queen opens parliament. The tails of these stallions, the blacks and cream-colored, all reach to and almost sweep the ground, with the exception of one big black animal, whose brevity of appendage is made up on state occasions by the addition of a false tail.

The harness for ordinary use is of black leather with elaborate bright brass trimmings, that for state occasions is also of black leather, the crowns and coats-of-arms, in solid metal, being heavily and richly gilded. The harness is kept in perfect condition, and kept on show, protected by glass doors and windows. You may see and admire the royal reins, but they are not to be handled by common fingers.

Among the carriages there is one kept for its past history and glory, not for present use—a gaudy, gilded, theatrical-looking vehicle, the weight of which is four tons, the great, heavily-tired wheels of which measure six feet in diameter, the whole being of the respectable age of one hundred and thirty years. The most beautiful feature of this curious relic of by-gone days is the eight pictures set in as many panels, painted by Cipriani, an Italian artist famous in his day.

But the carriages for Her Majesty's ordinary use and the carriage which is reserved for state occasions, which is drawn by the eight cream horses, are models of comfort, luxury and beauty. They are upholstered with dark blue cloth, the only interior ornaments being of worsted fringe matching the cloth in color. The wheels and body are dark blue, the panels being painted in a lighter shade, the centre of each door panel relieved by the royal crest of arms painted in rich colors, but not larger in size than a silver dollar. The carriages are hung on C springs and yield from any point to the slightest touch.

I ventured the remark to one of the footmen in charge that when Her Majesty places her foot on the step her weight must make quite a depression of the springs. "Does it," said the royal flunky; "you should stand 'ere when the Duchess of Teck gets in. The Queen's cousin is a werry heavy woman, God bless her. If you was to see her get in you *would* see a depression, or whatever you call it."

You will make a mistake if on leaving the Mews you do not drop a shilling into the ready palm of both coachman and footman.

A QUESTION OF HATS.

Americans treat women better, both at home and abroad than they are treated elsewhere, and they certainly show the sex more deference and respect in public and private than women are accustomed to receive in many older countries.

An American seldom addresses one of the gentler sex with his head covered, unless it is in the open air; and while this is also the custom in some European countries—in France and Switzerland, for instance—it is not nearly so common in Germany or Great Britain.

Englishmen with whom I have talked do not seem to notice such things, but I know from long and careful observation, that men in London sit with their heads covered during the whole of a theatrical performance. They occupy seats in "the pit," to be sure, but "the pit" in London is compared by some with the back rows of the parquette in American theatres.

Should this meet the eye of a barrister, he might charge me with being too general in my remarks. If he demands, in his "answer" to this "complaint," a "bill of particulars," I will mention, among places where I saw men sit covered during the whole evening, the Savoy Theatre, when "The Gondoliers" was played, and the Shaftesbury Theatre, where Willard performed in "Judah" in September, 1890.

At a Covent Garden concert in the same year, I saw four or five hundred persons on the floor (men and women) and not more than six men carried their hats in their hands. I remember remarking at the time that one-third of the number of hats were of silk plush ("top hats"), one-third were derbys of a brownish hue, the other third were mixed—all sorts.

Even in the dress circle at a Covent Garden concert some men wear their hats the whole evening—white hats, derbys, and heavy silk hats—and this in warm weather, too. It no doubt is the custom; at any rate such was the case on a certain "American night" (summer of 1890) when American airs were played, Mrs. Alice Shaw, the beautiful whistler, being the special attraction among the solo performers.

And when men at London theatres do remove their hats, they seem to do it reluctantly. They will enter a theatre and enter a box, remove their overcoat and gloves, take out opera glass, and spread the play bill before them, and then, as'a last thought, if they think about it at all, the hat will be slowly removed; they seem to be unwilling to part with it. How different in American theatres, where every man quickly doffs his hat the moment he enters the door of the auditorium. It is all the more noticeable in London theatres because the women are obliged to remove their hats before entering, and excepting at the Lyceum, the Savoy, and possibly one or two other houses, they are obliged to pay for their care.

At third and second-class London restaurants, men wear their hats as do people of the same class elsewhere, but some men in England not only carry their hats into the dining-room of a first-class hotel, but carry them on their heads until they take their seats; the presence of women makes no difference.

The editor of the New York *Press* says: "There is no surer test of a nation's sense of courtesy than its treatment of women. Judged by this standard, the people of the United States stand above those of any other nation on the face of the globe."

LONDON ODDITIES.

It serves the purpose of correspondents as well as of the postal authorities to add the postal district initials in addressing letters to London—as for instance, C., indicating central, or S. W., Southwest. There are eight of these districts, and the necessity for adding the initials will be seen when one learns that in London there are no less than thirty-five King streets, thirty Queen streets, eighteen York streets, a Victoria Park in the extreme east, one Queen Victoria street, a Victoria railway station in the Southwestern district, a Hotel Victoria in the western central and a Victoria Hotel in quite another district.

The postal system in London is as near perfection as it is possible to make it. Few letters go astray, and the delivery is prompt, there being from six to twelve deliveries daily; but by neglecting to add the initial letter of the district a letter may be delayed several hours. There are three thousand offices and pillar boxes in London, but in addressing letters take care and take into consideration that there are nearly six millions of people in London, that the streets and squares cover eight thousand acres, and within a radius of fifteen miles of Charing Cross seven hundred square miles are covered. Correspondence between England and the United States also shows wonderful increase. Ten years ago the number of letters which annually passed between the two countries was eight millions; at present the number is twenty-four millions. Reduction of postage rates has of course had something to do with this great increase and it will bear further reduction.

I happened to be near Euston station and wanted to go to my hotel in Northumberland avenue. I stepped into a hansom, and not wishing to be taken for a stranger I simply said "Victoria Hotel." In five minutes Mr. Cabbie pulled up in front of what seemed to be a gin palace, bearing the sign plain enough, "Victoria Hotel." "I want the hotel in Northumberland avenue," I said to the driver. "Then why didn't you say Hotel Victoria," was the sharp response, and cabbie charged me a fare and a half to emphasize the distinction.

The growth of London is something marvelous. More than ten thousand houses annually, or, it may be roughly stated, one thousand houses every month, are added to London. In August of 1889, 754,464 houses were supplied with water by the water companies, or 11,113 below the number in the same month of 1890. In September, 1890, the companies had to supply 10,976 houses more than in September of 1889. In August of that year 765,577 houses were supplied with water, and in September, 1891, that number had increased to 766,797.

The London police are a pleasant, polite set of men, and if they do not refuse the price of a pint of beer for a slight service, neither will they refuse to answer any question, respectfully and satisfactorily. The contrast is very striking between these good-tempered, obliging officers, and the sullen, saucy, sour-visaged, tobacco-chewing New York policeman who is just as ready to answer with his club, which he carries exposed, as he is with his uncivil tongue. London policemen are paid from six to seven and a half dollars per week: New York policemen from sixteen to twenty-four dollars weekly. A London police sergeant gets only ten dollars a week.

SIXPENCE FOR A PLAY BILL.—At the Prince of Wales Theatre and at the Shaftesbury you are charged sixpence for a bill of the play, and at the majority of London theatres you pay for a programme. The exceptions are Irving's Lyceum and D'Oyly Carte's Savoy, where no employee is allowed to accept a fee of any kind—not if the manager knows it. That does not say, however, that a "tip" for a programme is unexpected, even at the two houses named.

CIVILITY AND SERVILITY.—There's a difference between civility and servility. You are pleased to have an omnibus conductor audibly "thank you" when you hand him your fare, but in the London shops a saleswoman will do the same thing even when you make no purchase. At the pleasant Nayland Rock Hotel in Margate, on the south coast of England, a waiter will thank you for allowing him to put a clean plate before you, or when he hands you a glass of water—if you can get such a thing as water at your meals in an English hotel. It is not obtainable without a little trouble ; everybody drinks wine.

SOOT, SOOT, EVERYWHERE.—Owing to the use of soft coal in London, white buildings are soon changed into black ones, partially. This change, especially where one side of a set of Corinthian columns, for instance, remains the original color, and the other side has gradually turned very dark, gives some of the churches and public buildings a picturesque and pleasing appearance. Yellow brick is very largely used, but it soon changes color. If you place a tumbler of water outside your window at night with the idea of keeping it cool, for you rarely see a piece of ice, you will find a number of tiny globules of soot floating on the surface of the water in the morning. And it is exceedingly difficult in London to make weather prognostications, the sun being usually hidden or half-hidden by London smoke, if not by fog.

EXCHANGING COMPLIMENTS.—Englishmen say "as drunk as a Scotchman," and Scotchmen have a saying "as durr as an Englishman." "Durr" implies something more than quiet : it means surly, sullen. It cannot be denied that English tourists are unusually quiet : they seldom speak without having been formally introduced. That reminds me that two or three years ago I was traveling on the Midland road from London to Liverpool, and I happened to make some casual remark to a fellow traveler who was a stranger to me. The gentleman replied very briefly but courteously, and then added : "Beg pardon, you hail from the other side, do you not?" "Yes, but why do you ask?" "If I didn't detect it in your accent," said my neighbor, "I should know it because you addressed me. I have been traveling between London and Liverpool now for many years, and I am never spoken to but by an American, and I rather like it."

There are no "cross-walks," as we call them, in the cities of Great Britain ; none are needed. Nor does anybody cross the street at right angles, as we do in New York. Everybody crosses diagonally, from corner to corner, or crosses in the middle of the block. The road-ways are so smooth and well paved that all parts are alike, and it is never necessary to pick your way. In New York, besides exercising great vigilance to prevent being knocked down and run over by vehicles, you must always keep one eye on the ground while crossing. You may be upset by a car track, or you may step between two stone blocks that are a foot apart, more or less.

AS TO OYSTERS.—English oysters still retain their flavor, a great deal of flavor ; in fact they have entirely too much—that is to say, too much for anybody whose palate is not accustomed to the peculiar taste. You can get oysters as low as a shilling a dozen, but choice "Whitstables," that have a strong, coppery flavor, come as high as four shillings a dozen. For the uneducated American palate, Chesapeake oysters, or the Great South Bay blue points are good enough.

SERVANTS' WAGES.—Servant girls' wages in England are not nearly so high as they are in the United States. Even hotel chambermaids, who are paid better than family servants, only receive fourteen pounds sterling a year—about ninety dollars, but each one is allowed a fortnight's holiday (with pay) at the end of the summer. And the "tips" they receive from the guests are well worth consideration.

There are differences between the habits of London and New York women and here is one of the minor points: New York women go "shopping," that is to say they go into one store after another to examine the goods, as a diversion or pastime; English women never enter a shop without the intention to purchase; they make a business and not a pastime of replenishing their wardrobe. To go on a shopping tour American women often wear fine gowns and rich jewelry; English women on the contrary, dress very plainly when engaged in their business of purchasing. They reserve their fine clothes for the opera or for receptions, wearing no extra finery even for ordinary visiting. They are not seen parading the streets in silks and satins, and that is why some American writers who do not observe closely say that "English women in the street dress in dowdy style."

NO "FORELADIES" IN LONDON.—At the great dry-goods house and outfitting establishment of Debenham & Freebody, in Wigmore street, not far from the Langham Hotel, all the saleswomen are expected, nay, are obliged to dress in black. They number two hundred, but not a "saleslady" nor a "forelady" among them. They make derision of these terms, which are so commonly heard in New York. The firm also employs six or seven hundred young men. All the unmarried employees live on the premises, and this plan is found to operate satisfactorily to all concerned. The young men wear black coat, waistcoat and necktie. Many years ago salesmen in London dry goods houses were not allowed to wear a moustache, but there is more liberty now and they can adorn their faces as fancy dictates.

You don't hear the words, corsets, dresses nor pounds, in London shops of the first class, such as Kate Reily's, Debenham & Freebody's or Redfern's. They have gone back to the old-fashioned term—stays, gowns and guineas. English merchants favor the last term because a guinea is worth a shilling more than a pound.

CUSTOMS IN ART GALLERIES ABROAD AND AT HOME.—The English National Gallery, in Trafalgar square, London, like our Metropolitan Museum of Art and like nearly all galleries in different parts of the world, is only open free on certain days of the week, while the great French collection at the Louvre, in Paris (probably the largest and most valuable collection of pictures under one roof) is always free, and may be visited without application to any circumlocution office. The Louvre is open six days of every week in the year; only on Mondays are the public not admitted, the officers reserving Monday for repairs and cleaning. In nearly all of the public galleries of Europe, as in the Corcoran gallery in Washington, you are obliged to leave your umbrella or walking stick in charge of an official at the door and for the care of such an article a fee is charged in some places; at the Louvre you may carry into the galleries as many umbrellas and bundles as you please. This is not always an advantage: for my part I am only too glad to be relieved of my umbrella and overcoat on such occasions. It seems strange that men while viewing pictures in the foreign galleries should persist in wearing their hats—it seems strange to a New Yorker; the custom being so different at our Academy of Design.

POVERTY AND CHARITY IN ENGLAND.

The drinking habit among men and among women and girls still remains the curse of Great Britain, and its companion, poverty, is everywhere. But if the poverty is striking and awful to behold, its next-door neighbor, charity, God be praised, aims to keep pace with it. Hospitals and other philanthropic institutions supported by voluntary contributions, are to be seen almost wherever the eye turns in the United Kingdom.

The patriotic and other public funds, to meet special emergencies at home and abroad, may well challenge the world's admiration, not only for the princely amounts subscribed, but also for the hearty and expeditious way in which the funds are raised. The charitable institutions of the city of London number upwards of one thousand, and simply of asylums for the aged (colleges, hospitals and almshouses), there are one hundred and twenty distinct institutions.

But to return to the drinking habit, which presents itself before you constantly: I was riding up to London from Margate with a hotel-keeper, at whose house, on the edge of the surf, I had been staying for a week, and I remarked that the drinking water at Margate was of good quality. "Is it?" said Mr. Knaggs, for this is the name of the agreeable gentleman who presided for three years over the destinies of the Nayland Rock Hotel. "Is it?" said mine host. "Well, you know more about it than I do, for I've never tasted it."

On Sunday, while at dinner at Philp's Cockburn Hotel, Edinburgh, just before dessert was served, a small box was passed around the table by a waiter and into it people were dropping sixpences, shillings and pieces of higher denomination. At once it occurred to me, here's another overcharge or extra I had not counted on, and I began inwardly to rebel. "What's this for?" I blurted out in a rather injured tone. "Collection for the Orphan School, sir," and I gladly added my mite. Afterwards I saw money boxes in hotels and restaurants in other parts of Scotland and in England labelled, for example, "For Charing Cross Hospital; funds urgently needed," etc. Little boys and young women go about the busy and better parts of London on Sundays with boxes in their hands, begging you to "drop a penny in" for this charity or that—and you find it very hard, indeed, in London to keep any coppers in your pocket, so strong are the appeals. On hospital days the number of hospital boxes is largely increased temporarily. At this time sheets are spread in churchyards, into which people throw their spare change liberally.

"The People's Palace," which was opened by the Queen in jubilee year, is a noble illustration of the charitable English heart. The "People's Palace" is situated in one of the poorer quarters of London, and, as everybody knows, is the realization of an ideal conception of Walter Besant in his novel, "All Sorts and Conditions of Men." The palace includes a well-stocked library; a reading-room, supplied with papers from all parts of the world; a large swimming bath and a hall for musical and literary entertainments. In the basement of one of the main buildings boys are taught trades by which they may earn their living. That the recipients of all this good may not feel that they are objects of cold charity, a slight charge per month is made for those who use the reading-room, library, swimming bath, etc., and there is a nominal charge, about four cents each person, for admission to the concerts and lectures, which are given gratuitously by musicians and lecturers of celebrity.

I visited that part of the Whitechapel neighborhood which "Jack the Ripper" made infamous as the scene of his murders. It was a vile place three years ago, but the scene has been changed as if by a fairy hand. The Baroness Rothschild opened wide her heart and purse and erected here, for the poor of this unfortunate quarter, blocks of modern model tenements. These she lets at very low rents, asking only three per cent. return for her investment. In connection with the tenements the noble woman has built a well-appointed "Club and Library," with billiard-room, etc., for the amusement of her tenants. These premises are in charge of a custodian and his wife, who are paid for their services by the Baroness; and for the use of the "Club and Library" a merely nominal charge is made to any of the tenants who avail themselves of the privilege. It is not sectarian. In England they believe in "Faith, Hope and Charity," and of these three that "the greatest is Charity."

WHERE IS CHARING CROSS?

You hear a great deal about Charing Cross in London, but you may look in vain for a street sign bearing that name. Very few people in London know exactly where it is, nor does even the policeman on the "beat" know. Strange to say, neither the Charing Cross Hospital, the Charing Cross Station, nor the Charing Cross Hotel is in Charing Cross. Much as it is talked about, it is a very short street, extending easterly only from Cockspur street, then southerly, past the equestrian statue of Charles I. to Scotland Yard or Whitehall. Low's Exchange is in Charing Cross, and within two or three hundred feet of that spot (No. 57), is the very centre of the city of London. From this spot cab fares are reckoned. Start from here and you can ride anywhere, within a radius of two miles, for one shilling. Low's Exchange, by the way, is a very popular rendezvous in London for Americans. It is where they "most congregate," and it offers many conveniences for travellers.

If you are traveling on the other side make this your headquarters. Telegrams, letters, and even printed matter are forwarded to you with the utmost promptness. A special work of the house is the securing of state rooms on board steamers. It saves you much worry and bother, and the service of this agency costs you nothing, Mr. Low getting his pay from the steamship companies. Edwin H. Low served his apprenticeship, as it were, to this business, in the office of the National Steamship Company in New York, many years ago, and since then he has had large experience. The headquarters of the concern are at 947 Broadway, and Mr. Low may be seen sometimes at his New York house, at other times in London, but there is a very capable man who acts as general manager for Mr. Low in Charing Cross — Mr. George Glanvill, who served Mr. Gillig for many years at the American Exchange, 449 Strand. By all means register at Low's.

MARGATE,

AN ENGLISH WATERING PLACE.

I was ill in London, at the Windsor Hotel in the summer of 1890, and as my friend Dr. Walter M. Fleming of New York happened to be in London at the time, at the Savoy Hotel, I sent for him. The fact is that I had been receiving too much "attention" from my friends —dinners, drives, concerts, theatres, suppers, etc., all of which resulted in physical and nervous exhaustion.

Dr. Fleming's prescription was simple—"rest and a change of air," but as this was Dr. Fleming's first visit to England, I began to question my friends and others as to the best pharmacy at which to have the prescription filled. The proprietor of the Windsor Hotel, Mr. J. R. Cleave, said "Margate;" so, too, said the intelligent manager of the house, Mr. Mann. An old and trusted friend wrote me, "Don't go to Margate, go to Brighton or to Hastings." Thus opinions differed. I knew all about Brighton and wanted to see a place new to me. I was much inclined to go to Hastings, but a concensus of opinion prevailed in favor of Margate.

"There's a beautiful air at Margate," is the response of everyone in England to whom you speak of that place, from the boys at Low's exchange in Charing Cross to Mr. Richard Whiteing, editor of the London Daily News. This remark was also made to me by Major Arthur Griffiths, an English author and *littérateur*, who is known and esteemed on both sides of the Atlantic. So to Margate I went.

Margate is on the south coast of England, seventy-five miles from London, whence it is reached by the London,

Chatham and Dover Railway. This is the road celebrated for the beautiful rural scenery that borders it; it passes through the prettiest parts of Kent, "the garden of England," through Rochester and Canterbury, famous for their cathedrals, and other places of historic and scenic interest. You may also reach Margate by steamer from London Bridge. It is a pleasant sail on the Thames of ninety-three miles.

Having arrived at Margate, you can make it the starting point for many a delightful excursion. Boulogne on the French coast, for instance, across the channel, is directly opposite Margate; steamer fare round trip, six shillings—a dollar and a half.

Other pleasant excursions are made to Canterbury and to Ramsgate. To these places run "pleasure vans" accommodating twenty persons and the fare ranges from threepence to a shilling, according to the style of vehicle. If you do not care to patronize the pleasure vans, you may hire a victoria at two shillings per hour. Canterbury is the site of the famous cathedral. At Ramsgate lived the Jewish philanthropist, Sir Moses Montefiore, for nearly the length of his long and useful life—one hundred years.

Another interesting excursion is to the old-fashioned village of Broadstairs, for many years the home of Charles Dickens. The house Dickens occupied and which he called "Bleak House," still stands on its commanding site at the top of the cliffs directly overlooking the sea. A description of Bleak House, with illustration, appeared in the Home Journal in January, 1891, and has been widely copied in this country as well as in England. Broadstairs is only a five-mile drive from Margate, fare by victoria four shillings.

Few Americans who cross the ocean go to Margate, but they may spend a couple of days or a couple of weeks there with advantage. Margate is a town with a history. Its foremost historical feature is the Church of

St. John, built in 1050. It has seen the rise of Norman, Plantagenet and Tudor dynasties and still stands, the oldest of England's possessions. In the time of Queen Anne, according to the chronicler, to be buried in a sheet cost sixpence, and a shilling was the extravagant price of a coffin, but the honor of being buried from St. John's Church cost two shillings more! Marriage banns were to be had at St. John's for three-and-six.

Modern Margate is one of England's most popular watering-places. There are many pleasant walks and some fine buildings. One of the pleasure resorts is the ocean pier. Here, three times a week, a large band of picked musicians perform a good programme giving a promenade concert directly over the breakers.

It is the boast of the Britisher that his government is "parental;" it not only assumes to take charge of the individual, but it does in many particulars compel him to take care of himself. If, for instance, you are caught boarding or leaving a moving train you are fined "forty shillings" (ten dollars)—a favorite sum for a fine, by the way, is that same forty shillings.

The pier at Margate would seem to be an exception to the rule of safety; it cannot be called absolutely safe at night. The boat landing below is reached by several flights of wide stairs, and the lowest flight is open and unguarded, not only in daytime but also at night. In addition to this the lower part of the pier is not lighted at all, and it would be the easiest thing in the world on a dark night to walk off by accident into the water. Why more accidents and loss of life do not occur is surprising. Twopence admits you to the pier, and it is a popular democratic resort.

At night the scene near the pier is a lively one. Street restaurateurs, their barrows ablaze with flambeaux, line the highway and drive quite a business selling plates of oysters, mussels, cockles and snails, which are more or less tempting.

MARGATE.

MARGATE.

If you are fond of sea bathing by all means go to Margate. There is no high-rolling surf, but if you are a swimmer you will be all the better pleased. There are no ropes to lay hold of, none are necessary; you bathe in perfect safety and comfort, and, as at all English resorts, you bathe from a "machine."

In America bathing facilities consist of long rows of commodious wooden boxes placed on the beach at some distance from the surf. You purchase a bathing ticket for twenty-five or fifty cents, the price depending on whether you prefer a woolen to a cotton costume. You receive the suit and the key of your box. Then you put your valuables in an envelope sealed by yourself and hand them to the custodian, who places them in a separate box in an enormous safe, returning you a check tied to a rubber band, which latter you pass over your head and wear while bathing. You proceed to your "house," as we call it, disrobe and don your scant suit, lock your door and walk out and down to the edge of the water, where, as fancy dictates, you loll around on the beach, talking to your friends, or you plunge immediately into the breakers only to come out, dry yourself in the sun, cut up capers on the sand, chat or smoke, repeating the process *ad libitum.* Of course men and women bathe together.

Not so in England. There you bathe from "machines," small wooden houses, five feet square by ten feet high, mounted on four wheels. They have entrances back and front, each approached by a low flight of steps. You enter by one door in street costume, and having disrobed and donned your bathing garments, you give the signal, a horse is attached to the "machine" which is drawn a short distance into the water. You step down and out, disport yourself in the water as long as you please and reënter your box, to emerge therefrom once more in everyday habiliments. No lolling about the beach, no unseemly display of person; all is conducted in a proper, staid and exemplary manner—on the beach.

And in sooth, why should you walk around and smoke and chat with your friends on this occasion, in a costume, or lack of costume, which if worn at other times or places would land you in jail for exposure of person? This with reference to the American custom or costume.

In England it is worse in some respects, for while the women dress as they do here, the men bathe in a nude state, so to speak. They wear small trunks or loin cloths only, and men and women bathe together indiscriminately. Notices are posted in prominent places near the beach, boldly printed and bearing the English coat of arms, to the effect that in the water men and women must remain separate, and further that you will be fined forty shillings (of course forty shillings) if you are found nearer to a female than one hundred yards; but it is a dead letter law, and is entirely disregarded. I am not the most prudish man in the world, but I confess to having been shocked. Trunks did not suit me; I preferred and obtained a bathing costume which is to be had upon special application.

The beach is hard and smooth, broad and gently sloping. The bluff at Long Branch is not to be mentioned, scarcely, with the bold, beautiful white chalk cliffs that rise abruptly and picturesquely from the beach at Margate to a height of seventy-five feet. Along this bluff are miles of grassy, serpentine walks, gardens prettily laid out, dotted with summer houses and bounded by hedges and clover fields—a beautiful, natural landscape, artificially enhanced.

The favorite bathing place on the beach is managed by Charlotte Pettman. It is reached by a "coast guard" cutting in the cliff, an inclined passageway sloping from the road to the beach under the bridge. It is a sort of artificial cañon. Bathers are charged sixpence each, "six baths for two-and-six, twelve for four-and-six."

Mrs. Pettman advertises her baths by a circular which contains the following touching verse, no doubt assisting trade materially.

> "I pitied the dove, for my bosom was tender,
> I pitied the sigh that she gave to the wind;
> But I ne'er shall forget the superlative splendor
> Of Charlotte's sea baths, the pride of mankind."

In his early days of struggle the great Charles Dickens, for a few shillings, penned these lines as a "puff" of Day & Martin's blacking.

So far as the waves are concerned, the cliff is as solid as it appears to be, but it has yielded to the hand of man, and at Charlotte Pettman's baths there is a statue sculptured in the cliff, entitled "My first plunge." It is the life-size figure of a young and beautiful girl in bathing costume, just about to take "a header" from the platform. It is by Priestman, an English artist. The door is opened to art lovers for twopence each, or as much more as the generously disposed may be inclined to give, the proceeds being handed over to a local hospital.

One of Margate's architectural features, as seen in the accompanying illustration, is its handsome clock-tower, standing in a conspicuous position on the Marine drive. It was erected in honor of the Queen's Jubilee in 1887, and has a musical chime of bells.

Like Brighton and some other seaside resorts, Margate is democratic in the height of summer, but select in the autumn. In olden times the season commenced in June and continued until October. Margate offers every inducement to a prolonged season. While London is miserable under November fogs and humid atmosphere, Margate is brilliant with glorious days and bright skies; fine weather from August until Christmas.

Americans, of course, must flock to the largest hotel. They like size, and many of them patronize the Cliftonville Hotel, which, to be sure, is a large establishment in the most fashionable, and certainly the most attractive part of the town, near the grand cliffs, and overlooking the sea—a splendid site and a beautiful house exteriorly, but not as well kept as an Amerian host might care for it.

The White Hart Hotel, on the principal street, is a commercial house, and has a comfortable appearance from the outside, but the Nayland Rock Hotel, not far from the two railway stations, yet overlooking the sea, and from the windows of which you may toss a biscuit into the water (provided you have the biscuit), is to my knowledge a well-appointed hotel, with bedrooms as clean and comfortable and dining-room as cheerful as any hotel in the world. The cuisine is of the best. If great variety be absent, quality is present. The food is choice, and served in a neat, tempting and scrupulously clean manner.

European hotels, as a rule, are kept on the European plan ; at the Nayland Rock you have your choice. If you choose the American plan, the terms are very low for the accommodation afforded. Two dollars and a half a day secures you pleasant room, three good meals, lights and service. There are no extras. The wines are of first quality.

But I almost forgot an important item. I went to Margate for health and rest ; I found both there. After one week I returned to London "like a lion refreshed," and I shall always say, as everybody in London says, "there's a beautiful air at Margate."

TWO BRIGHTON HOTELS.

The company that owns the Grand Hotel and the Métropole in London, opened in March, 1890, a magnificent house at Brighton, on the English southern sea coast. "Magnificent" is the word. It is built of stone; it faces the sea; it has an acre or two at the back laid out in gardens, tennis courts, and pretty walks, after the style of the United States Hotel at Saratoga; there is a separate building on the grounds for a ball-room, in this respect resembling the Grand Union Hotel at the same American spa; the elegant drawing-room on the ground floor looks on the King's Road and the ocean; the library, which faces the garden, contains a large and choice selection of books by leading authors, and in the basement there are Turkish and Russian baths fitted up with a luxury and perfection of appointment not equalled in any other hotel. The proprietors have availed themselves of all the latest ideas in the construction and furnishing of hotels, and nothing that money can supply, or good taste can suggest, has been left undone to make the Métropole at Brighton what it is—one of the most beautiful and luxurious hotels in the world. It is said to accommodate six or seven hundred guests.

Besides this hotel, and the Grand and Métropole hotels in London, the same company owns another hotel in London, "The First Avenue," in Holborn; also the Burlington at Eastbourne; the Royal Pier Hotel at Ryde, Isle of Wight; the Métropole at Monte Carlo; and the Métropole at Cannes—all of them luxurious establishments.

TWO BRIGHTON HOTELS.

Brighton attracts visitors the year round ; in fact it is a city of no mean size, having a permanent population numbering an eighth of a million. It enjoys two seasons—one for the *hoi polloi*, which begins in June and lasts three months, and another for the fashionable world, which begins in September and continues till near Christmas. During the second season the prices at Brighton are greatly increased.

I entered one of the leading hotels one day about lunch time, and as is my custom before engaging rooms or partaking of a meal at an English hotel, I asked: " What is the charge for a *table d'hôte* lunch here? " " Two-and-six," replied the porter. As for seeing the lessee or manager of an English hotel, you can almost as easily secure an audience with the czar of all the Russias.

But to return to my muttons—or to the lunch, which, truth to tell, was good in quality and nicely served. My daughter heard the following conversation between the head waiter and the said porter as we were passing in to the " coffee-room" Quoth the former :—" How much did you tell these people for lunch ? " " Two-and-six," replied that blue-coated, gold-embroidered official. " That's wrong," remarked the head waiter, who almost lost his head as well as his temper. " Three shillings is the price to strangers," and three shillings each we had to pay.

This reminds me of the old story of the Englishman who was heard to remark about a man passing, who had a foreign look : " ' Ere's a stranger, Bill, 'eave 'arf a brick at 'im."

That they call these apartments in English hotels " Coffee Rooms," when they never serve in them a cup of coffee after dinner without a separate and extra charge, is rather exasperating.

The porters and officials at some English hotels are not, though it appears as if they were, in league with

TWO BRIGHTON HOTELS.

the cabmen. If you ask them about rates just before taking a drive they will occasionally mislead you and name a higher rate than the usual or legal one. For instance, I asked the clerk at another hotel in Brighton, what was the fare by the hour for a drive in an open cab or victoria holding two persons. "Four shillings per hour," quickly responded my misinformant. I knew better, for this was not my first visit to Brighton, but said nothing. To a cabman with a good-looking victoria who stood immediately opposite the hotel entrance I popped this question: "What will you charge us for an hour's drive along the beach and about the town?" "Two-and-six," briskly replied cabbie and we drove about the pretty place for a whole hour for the half crown.

A VISIT TO BLEAK HOUSE.

Bleak House, the scene of the novel of that name, is near the village of St. Albans, about twenty miles from London, and is described in the early part of the story as an "old-fashioned house with three peaks in the roof in front and a circular sweep leading to the porch." That there was more than one Bleak House in the mind of Dickens "there can be no possible probable manner of doubt," as Gilbert sings in "The Gondoliers," because at the close of the story one of the characters in it is made to say, "Both houses are your home, my dear, but the older Bleak House claims priority."

But the "Bleak House" which was for many years the home of Charles Dickens, and where he wrote many of his novels, was so named by the author after his famous story. It is located in the old-fashioned village of Broadstairs, on the North Sea, in the county of Kent, the garden of England, and is seventy-two miles from London, on the London, Chatham and Dover Railway. The population is given in the latest census as two thousand two hundred and sixty-three.

The house was formerly called Fort House, from its proximity to the British fortifications on the coast. It stands directly on the top of the chalk cliffs, seventy-five feet above the water, quite alone, and so near to the edge that from the portico a stone might be easily thrown into the surf—what little surf there is. It com-

BLEAK HOUSE.

mands a wide view of the ocean. In the southwest it looks toward Ramsgate, a seaside pleasure resort, distant five miles ; in the northeast toward Kingsgate. The house is appropriately named, for it is indeed bleak from Christmas until April, when the cold, biting northeast winds, for which these parts are noted, blow with all their might.

It was natural for Dickens to select such a spot for a residence. If he was not actuatly fond of the sea, he certainly had a great liking for the sea-coast, with which were associated the earliest memories of his childhood. It will be remembered that he was born at Portsmouth, a fortified seaport town, and the principal naval station of Great Britain, about one hundred miles southwest of London. Dickens lived at Portsmouth until he arrived at his majority. At Portsmouth he studied law, but he found Blackstone and Coke rather dry reading, and so went to London where, as every body knows, he entered upon his literary career by reporting parliamentary debates for the *Morning Chronicle*.

Bleak House is a plain, substantial, compact, three-story structure of burnt brick. It has grounds of one and a quarter acres in extent, and the property is what is called in England "freehold ;" value, two thousand seven hundred pounds sterling. A stone wall five feet high, encloses the house on two sides. One side of the house is a flat, blank wall, evidently planned so that an extension could be easily made, and the lower part of the front is protected by plain iron railings. The entrance is by a low flight of five steps leading up to a portico and doorway supported by Doric columns. Next the doorway, on the first story, a semi-circular bay window projects, and on the second story are two deep windows which open upon a pretty ornamental iron balcony, having a curved, sloping roof. A great deal of ivy softens the bareness of the architecture. It climbs up the walls and around the bay windows.

Dickens was very partial to the ivy plant, as his lyric, "The Ivy Green," testifies. He wrote several lyrics, but "The Ivy Green" which appeared originally in "Pickwick Papers" is the only one that has become familiar. It was first published as a song in the United States, and when a London publisher wished to reproduce it in England, Dickens refused the privilege except on the condition that the publisher pay ten guineas to the composer, Henry Russell.

Dickens was more thoughtful concerning Henry Russell's rights than this English composer is of the rights of others. I well remember that my predecessor on the *Home Journal*, the much beloved poet, George P. Morris, had a grudge against Russell, because Russell, in England, claimed to be the author of the words, "Woodman, Spare that Tree," as well as the composer of the music; and it is my humble opinion that the music in merit is far below Morris's poetry. The sentiment is beautiful, the words breathe a true, manly spirit and are full of deep feeling, while the music is plaintive, weak, childish — namby-pamby expresses it.

Russell did better with the English poet Mackay's song, "Cheer, Boys, Cheer," making it go with life and spirit, and he set appropriate music to our own Epes Sargent's song, "A Life on the Ocean Wave," in which you may fancy you almost see the good old sailing ship bowling along before the wind. Henry Russell, who, by the way, is a father of Clark Russell, the novelist, is still living in London—February, 1892.

As to the melody, "The Ivy Green," an astute critic says: "It seems to me the composer has failed to catch the poet's meaning. Dickens's words are as sombre and tender as the vine that deepens the shâdows and softens the ruggedness of decaying grandeur; while Russell's music is as free and sturdy as the hardiest oak." The song opens with this stanza:

> A dainty plant is the ivy green
>   That creepeth o'er ruins old,
> Of rich choice food are his meals, I ween,
>   In his cell so lone and cold ;
> The wall must be crumbled, the stones decayed,
>   To pleasure his dainty whim,
> And the mould'ring dust that years have made,
>   Is a merry meal for him.
> Creeping where no life is seen,
>   A rare old plant is the ivy green.

The house is about fifty years old, and contains ten rooms. Dickens's study was on the second floor, front. It has a southeastern outlook ; he was fond of the rising sun. The furniture and appointments of the room, which the writer saw in the autumn of 1891, remain as when Dickens left them—table with telescope, bookcase, plain wooden armchair, etc.—a very simply furnished study. He did not die at Bleak House, however, but at a short distance from it, on June 9, 1870, at Gads' Hill, " Higham by Rochester, Kent," as he was in the habit of dating from.

Dickens, at Bleak House, was a tenant of a Mr. Fosbury, but the house was sold after Dickens's death, and is at present owned in Broadstairs by " W. S. Blackburn, house and estate agent, undertaker, builder and decorator, and upholsterer and mover of furniture," by which man-of-many-trades the house was leased for a very short term to a Mrs. Whitehead, sister of the vicar of St. Peter's of Broadstairs, at an annual rent of six hundred dollars. Mr. Blackburn now offers the property for sale. It would make a cool and charming summer retreat for some American prince. Or let some large-hearted and large-pursed man like George W. Childs buy the precious property and present it to the village of Broadstairs.

BLEAK HOUSE FROM THE NORTH SEA.

TAKIN' NOTES
IN EDINBORO' TOWN.

Singular that more Americans do not "take in" Scotland when they are making the grand tour. Its historic interest and its scenic beauty are great. Glasgow is reached direct from New York by the fine fleet of Anchor boats, numbered among which are the "Furnessia," the "Devonia" and the "City of Rome." Excepting the last named the Scotch boats are slow in these days of "racers" and "greyhounds," but they are very comfortable vessels, as I know, from experience, and I have crossed in seven days by the "Rome"—crossed, that is, from Queenstown to New York.

If you don't care about bustling, busy Glasgow, with its smoke and its dirt, bonnie Edinburgh is distant only sixty-five minutes by express trains of the Caledonian railway, one of the best built and best equipped roads in Great Britain.

It hasn't the commerce of Glasgow, not being a seaport, but it is the cleanest city I ever visited, and one of the most beautiful. Many travellers consider London the most interesting city in the world, but to a casual observer, the four most attractive cities in Europe are Rome, Paris, Brussels and Edinburgh.

The whole city is built of granite and freestone. You don't see a brick excepting in a very few and very tall factory chimneys. To some eyes this is monotonous; to mine it is pleasing. It looks, and it is, substantial, solid and strong.

Don't come at any time, not even in August, without winter clothing. The winds are keen and cutting.

Umbrella and "waterproof" are indispensable; overshoes, also, if it is your habit to wear them, for "the rain it raineth every day"—so to speak. This is not the remark of a hasty tourist. I have been making trips to Scotland for the past twenty years and I have stayed there for weeks at a time.

It is cool here and rain is frequent, but everything in this life has its compensation. This is the twentieth day of August, 1891, and we have strawberries for breakfast every morning and fresh green peas are in season. Large, luscious strawberries and raspberries sixpence a quart. Edinburgh, remember, is four hundred miles north of London. The twilight is long and late, I was reading a badly-printed Scotch newspaper this evening by daylight at half-past eight.

Labor is cheap here, and yet boys do men's work, such as driving carts and sweeping the streets.

The drives in and about Edinburgh are very attractive, and there are no better roads anywhere.

There are tram-cars in the city: fare, inside, two pence; "on top," one penny. There are also two lines of cable cars.

In a "distillery agent's" window, in Princes street, I saw flasks of wine marked "two shillings." I stepped in and bought a flask. "One penny more," remarked the salesman. "For what," said I, inquiringly. "For the cork." When I reached my hotel I applied a corkscrew; it wouldn't budge. The penny "cork" was a glass stopper with a "worm," to screw on and off.

It strikes a stranger as rather odd to see men and boys carry so much on their heads and to see them balance their loads with such nicety. Instead of using small, light push carts, or delivering goods in baskets hanging on the arm, as is done in New York, Edinburgh boys use a tray or flat board with an edge turned up, in which they carry vegetables, meat, poultry, fruit, etc. This tray is placed on the head and is scarcely ever touched by the hand except to load or unload. The head in Edinburgh is made to do good physical service.

The house still stands, and is likely to stand for centuries, in which Walter Scott lived for years, and in which he wrote several of his novels. It is of granite, with a rounded (swelled) front, three stories high and about thirty feet wide. You must look it up when you go to Edinburgh—No. 39 Castle street. It is now used for office purposes, and is tenanted by doctors, lawyers, civil engineers and the like. In the transom window, over the door, you will see a small marble bust of the novelist.

Princes street, the principal street, is not very long, only about one mile, but as far as it goes it is not easily surpassed in any city. On one side are the principal hotels and business blocks, all of granite or freestone; on the other side are the handsome Princes Gardens with monuments and the magnificent Art Institute in the foreground, and in the background such buildings as the Castle, several churches and the Bank of Scotland.

The gardens, with their terraces, gravel walks, fountains, rustic seats, lawns and flower-beds are uncommonly attractive. It would seem that nowhere are the flowers brought to a higher state of cultivation than in the Princes Gardens.

Blackwood has a large but very quiet-looking shop in George street, not so crowded a thoroughfare as Princes street, but in which a very select business is transacted.

Thomas Nelson & Sons have the largest book publishing establishment in Scotland—I was going to say in Great Britain. Their business buildings cover a vast space of ground, and Mr. Nelson's residence, not far from Holyrood Palace and Arthur's Seat, is one of the most attractive private citizens' residences in this part of the country. It was only two or three years ago, so a coachman informed me, that Mr. Nelson gave ten thousand pounds to restore the front of the castle.

David Douglas, whose retail house is at No. 9 Castle

street, makes a specialty of publishing and republishing works of American authors, and finds his profit in it. You may pick up on his counters almost anything of Longfellow, Holmes, Lowell, Howells, Winter and Aldrich. Winter's "Shakespeare in England" and his latest work, "Gray Days and Gold," were both published by Douglas, duplicate plates being sent over to Macmillan of New York.

Talk of books being expensive in England: these very books by Winter which Macmillan sells in New York at seventy-five cents each, Douglas publishes at two shillings; in paper covers for one shilling—twenty-five cents.

Douglas's people tell me that Winter's books find a ready sale in Great Britain. The critics and the reading public are delighted with his sketches of English and Scotch scenery, and especially with his scholarly and beautiful descriptions of Stratford-on-Avon and Shakespeare's country. They think that no author has written with more reverence and feeling about Shakespeare. They find "his language poetical and his style artistic, with a Meissonier-like finish."

FRUITS AND FLOWERS.—In Scotland herrings are always sold by pairs, haddocks by threes. In England and Scotland fruit is sold by the pound, so are vegetables: and this fair and excellent method proves satisfactory to buyer and seller. Flowers and fruit are sold in the same shop: the signs read, "fruiterer and florist." Flowers are very high in price. They use growing flowers and living plants in pots very freely to decorate the dinner table, but this idea, which is pretty enough in its way, is carried too far in hotel dining-rooms. So many tall plants make the table look dark and heavy, and the broad leaves prevent you from seeing your neighbor or chatting with a friend on the other side of the table, for in some hotels they still persist in using the old-fashioned long tables which are neither home-like nor comfortable. Choice fruit, being either imported from the warmer climates or grown under glass, is very expensive in the British kingdom. You pay sixpence or a shilling for a peach or nectarine; two shillings each for choice varieties. The largest and handsomest peach ever grown, possibly, or certainly ever shown, was exhibited last summer in a shop window in Buchanan street, Glasgow. It weighed eighteen ounces, price three-and-sixpence.

The capital of Scotland is always spelled Edinburgh, but is always pronounced Edinboro'.

In the stamp department of the post-office in Edinburgh there is a shallow indentation about four inches square in the table, in which a piece of felt is kept constantly damp, Instead of putting the stamp on your tongue you pass it over the piece of felt before placing it on the envelope. Small matter, but very convenient, and shows thoughtfulness on the part of the authorities.

STREET RELIGION.—There's a great deal of poverty and drunkenness in Edinburgh, but there is also a great deal of religion. All the churches are well attended on Sunday, and there are preaching, praying and singing in the public streets. Church choirs, men and women, stand and sing in the public highways. In the lower quarters of the city they attract people with a harmonium, which is wheeled about from place to place. Passers-by stop, join in the singing, and in fine weather uncover their heads. The singers are not paid for their services.

THE DOGS.—Here's a hint for the society which Mr. Henry Bergh founded:—On the sidewalk in front of large shops and public buildings in Glasgow and Edinburgh they place small earthenware or iron vessels filled with water for passing dogs. The vessel is simply and legibly marked "DOG." Probably the dogs cannot read, but they seem to know or to "nose out" the shops where such a humane practice is carried out. But a certain Scotch editor contends that Scotch dogs can read.

INDIA RUBBER PAVEMENT.—The attention of every stranger who walks in Princes street, Edinburgh, is immediately arrested as soon as he gets in front of a certain shop, nearly opposite the castle, where rubber goods are sold. His attention is arrested because he finds himself on a yielding pavement. It is a rubber "sidewalk" (as we say in New York), and was laid there by the enterprising shopkeeper. It is very pleasant and comfortable to walk on, and so durable that the authorities have talked about putting down rubber pavements on both sides of Princes street.

GLASGOW UNIVERSITY. — There is not much for the tourist to see in Glasgow except the university, the cathedral, founded in the fourteenth century, and the municipal buildings. But the first-named is worth walking many miles to visit, if one is interested in such things. I spent several hours in the university with pleasure and profit. This university, Glasgow people claim, is the finest in Scotland. It accommodates twenty-three hundred students, who pay on an average of forty pounds a year. It is generously endowed. The buildings are of granite and present a noble appearance, standing on very high ground in their own large park, which is beautifully laid out with terraces, flower beds and gravel walks. There are some grand old trees in the park, and a pretty winding lake, over which are thrown many picturesque bridges. Though it is a seat of learning, you will not expect the services of a college professor as a cicerone, but you might naturally expect to hear fair English spoken. The liveried servant who guides you will tell you, with strong aspirations, of the "helementary" classes and the "school of harts." In decribing the *modus operandi* of taking the gold medal, the graduate sitting in a very high-backed chair, which is several hundred years old, you will be told "it's a very 'igh honor."

In the " Edinburgh Café," a fairish kind of restaurant

in Princes street, opposite the Scott monument, a penny is charged for the privilege of washing your hands, and a penny for the use of a napkin. The majority of this café's customers, however, if the truth must be told, make a *mouchoir* serve for a *serviette*.

SLIPPERS SUPPLIED FREE.—If you go to Philp's Cockburn (pronounced Coburn) Hotel in Edinburgh, it matters not if you have forgotten to pack your slippers in your portmanteau, for the porter will provide you with a pair. One hundred pairs of red morocco slippers are kept at this hotel for the use of guests. A foot of any size can be accommodated, and there is no charge.

Smoking is not allowed in bedrooms of Scotch hotels, and a notice to that effect is posted in each room. "Smoking rooms" are provided, and only such apartment may be used for this purpose. They are both smoky and dingy.

AN EDINBURGH DOLLAR DINNER.—I have dined at the leading hotels in New York, at "The States," in Saratoga, the Breslin, at Lake Hopatcong, and my experience includes the leading hotels in the principal European capitals, and the leading hotels in the Southern and far Western States, as far as California, yet I can say that the *table d'hôte* dinner served at Philp's Cockburn Hotel, Edinburgh (on Sunday, August 24, 1890), will rank with the fare at any of these houses, and it excels the table d'hôte at some high-priced hotels in London and Paris. And the price charged for this dinner was very moderate—only four shillings, about one dollar. The dinner included grouse, peaches, strawberries and nectarines, and from the hare soup down to the dessert, everything was well cooked and nicely served. The charge is remarkably moderate when it is understood that this is a "temperance house," and when you know that the choice fruit is grown under glass at high cost. The dinner would have been perfect with *café noir* at the close, but this is not served in British hotels without additional charge.

THE BURNS MONUMENT.

If Baltimore is the monumental city of the United States, Edinburgh may surely be called the monumental city of the United Kingdom. The majority of its public buildings, of freestone or granite, are noble structures standing on hills in the heart of the city, and for their situation alone would command admiration—the old Castle, Nelson moument, the city prison, the National Gallery, the Bank of Scotland, etc. No bank in the world occupies a more commandiug site than the one just named. Owing to the peculiar natural formation of the land upon which the city is built, an observer may stand in one spot in Edinburgh (say the Waverly Gardens) and see a greater number of splendid buildings at a glance than may be seen simultaneously from the level in any other city.

Not among the largest by any means but among the most interesting must be reckoned the Burns monument, which occupies a high position near its still higher neighbor, the Nelson monument, on Calton Hill. The Burns monument was built in 1830 for the purpose of containing a marble statue of the poet by Flaxman. The building, of freestone, is a circular temple on a quadrangular basement surrounded by a peristyle of twelve Corinthian columns which support an entablature and cornice. Over this is a cupola, a restoration of the monument of Lysicrates at Athens. The whole is surmounted by a tripod supported by winged griffins. The extreme height of the structure is fifty feet, the twelve outside columns are fourteen feet high and the twelve inside columns are ten feet high. The latter are of freestone painted to represent variegated marble. The cost of the monument and statue was three thousand three hundred pounds sterling (about sixteen thousand five hundred dollars)—not a large sum considering the result attained.

Besides the statue of the poet, the monument holds a number of relics—letters written by or to Burns, the worm-eaten three legged stool upon which the poet sat in 1786 and '87 while correcting the proofs of his poems, and other things of interest. One of the most interesting letters is that subjoined. As is well known, the poet spelled his name Burness (his family name) until the publication of his poems in 1786. The letter is thus addressed:

To
    Mr. James Burness,
        Writer, Montrose.

My Dear Cousin:
When you offered me money assistance, little did I think I should want it so soon. A rascal of a haberdasher to whom I owe a considerable bill, taking into his head that I am dying, has commenced a process against me and will infallibly put my emaciated body into jail. Will you be so good as to accommodate me, and that by return of post, with ten pounds. O, James, did you know the pride of my heart you would feel doubly for me. Alas, I am not used to beg. The worse of it is my health was coming about finely, you know, and my physician assures me that melancholy and low spirits are half my disease. Guess then my horrors since this business began. If I had it settled I would be, I think, quite well in a manner. O, do not disappoint me.

Among other relics preserved in frames and hung on the walls is the printed newspaper report of Burns's death. This occurred at Dumfries, July 21, 1796, and the report appeared in the London *Herald* of July 27— nearly one week after. The London *Herald* of that day was a very small sheet, about fifteen inches long and only four columns wide, price fourpence halfpenny a copy. The obituary notice is unique and is worth reproducing to-day:

DEATH OF MR. ROBERT BURNS,
THE CELEBRATED POET.

On the twenty-first instant died at Dumfries, after a lingering illness, the celebrated Robert Burns. His poetical compositions, distinguished equally by the force of native humor, by the warmth and tenderness of passion, and by the glowing touches of a descriptive pencil, will remain a lasting monument of the vigor and versatility of a mind, guided only by the light of nature and the inspirations of genius. The public, to whose amusement he so largely contributed, will learn with regret that the last months of his short life were spent in sickness and indigence, and his widow and five infant children, and in the hourly expectation of a sixth, is now left without any resource but what she may hope from the regard due to the memory of her husband.

Apropos to the subject come these remarks in the New York *Sun:*

It is better to write a little book that is full of heart and brains than a big book that lacks both. Probably there is no writer but Robert Burns who has made such broad and enduring renown as his through a book as small as his. This thought arose while taking a glimpse of a new statue of the bard that is to be erected in a city out West. There is a statue of Burns in our Central Park; there is another up at Albany; there is at least one in Australia, and there are several statues of him in the British Isles. All that he wrote appears as a tiny volume in the latest edition of his works; much of it is in a dialect that is hard to be understood by English-speaking people, and he died in obscurity about one hundred years ago. Yet there are probably as many public statues of him in various parts of the globe as there are of Shakespeare, who wrote voluminously.

Monuments, however, are not Edinburgh's only attractions, but do not count on seeing the sights there on Sunday. The day is closely and strictly observed.

London is surely quiet enough on a Sunday, but it is gayety itself when compared with the capital of Scotland. Not a shop is open; even the drug shops are open only during two hours. Everything is shut as tight as a drum in Edinburgh except the churches, and to these you must either walk or hire a carriage, for not the wheel of an omnibus or car turns on Sunday.

THE BURNS MONUMENT.

RIGHT REVEREND THE MODERATOR,
JAMES MACGREGOR, D. D.

In September, 1890, I had the privilege of listening to England's foremost preacher, Rev. C. H. Spurgeon, in his Tabernacle at Newington Butts, in London; and one year later, on Sunday, September 16, 1891, happening to be in Edinburgh, I made it a point to hear the Rev. James Macgregor, the leading light of the Scotch Presbyterian Church.

Americans mostly flock to St. Giles's in Canongate, on account of its age and historical associations. They attend divine service there early in the morning with the soldiers from the old castle. But I wanted to hear a great preacher, so I repaired to Synod Hall, which the members of St. Cuthbert's parish were using as a temporary place of worship.

The extensive alterations, internally and externally, which were then making in St. Cuthbert's Church, will render it, in some respects, worthy of the site, and of its long and honorable history. The present structure dates from the year 1775. Only the tower and spire of the old church will be retained, and the new edifice, which will not be finished until the autumn of 1892, will accommodate a much larger number of people than the former building did.

It is a notable fact that on the spot where the building stands—under the Castle Rock of Edinburgh—Christian worship has been continuously maintained for more than a thousand years. It is, indeed, one of the very oldest shrines in Scotland, hallowed by the prayers of the faithful, which have arisen from it for century upon century.

Originally a mere Culdee cell, dedicated to the memory of Cuthbert, the monk of Lindisfarne, it has passed through a variety of forms. Changing with the revolutions of Scottish history, it has been Roman Catholic, Presbyterian, Episcopalian, and finally Presbyterian.

The whole aspect of the place where it rose has changed. The Nor' Loch, which stretched away from it eastward under the Castle Rock, has disappeared; the sweep of undulating country has been transformed into wide streets; a great city has arisen around it; and it still remains what it has been for ages, a centre of Christian influence to a wide community.

It is interesting as a piece of religious history to note that within little more than a stone's throw of the site of the present structure is the spot where the first General Assembly was held on the 20th of December, 1560. It consisted of forty-two members, of whom only six were ministers. The first name on the roll is that of "John Knox." It was a fully equipped Ecclesiastical Convention, and at once proceeded to important business. There is no parallel instance of a court with such authority springing so suddenly into being. That authority was almost sovereign. It was based on the sanction and support of the popular will. With a power to which the Scottish Parliament never attained, it was the representative assembly of the Scottish people, embracing within it from the very beginning the pith of the nation's manhood. The General Assembly was simply the Scotch people convened, through their natural representatives, to settle their own religious affairs. And they did it effectually. Never was a change so radical and so beneficial effected in as brief a space of time as that accomplished by the Scottish Reformation.

So much for the past. Synod Hall, which, as I have said, was temporarily occupied by the congregation of St. Cuthbert's, is a large freestone building occupying a prominent site in Castle Terrace opposite the back of the Castle. It accommodates about twenty-five hundred people. A bold placard in the vestibule informed the hundreds of strangers in and about the vestibule that they would be admitted into the body of the church a few minutes before the services commenced. The "strangers" waited with all the patience they could command, and when the sign was made by one of the deacons, they flocked in, a large space at the back of the house being set apart for them. Soon every seat was occupied and people were requested to please sit closer together. Then, when there was not an inch of room to spare on the benches, chairs were placed in the aisles.

Dr. James Macgregor, the present minister, was appointed Moderator of the General Assembly for the current year in May, 1891. He has been connected with St. Cuthbert's for fourteen years, having succeeded Dr. Barclay, now in Montreal. St. Cuthbert's, or, as it is also called, the "West End Church," is not given to making changes oftener than is necessary. Dr. Barclay is said to be the only man who ever left St. Cuthbert's; his predecessors all died at their posts.

In Synod Hall there is no organ; the music was supplied by the congregation and a choir. St. Cuthbert's usually rejoices in a large choir, but on the occasion of my visit many of its members were "away on their holidays," as they call their vacation in Great Britain. The choir on that Sunday numbered fifteen—three men and twelve of the gentler sex.

Mr. Edie, a promising and rather brilliant man under thirty, who has a clear voice and a Scotch accent is assistant to Dr. Macgregor. The first selection of song which he gave out was the 129th Psalm:

> Lord of the worlds above
>   How pleasant and how fair
> The dwellings of Thy love,
>   The earthly temples are.

Then Mr. Edie read the 62d Chapter of Isaiah. The next selection for the congregation was the 102d Psalm, 6th Verse: "And God in His glory shall appear;" and then the 356th Hymn: "Te Deum Laudamus."

Mr. Edie concluded his part of the services with a fervent and beautiful prayer in which, after the Queen, Prince of Wales, the princess, the judges and magistrates of great Britain were enumerated, special mention was made of the President and people of the United States; of "our wandering brethren, the children of Israel; of our Catholic brethren; bless all honorable business men; bless our friends and also those who have wronged us."

Dr. Macgregor, who then rose from a chair, took his text from the 4th Chapter, 1st Verse, of "Hosea:" "Hear the word of the Lord, ye children of Israel,"

Then followed a brilliant discourse on the history of the Jewish race, in which, incidentally, much information was conveyed, the main ideas being: first, that the government of Great Britain should use its influence in behalf of the Russian refugees; second that the Christian people owe much to the Jews and should therefore be most charitable toward them.

The minister paid a high tribute to the chosen people and their characteristics. He said that the countries which abused them most, Spain and Portugal, had been least prosperous, and it would be strange, indeed, if Russia suffered not for its inhuman persecution of them; that, in fact, it was suffering.

Notwithstanding that they had been downtrodden for centuries, the Jews were vastly stronger in numbers to-day than ever before in the history of the world, numbering at the present time twelve millions.

The speaker showed that the decline of Jerusalem was owing to the comparatively small number of Jews there in later years, and he strongly advocated their return.

To quote the doctor almost verbatim: "I may be criticised for criticising Russia. Some may say: 'Let each country look after its own affairs, and it will have enough to do. It is none of England's business what Russia does,' but I say it is the business of every civilized country, of every civilized man; it is your business and my business; it affects each and every one of us; it hurts you and me, and it is to be hoped that Great Britain will lift up its voice and use its influence in behalf of these much injured refugees."

If this discourse had been especially prepared to deliver before a strictly and exclusively Jewish assemblage, it could not have been more complimentary to their people. One of its "points" was thus worded: "There must be something wrong with that man's head—with that man's heart who despises the Jews."

Dr. Macgregor has the title of one of Her Majesty's chaplains; he is a member of the Hon. Royal Scottish Academy, and a member of the Royal Society of Edinburgh, but a self-made man withal. He is not ashamed

RIGHT REVEREND THE MODERATOR. 121

to acknowledge that his parents were poor and modest. He may have lacked early advantages, but he certainly has made the best of his later opportunies. He is a man of fine intellect ; a ripe scholar, with broad and liberal views. His language is choice, and yet the fine phrases and well selected words seem to follow each other with great ease. His diction is neither stilted nor is it too simple but that of an intellectual man who is addressing intelligent people.

His voice, notwithstanding a certain and unmistakable nasal quality, is penetrating—and his elocutionary powers are great. I was on the last bench, with my back against the wall, and I heard almost every word. I could not follow the speaker quickly on account of his strong Scottish accent—"murdering" became "mu*rr*-de*rr*ing," with a most decided roll of the *r*, and "Turks" came to me in two syllables, something like "Turreks," while "earth" was changed to "airth," with the *r* in the middle by no means slighted.

The speaker's facial expressions were a study, and his gesticulations at times strikingly dramatic. He appealed in tender and pathetic tones to the hearts of his hearers, with hands uplifted as if in supplication, and then again he would raise his head and fold his arms across his chest in a Napoleonic, defiant attitude when combating the arguments of an imaginary adversary.

In fact, he does not seem to be addressing a large audience, but talking to and debating with but one person, and each person in the congregation might imagine that he was that one. He takes both sides in the debate, and makes both effective, but he carries the day for his own because he is on the side of right.

Dr. Macgregor closed the service with Hymn 117 :

> Arm of the Lord, awake, awake !
> Put on Thy strength, the nations shake ;
> And let the world, adoring see
> Triumphs of mercy wrought by Thee.

When the moderator is in the pulpit you do not notice that he is below the medium height; only when he steps down, and when you stand by his side, do you observe that he is small of stature—not much over five feet. His eye has a most kindly expression, his voice is pleasing in conversation, and his manner gracious and gentle. The accompanying portrait is reproduced from a photograph made by John Moffatt, 125 Princes street, Edinburgh.

On the day I had the good fortune to be present, there were in the congregation many prominent members of the Archæological Society of Scotland, who were on a temporary visit to Edinburgh, including the Bishop of Carlisle and the Earl of Percy, heir to the dukedom of Northumberland.

After the service I had the honor of being presented to Dr. Macgregor by a member of this society, in "The Moderator's Room," so inscribed on the door. Upon hearing that I was "from the States," he immediately expressed his great admiration for the country and its form of government. He seemed to be well-informed regarding our people and the country, and said that one of his cherished hopes was to make us a visit.

CROSSING THE CHANNEL.

There are many ways of "crossing" between the Continent and the English coast, or *vice versa*. The best steamers between England and Holland are those which go from Rotterdam to Harwich. Harwich (Anglice, Harridge) is about a two hours' run up to London. I have tried the different ways of crossing from the French coast to England—via Newhaven and Dieppe, Folkstone and Boulogne, and Calais and Dover. The last route is by far the best. It would be preferred over all others, if for only one reason, because it is the shortest, the English Channel being "disagreeable" at least one half the year. The Calais and Dover boats are advertised to make the trip between the two points "in seventy minutes," and they do actually make it in one hour and a quarter. The other routes are much longer. No small craft that ply on the English waters are as beautiful in their appointments as our Hudson river boats, or those for instance of the Fall River line, but they are staunch and swift, and they are manned by as brave a set of seamen as ever trod a deck. The English boats are proof against wind and wave, the only danger being from fire or fog, but as they are officered by skillful and experienced navigators, and are very carefully handled, the danger is reduced to a minimum.

PARIS HOTELS.

Paris is not in the least behind other cities in the number of its hotels nor in the variety of accommodations offered. Your choice must depend first upon the length of your purse; second, upon the length of your stay; third, the purpose of your visit. The number in the party and their individual tastes and requirements must also be taken into account.

I have not passed near so much time in Paris as in London. The most I can do is to suggest a few of the choicest hotels and *pensions* with which I am acquainted, giving their rates and distinctive features.

For information as to Where to Dine in Paris I must refer the reader to a chapter further on, entitled "The Restaurants of Paris," by that facile magazinist and connoisseur in many arts, Mr. Theodore Child. It first appeared in a book entitled "Living Paris," which was published in London three years ago by Ward & Downey, and is the most complete and comprehensive Guide to Paris I have ever seen.

THE GRAND HOTEL.

The Grand Hotel is one of the largest and most expensive. It is grand in size; grand in appointments. It is not a cheap house in any sense of that term, and possibly for that reason is largely patronized by Americans. The building occupies a square block facing that magnificent street, l'Avenue de l' Opéra, diagonally across from the Grand Opera House. It encloses a large courtyard with fountains and parterres. The *caves* of the Grand are ranked as one of the sights of Paris ; they are stocked with the choicest of wines. Rooms from six francs per day : table d'hôte dinner, seven francs.

HOTEL CONTINENTAL.

The Continental, on the corner of the rue de Rivoli and rue Castiglione, is opposite the gardens of the Tuileries. Near by are Hotel des Invalides, the Madeleine, the Eiffel Tower and other interesting buildings. It is large and elegant—grander than the Grand. The grounds, with the structure and furnishing are said to have cost a few millions of francs, and it may be readily believed. Some of the rooms are palatial in size, furniture and decorations.

The rates at the Continental are a little lower than at the Grand. They range all the way from five francs to thirty-five francs per day for room ; lights and attendance extra. Breakfast of coffee, chocolate or tea with rolls, from one to two francs ; breakfast proper, or *déjeuner à la fourchette*, five francs, wine and coffee included. Table d'hôte dinner, seven francs. At all Paris hotels wine is included in the charge for dinner, but at the Continental on Sundays, champagne as well as *vin ordinaire* is served free, but not, as in the case of the latter, in unlimited quantity.

HOTEL MEURICE.

Smaller than these two hotels and for that reason thought by some to be more select is the Hotel Meurice, in rue de Rivoli. It is near rue Castiglione and opposite the Tuileries gardens, altogether a beautiful location. Issuing from the handsome courtyard and turning to the left, a few minutes walk brings you to the Palais Royal and the Louvre galleries ; or turning to the right a few steps bring you past the hotel Continental, to Place de la Concorde and the Champs Élysées. It may seem strange to those who have not lived in continental hotels, to note that the hotel Meurice is scrupulously clean. You observe this in its beautiful courtyard, in its handsome dining-room and in the neatly kept bedrooms.

The hotel is patronized by leading New York families and by the best English society, and it ranks as does the Brunswick or the Victoria in New York. The *cuisine* of the house is famous and its cellars contain rare wines. Hotel Meurice was established in 1815 and its present proprietor has kept it for more than thirty years. If your stay in Paris is to cover a week or more, you—and especially the ladies of your party—will find this hotel a thoroughly agreeably place of sojourn ; Baedeker counsels avoiding the largest hotels if you are accompanied by ladies. Hotel Meurice has electric light, and new plumbing was put in a few years ago. It accommodates two hundred guests. Single rooms from five francs per day ; apartments from fifteen to one hundred francs. Table d'hôte dinner, at six P.M., six francs. Proprietor, H. Schëurich ; address, 228 rue de Rivoli.

HOTEL CHATHAM.

Hotel Chatham is justly famed as one of the most elegantly appointed of Paris hotels. I have known it for twenty years, and for twenty-five years it has been the temporary home of travellers of all nations,—those who demand the best hotel accommodations. Hotel Chatham occupies a central location, near the Opéra, rue de la Paix, the theatres, and the best shopping streets. Once inside the house, however, and an air of tranquility reigns that is in marked contrast to the busy life of the city, in the midst of which the hotel is situated. The first feature of the Hotel Chatham that attracts attention is the large, light, and spacious courtyard, fifty by one hundred feet. It makes an impression that gains in favor when you see the apartments. The grand salon, the reading-room and café look out upon this courtyard, which is embellished with plants and flowers,

The sleeping apartments are beautifully furnished, have plenty of light and good ventilation. There are elegant suites, also choice single and double rooms. The decorations are in good taste. In the best apartments the walls are not hung with paper, but are covered with stuffs—a mixture of worsted and soft silks. Hot and cold water on every floor. Two features especially commend themselves to those who are acquainted with foreign hotels; there are two Otis elevators, and the house is lighted throughout by electricity—shedding a light in the rooms, not of one *bougie*, but of twenty. The cuisine represents the perfection of the culinary art, and the wine-cellars are celebrated for their famous vintages.

The Hotel Chatham is the home of the best people and many Americans annually seek its hospitality. The Harpers, for instance, members of the great publishing house, are among its regular guests. The present proprietor is M. H. Holzschuch, son of the late owner, under whom the house acquired its wide fame. Hotel Chatham is at 17 and 19 rue Daunou, between rue de la Paix and Boulevard des Capucines.

HOTEL BINDA.

Everybody in Paris knows the Hotel Binda, and it is known by a great many people who have never been in Paris. With New Yorkers the house is a favorite because it is kept by Mr. Charles Binda who for years was manager of Delmonico's, and this settles at once and satisfactorily the important question of *cuisine*. The house was opened in 1878. It is solidly built of stone, five stories high, and is an imposing structure. It stands in rue de l'Echelle, on a corner of the avenue de l'Opéra, the principal business street of Paris, and probably the handsomest shopping street in the world. It is most conveniently located for the principal places of interest—the Grand Opera, Palais Royal, the Louvre galleries, etc. One minute's walk brings you to the rue de Rivoli, that wide open street, one side of which is flanked by the open and beautiful gardens of the Tuileries.

If in the heat of a summer day in walking to Place Vendome or to the Champs Élysées, you wish to avoid sunny rue de Rivoli, shade is at your very door in the narrow but picturesque rue St. Honoré, which, with its little shops, its hotels, old churches, etc., is a feature of outdoor life in Paris.

The Grand Opera is at the other end of the Avenue de l'Opéra, a short walk. But omnibuses pass the door, by which you can reach any part of Paris at the expense of a few sous. And, for that matter, it is only a thirty-cent cab fare to the Grand Opera, to the offices of the American Minister, Whitelaw Reid, in Avenue Hoche, or to the Anglo-American Bank on the corner of Chaussée d'Antin and rue Meyerbeer. *Cocher* will go fast enough if by the course and slow enough (too slow) if by the hour.

Instead of a courtyard such as many hotels in Paris have, and which in some cases are useless, the space on the ground floor is used by the Binda for a grand, glass-enclosed reception and reading-room, beautifully lighted by day and by night. There is also a grand drawing-room and a smoking-room, which unlike the dingy rooms turned over to the use of men in some English hotels is, in the Binda, a very bright and attractive apartment.

All the apartments are comfortably and tastefully furnished, but some of the rooms are furnished in palatial style. There are baths on every floor and some rooms have running water. Of course there are electric lights and an *ascenseur*, Anglice "lift." But for all its grandeur, one may live at the Binda at moderate cost.

If you know about how wide you wish to open your purse in selecting apartments you can tell as precisely as you could in an American hotel how much your bill will amount to for a stay of five days or five weeks. Single rooms may be had from seven to twelve francs per day; double rooms from fourteen to thirty francs. Special rates, lower than these, are made to guests remaining a length of time. Here is the tariff for the dining-room: Plain breakfast (tea or chocolate) 1f. 50c., about 30 cents; table d'hôte dinner, served at separate tables, 6f., servant's board 6f. per day. No charge is made for attendance.

That Charles Binda is proprietor is guarantee that the table is equal to the Cambridge in New York, or the Albemarle in London, and these satisfy the most fastidious. Mr. Binda is famous for his *cuisine*, but he prides himself most upon the quality of his guests. He demands that above and beyond everything else his house shall be select, and it is so in the fullest sense. You may meet crowned heads and princes there. Hon. Thomas L. James, one of New York's honored and honorable citizens, with his charming family, stayed at the Binda while he was in Paris last summer, and I also saw Judge Dittenhoefer, the family of Vice-Consul

Hooper, and other well-known Americans in the reading-room. Yes, the Binda is a select family hotel. Address No. 11 rue de l'Echelle.

HOTEL ANGLO-FRANÇAIS.

There are several comparatively small but decidedly pleasant hotels in rue Castiglione—Hotel Liverpool, Hotel Balmoral and Hotel Anglo-Français. The last-named is especially to be commended for its choice location, the comfort and cleanliness of its rooms, its appetizing cuisine, and its remarkably moderate charges. It is in rue Castiglione, directly opposite the Continental; two blocks one way from the Column Vendome, two blocks from the Place de la Concorde, near the Champs Élysées, and only a few hundred feet from the beautiful gardens of the Tuileries.

Like the majority of Paris hotels, the Anglo-Français is entered by a court-yard, but unlike some of them, the ventilation and lighting of the house are good. It has ample room for more than one hundred guests, and they can be made very comfortable.

The house is kept on the American as well as on the European plan. If you adopt the system which prevails abroad, you may hire a single room as low as four francs per day, or a double room from seven francs per day; breakfast, three francs; luncheon, four francs; table d'hôte dinner, six francs. This figure includes good wine in *quantum sufficit*, as a medical man might say. As at nearly all Continental hotels, "service" is charged. In this instance it is one franc per day; and you pay for lights—item seventy-five centimes, about fifteen cents.

But if you wish to be relieved of all this detail and save the bother of reckoning, you can stay at the Anglo-

Français, and your whole bill per day for board, lodging, lights, wine, etc., will be the moderate sum of fifteen francs (three dollars), which, considering the appointments of the house, the excellent table and the attention you receive, is an uncommonly low rate.

The proprietor is a gentleman of decidedly pleasant and courteous manners, who, having lived in England for twenty years, is perfectly at home in the English language as well as his native tongue.

If you desire to mix with an ultra-fashionable set, the Bristol is your house ; if you want to see and be with Americans only, then select the Grand. The Continental is the place for those who would feast their eyes on palatial salons : at the Anglo-Français you will get into the company of good people from different countries, you can be quiet and comfortable and made to feel at home, as is to be expected in a smaller house. Moreover, your purse will be lightly drawn upon in accordance with the figures given above. Proprietor, Paul Vargues ; address, No. 6 rue Castiglione.

HOTEL DE LILLE ET D' ALBION, in rue St. Honoré is not a very large house, but it is ranked among the best, although its charges are quite moderate. It has baths, lift, electric light and English billiard tables, its modern contrivances including telephonic communication with the leading European cities. The sanitary arrangements are said to be perfect. The location is central for shopping, for places of amusement and points of interest, being near Place Vendome, Tuileries Gardens and the Opera. Mail address, 223 rue St. Honoré : telegraph address, Lillalbion, Paris.

HOTEL BRISTOL AND HOTEL DU RHIN both front on the Place Vendome ; you can't miss them : they are near the tall and graceful Column Vendome which pierces the sky from the centre of the square. There is no question as to the excellence of either of these houses. Both are patronized by a select class of patrons ; the former is the home of the Prince of Wales when he visits Paris.

HOTEL LIVERPOOL is patronized by the Astors. To Americans this information conveys more than could be detailed in a whole page of description. It is situated at 11 rue Castiglione, a wide and fashionable thoroughfare leading from Place Vendome to the Tuileries Gardens. The house was recently newly fitted up and has a hydraulic lift. There are large apartments for families making a more or less prolonged stay ; smaller apartments for transient guests.

HOTEL DE L'ATHÉNÉE. Of hotels just as select as any of those mentioned, there are a score or more. Among them may be mentioned the Hotel de l'Athénée, 15 rue Scribe. It was recently enlarged, the whole of the Théâtre de l'Athénée having been added, and the former dining-room is now converted into a reading room. There are two bath-rooms on each floor. The appointments include a parlor, a reading room, a restaurant a la carte, and two private dining-rooms. There are 180 rooms in all, which rent from four francs to twenty francs a day, but there are not very many rooms in the house at four francs.

DES DEUX MONDES.—A comfortable family hotel, newly and tastefully furnished, is the Hotel des Deux Mondes, 22 Avenue de l'Opéra, facing full south. The charges are moderate and the table d'hôte good.

PRINCE ALBERT.—If price alone is a recommendation there is the Hotel du Prince Albert, 5 rue St. Hyacinthe, near the Tuileries. Rooms from 2 francs 50 centimes per day with even lower terms for the winter. The house seeks American patronage.

HOTEL BRIGHTON, 218 rue de Rivoli. Rooms from 6 francs per day : breakfast, 2 francs, dinner 7 francs. Proprietor, A. Bastianello.

HOTEL CAMPBELL.—This favorite house with an English name has changed hands, lately. Arthur Geissler is the new proprietor. It is at 61 and 63 Avenue de Friedland, a pleasant and fashionable location, near the grand drive of the Champs Élysées. The house is in a healthy condition and the rates are moderate, Hotel Campbell is easy to find ; it is close to the Arc de Triomphe.

PENSIONS OF THE FIRST CLASS.

But you are not forced to patronize any hotel, large or small; there are many very delightful *pensions* or boarding houses in Paris. These some people prefer, if their party includes ladies, or if they intend to make a protracted stay. A few of these *pensions* are presided over by American women.

THE LAFOND combines some of the best features of hotel and *pension*. It is at 14 rue de la Tremoille, near the Champs Élysées. It is called "a comfortable American home," and is made all the more comfortable by having a lift. Rates for two persons in one room, with three meals per day, 18 to 30 francs per day; single rooms, 10 to 15 francs per day; children and servants, half rates. These figures include all charges; the American plan. If you prefer the European plan, these rates prevail—breakfast, two to four francs; luncheon, three francs: dinner at 7 P.M., five francs. Cable address, Lafhotel, Paris.

HOTEL DE DIJON is situated in rue Canmartin, between the Opéra and the Madeleine. It is a family *pension*, and the charges range from 7 to 10 francs per day, according to rooms. Soirées are held every Friday with music, singing and dancing. The table d'hôte is good; there are reading, smoking and bath-rooms.

THE VAN PELT PENSION at 69 Boulevard St. Michel is kept by Mrs. E. L. Van Pelt, a Philadelphia woman who took with her to Paris the best American references. This place has many features which commend it to the stranger in Paris. Its location, facing the Luxembourg Gardens, is near the famous art schools and the Sorbonne, where free lectures are given, thus making this a desirable residence for students. It is within easy access by omnibus, cab or train to all parts of Paris and environs. The house stands on a corner, and all the rooms are exposed to the sun and air. A balcony surrounds the first floor. French is the language of the household, and a chaperon accompanies ladies to lectures, etc. There is a separate table for those who prefer to speak English.

AMERICAN FAMILY HOME.—This term is appropriately applied to the *pension de famille* presided over by a young French widow whose personal beauty and grace of manner are more than marked. Reference is made to Madame Veuve Léon Glatz, who is assisted in her duties by her sister. Both of them speak English with a pretty and piquant accent. The Glatz *pension* is in rue de Clichy, five minutes distant from St. Lazare Station and Park Monceau; ten minutes from la Madelaine and the Opera. It was built in 1885 and is sanitarily correct; supplied with pure spring water from the new water works of Paris. There is a really grand *salon* in which *musicales* are given weekly. In the rear of this is a large and handsome garden, neatly kept—a very pretty lounging place on summer evenings. There are baths in the house, the bedrooms are nicely furnished, the service is good, and last, and by no means least worthy of note is the table, which is liberally supplied; the best as to quality. But Madame Glatz at present has only room for thirty guests and her house is in such demand that you must engage rooms months, or at least weeks, in advance. Terms, 8 to 14 francs per day, which is the full charge; no extras, except, possibly, for lights. This is a favorite place with Americans of refinement: others are not admitted to Madame Glatz's charming family circle. Address, 45 rue de Clichy.

THE POWERS PENSION — One of the most desirable *pensions* in Paris, especially desirable for Americans, is kept not by a "charming Frenchwoman," nor by a "hearty" Britisher, but by a couple of cultivated, good Americans, well-known in New York—Mr. and Mrs. J. G. Powers, Jr. The house is in a high and delightful location, in the American quarter, 69 Avenue d'Antin, near the Champs Élysées. Mrs. Powers claims that it is "the most elegant and comfortable *pension* in Europe," and I, who have had some experience in hotels and *pensions* of the first rank, do not contradict the statement. I am not given to using the adjective "elegant" too freely, but elegant and tasteful are words that come to mind without summoning, in speaking of the Powers *pension*. The *salon* is a beautiful apartment; yes, uncommonly beautiful. It is on Monday evenings more particularly that this *salon* looks its best, when the receptions, with music, are held. The Powers *pension* is a select family home in the strictest sense of the term, and the rates for board are quite reasonable: pleasant rooms and three meals from ten francs per day. A lift was put in last autumn. Make a note of the address—69 Avenue d'Antin.

In the hotels mentioned the reader has a very wide latitude of choice and he may be guided by the facts and the figures set forth, so far as they go. As a last word I will add that if the reader "puts up" at the Hotel Chatham, Hotel Binda, or the Anglo-Français, or the *pensions* of Mr. and Mrs. Powers, Madame Veuve Glatz, or Mrs. Van Pelt, he will surely have no occasion to regret his choice of quarters.

THE RESTAURANTS OF PARIS.

BY THEODORE CHILD.

In order to anticipate criticism, and to avoid disappointment, it may be well to state at once that the art of cookery is in a terrible state of decadence in Paris. The men of the present generation do not seem to have the sentiment of the table; they know neither its varied resources nor its infinite refinements; their palates are dull, and they are content to eat rather than to dine. This decadence may be remarked both in private and in public establishments. The *gourmet* nowadays is a rarity, and a man of thirty years of age who knows how to order a dinner is a still greater rarity. One might discover many causes of this decline of a delicate art. The conditions of contemporary life, the hurry and unrest of modern Paris, doubtless do not conduce to the appreciation of fine cooking; but the chief cause of the decline of cookery in restaurants is the development of club life. The men of fashion, leisure, or wealth, who formerly would have lived at the restaurants, now dine at their clubs between two *séances* at the baccarat table, and the restaurants have thus lost that nucleus of regular and fastidious customers which, by its readiness to criticise and appreciate, obliged and encouraged the *chef* to keep up the traditions of the dainty palates of the past. At present the great restaurants of Paris depend for support as much on foreigners and on provincial people as on resident Parisians. The criticism of their cookery is less constant and less rigorous; the bills of fare are less varied than they were of old; the *amour propre* of the cooks is less; in a word, cookery has become nowadays more an industry than an art. Even in the most famous Parisian restaurants the visitor must not expect too much in the way either of viands or of wines.

In certain things, again, it must be remembered that the Parisian market is inferior to the markets of almost any town in England. The English visitor generally speaks disparagingly of the French oyster, for instance, doubtless because he is not accustomed to its flavor, and yet I know many connoisseurs who have travelled and dined in many lands who maintain that of all oysters the green Marennes (*Marennes vertes*) are the most delicate and delicious. The lovers of comparisons will ask what equivalents the French have for real turtle-soup, ox-tail, mulligatawny, and pea-soup with a sprinkling of dried mint and sippets. Is it their *bisque* or *purée* of crayfish, their *consommé de volaille*, their *Saint Germain*, or green pea-soup, their *Parmentier*, or thick potato-soup? But the traveller does not go to Paris to eat the food of his native land, but rather to enjoy the particular food of the country. Therefore, he must not expect to get fine salmon, or cod-fish, or turbot, or even mackerel in Paris. The city is too far away from the sea to have good salt-water fish. Salmon in Paris is dry and of poor flavor; fresh cod-fish is rarely seen, and the habits of the restaurants render it impossible to eat such salmon and turbot as there is in favorable conditions. In a London restaurant a whole salmon or a whole turbot is served hot like the joints; in a Paris restaurant; if you order boiled salmon or turbot, the cook cuts a slice off a parboiled fish, puts the slice in the pot, and boils it up for you. The result is unsatisfactory. As a rule, I should say, in a Parisian restaurant eat your salmon and your turbot cold, and prefer to both a red mullet (*rouget*), a sole, a trout, or some fresh-water fish.

A carefully prepared *matelotte d'anguilles*, which is not precisely the same as stewed eels, and *friture de Seine*, which need not be compared to whitebait, are both dishes not unworthy of the attention of the epicure.

The French are poor roasters; the roast beef and roast mutton in their restaurants cannot for a moment be compared with the joints at Simpson's or Blanchard's in London. Pies and puddings also are unknown to the French, with the exception of *pâtés de foie gras* and game pies. The French, again, eat their game very fresh and less cooked than the English. Generally, I think that the raw material of the Parisian restaurant cuisine is inferior to that of English restaurants; on the other hand, with the limitations referred to above, particularly as regards roasting, the preparation of the dishes is superior, and in the first-class restaurants unique. In the preparation and variety of vegetables the French lead the world; in the fabrication of sauces they are unsurpassed; in the serving and arrangement of a dinner they leave little to be desired.

But where can one go to dine in Paris? Which restaurants are the best, and what are the prices, and what is one to order? The subject is delicate and even dangerous, for although the critic has the right to declare a book or picture bad, pernicious, or abominable, and to pronounce its author to be unworthy of public attention, he dare not be so outspoken about the wretchedest restaurant-keeper who is licensed to poison his customers. I cannot tell you that such and such a restaurant in the Palais Royal is not to be frequented, or that such and such a gilded palace on the boulevard is an expensive delusion. I may, however, assure you that as prices run in Paris, it is impossible for a restaurateur to serve you with a healthy and honest plate of meat for less than one and a half francs, and you may therefore conclude that the restaurateurs who, for a fixed price, varying from one and a quarter to three francs, offer you a complete dinner of five courses—soup, fish, meat, two desserts, and half a bottle of wine—are probably in league with the honorable apothecaries, whose aid their customers must often need.

To the traveller I say avoid *prix fixe* dinners altogether, or, if you will satisfy your curiosity, go to the Dîner Européen at the corner of rue Lepelletier and the boulevard (price five francs), or to the table d'hôte dinners of those vast caravansaries, the Hôtel du Louvre, the Grand Hôtel, or the Hôtel Continental, where you dine for six, seven, or eight francs, and see specimens of men, women and children of all the countries of the world, and a profusion of linen, of silver plate, and luxurious surroundings which, for a time, will perhaps distract your attention from the insipidness of the roasts and the cheapness of the sauces.

The Bouillon Duval is an establishment which generally attracts the attention of the traveller. In every quarter of Paris you see one or two sober and respectable-looking façades painted dark red and lettered simply, "Établissement Duval." The Duval restaurants are wonderfully organized, exceedingly cheap, and all the food sold in them is good and genuine; these establishments now serve an average of three million meals a year. The visitor may often find it convenient in his wanderings about Paris to lunch in one of these Duval restaurants, if he is out of the way of any other well-known restaurant. In all of them he will find the food of the same quality, and the prices the same. As he enters, the doorkeeper will hand him a bulletin, on which all that he eats and drinks will be checked off, and which bulletin, when duly paid and stamped, will serve him as a passport when he leaves the establishment. The prices at the Duvals are very low; no dish costs more than one franc, and most of them only fifty or sixty centimes; wine costs twenty centimes a carafon, which is equivalent to one glassful, or one franc a bottle and upwards; coffee and cognac costs forty centimes. The Duval restaurant may be frequented with impunity, for nothing poisonous or deleterious is sold there; the only disadvantage is that the portions being very small, a hungry man, in order to satisfy his appetite, will need so many portions, that his bill will mount up to as much as if he had lunched or dined in an establishment of superior standing and comfort. The Bouillon Duval stands in the same relation to the regular restaurant as the omnibus or tram-car stands to the victoria; as somebody has said, *c'est l'omnibus du ventre.*

At length we come to the restaurants proper, the restaurants where one dines in the true sense of the term. It is commonly believed that the first-class restaurants in Paris are very dear. The Café Anglais, you will be told, charges twelve francs for a beefsteak for two, and fifteen francs for a Rouen duck. Yes, but the beefsteak in question is a Chateaubriand, a kernel of delicate meat cut in the heart of the *filet*,—meat that is sold at two and a half francs a pound by the butcher—and the duck costs eight or nine francs at the poulterer's. Good provisions in Paris are dear, and when one considers the heavy expenses of the first-class restaurants, one cannot complain of their charges.

As regards perfection of cooking, the Café Anglais heads the list. Its soups and sauces are exquisite; a sole "à l'Orly," "Colbert," "normande," "à la Joinville," or "au vin blanc," may be eaten there in perfection, and there is no restaurant in Paris where you can get a more delicate "sauce diable" served to a grilled fowl. The two great tests of a French kitchen are soups and sauces; if these are good, you may rest assured that everything else will be good.

In the same category with the Café Anglais, both as regards quality of food and price, may be placed Durand's, opposite the Madeleine, and Adolphe and Pellé behind the Opéra. Next come the Maison d'Or, the

Café de la Paix, Bignon, and the Café de Paris, in the Avenue de l'Opéra, Voisin in the rue Cambon, the old Véfour in the Palais Royal, the Père Lathuile, in the Avenue de Clichy, and Fayot, opposite the Luxembourg Palace. At all these restaurants you can dine delicately and drink as good wines as are still to be had in France. Voisin and Foyot, especially, have choice Burgundies of incomparable fineness.

The third category of restaurants includes the Café Riche, which years ago belonged to the first category; Brébant's, now a general Bouillon, at the corner of Boulevard Montmartre; Chevilliard, at the Rond-Point des Champs Élysées; Laurent, and Ledoyen, in the Champs Élysées; Champeaux, Place de la Bourse, where you dine in a perpetual winter garden; Edouard, Place Boieldieu, opposite the Opéra Comique; Wepler, Place Clichy; La Pérouse, on the Quai des Grands Augustins; Maire, at the corner of the Boulevard de Strasbourg and the Boulevard St. Denis; Marguery, next door to the Gymnase theatre; Perroncel, rue du Havre, opposite the Gare Saint Lazare. In the Bois du Boulogne the restaurants of Madrid, and of the Pavilion d'Armenonville are much frequented in the summer by gay and smart people : the prices are about the same as at the restaurants in town of the second category, that is to say, two can dine there modestly with ordinary wine for a louis.

I presume that the traveller comes to Paris to taste Parisian cooking, and therefore I shall not recommend him to try the pseudo-English cuisine of Weber or Lucas in the rue Royale and Place de la Madeleine, or the Russian restaurant in the rue Marivaux, or the Hungarian restaurant in the rue Rougemont. There remain then to be mentioned only a few special establishments, such as the Pied de Mouton near the Central Market, and the famous tripe restaurant in the rue Montorgueil. There are several restaurants in Paris which make a specialty of Bouillabaisse ; but I do not recommend that dish in Paris, for the simple reason that it is not the real article. In the Parisian Bouillabaisse several of the fish elements are wanting because they cannot bear transportation from the seaside. The traveller *gourmet* will prefer to wait until chance leads him to Marseilles, where the reigning chief of the great dynasty of Roubion will serve him this savoury dish on a balcony overlooking the blue Mediterranean. The café concerts in the Champs Élysées are also much frequented by open air diners in the summer. The spectacle is curious and amusing, but the *gourmet* will flee the promiscuity and bustle of their dear and mediocre cuisine.

To give precise details as to price is difficult. One may say generally that at the Café Anglais two persons can dine delicately and well without stint as to good wines or choice of dishes, for about two louis (forty francs). On the other hand, the single man who is prepared to spend not less than seven francs on his dinner may enter boldly any restaurant in Paris, from the Café Anglais downward, and dine for that sum on soup, one dish, cheese, and half a bottle of wine. For ten or twelve francs one may dine simply but abundantly almost anywhere, except at the very tip-top houses, such as the Café Anglais, Durand's, and Adolphe and Pellé's. By way of practical hints I will subjoin a few observations.

Beware of *hors d'œuvres* and baskets of fruit, for their influence on the total of your bill is alarming. If you are alone, resolutely refuse radishes and butter, or rather leave them untouched on the table before you ; if you have invited a friend to dinner, offer him *hors d'œuvres* and hope that he will refuse ; if you are with a lady, both *hors d'œuvres* and the basket of fruit are obligatory. Eve offered fruit to Adam ; the least we sons of Adam can do is to return the politeness.

The real *gourmet* eats by candle-light, because, as Nestor Roqueplan said, "rien n'est laid comme une sauce vue au soleil."

When you enter a restaurant refuse as a rule the place that is offered you. Choose your own table, and if it is breakfast-time secure a view through the window and a view of the whole restaurant, and if possible let the light strike on the table from your left hand.

Preserve your freedom of will, but do not try to impose it. You are the master, it is true, and yet to a certain extent you must obey. Consult, therefore, with the *maître d'hôtel*, consider what he recommends, and accept it if it be to your taste, for in the good restaurants there is no question of passing off stale food. The *maître d'hôtel* is flattered when you ask his advice, and it is his business to be acquainted with the special and daily resources of the larder. At places like the Café Anglais the written *menu* mentions only a few very ordinary dishes, and you will inspire respect by not asking for the *carte*. At Bignon's do not trouble yourself about the *carte*; ask advice of the portly Louis, and do not disdain his counsel. In cookery as in love much confidence is necessary.

Always ask for the wine list, *la carte des vins*, even if you end by selecting *vin ordinaire*. The richest people in the land drink *vin ordinaire* with their dinner, and dilute it with simple water. The traveller, therefore, need not fear to do likewise even in the most gorgeous restaurants. Champagne is not much drunk by French *gourmets*, and such champagnes as the Paris restaurants keep is sweeter than our people generally like. To the connoisseur in champagne I would say, "Do not drink champagne in France, for the best *crûs* are to be found in England and Russia." If you desire fine red or white wines you will find the nomenclature and the prices on the list; choose your Beaune, Pomard, Volnay, Nuits, or Moulin à Vent, your Tavel, Tonnerre, or Chambertin according to your taste and purse; consult confidentially with the butler, and mind that you always address him as *sommelier*, and not *garçon*. The *sommelier* is inferior to the *garçon* in the hierarchy of table service, as you will see from his more humble and respectful demeanor.

Ask for *l'addition*, and not either *la carte* or *la note*, which savours of provincialism. Verify your change rapidly, and see that no pieces lurk on the plate beneath the bill. Be liberal towards the waiter, for it is the *pourboire* that secures you a smile when you arrive and a smile when you leave, a helping hand when you are struggling into your overcoat, obliging and ready service, and the appearance, nay, even the reality of friendship. In the three categories of restaurants mentioned above do not give the waiter less than fifty centimes, however modest your bill, and the more delicate and satisfactory your dinner, the more liberal let your *pourboire* be, ranging from one franc up to five, calculated generally at the rate of five per cent. on the total of your bill.

THE ANGLO-AMERICAN BANKING CO.

When Americans have the facilities to execute a good idea they always possess the energy and the boldness to execute it in a fitting way. Thus instead of going into small quarters in an out of the way location, the Anglo-American Banking Company of Paris selected a large and imposing building, fronting on two broad streets. Then with a liberal outlay of money they proceeded to fit up the different floors in luxurious style. The site, on the corner of Chaussée d'Antin and Rue Meyerbeer, half a block from the Grand Opera, a step from the Grand Hotel, and near some of the leading boulevards, is at once choice, central and accessible.

The ground floor of the building, where money is exchanged and where letters of credit are cashed, is roomy and has a solid and business-like appearance, while the upper floors are furnished with an eye to convenience, comfort and beauty. It is here, on this second floor, where there are tastefully furnished rooms for ladies, where desks are at hand for clients to conduct their correspondence, and where the leading American, English and French papers are kept on file in charge of a prompt-serving and careful attendant.

The bank is now established on a firm basis; it has the confidence of the French people, and it promises to become an "institution" in Paris. It is convenient to keep a small account at the bank, drawing checks against it in making purchases in Paris. But the house can be used for any and every legitimate banking purpose, and Americans find it very useful as a place where their letters may be addressed, where their letters of credit are cashed and where they may meet friends. It has some of the features of a club, and although only established a few years is now quite a popular rendezvous for Americans. The Anglo-American bank itself issues letters of credit payable all over the world.

The officers of the American Banking Company are S. J. Gorman, of New York, president; J. L. Carr, vice-president; J. H. Hobson, of New York, general manager; Edmond Huerstel, secretary. Cable address, Anabaco, Paris.

AU BON MARCHÉ.

Everybody has heard of, and all who have been to Paris have visited Au Bon Marché, world-renowned of dry goods establishments. This great emporium was practically founded by Jacques-Aristide Boucicaut, who, beginning life in a small way in the dry goods business, became partner, and finally sole owner of the Bon Marché. Once above the rank of ordinary employee, he undertook to improve the moral and material condition of his fellow workmen. He inaugurated free classes in the arts and sciences, language, music, etc., and established a provident fund for long service in the establishment, supplied his employees with free medical attendance, and in many other forms, in addition to large outside charities and good works, evidenced more than enough of the spirit to entitle him to the appellation of philanthropist. At his death in 1877, the annual returns from his business exceeded sixteen millions of dollars. After his death his good works were continued by his widow, who, with an enormous fortune at her command, dispensed it in extended and elaborate charities, establishing the system of sharing of profits among her employees, creating a retiring pension fund, erecting and maintaining hospitals, and at her death disposing of millions of francs to churches, colleges, and other public institutions.

Mme. Boucicaut died ten years after her husband, but the Bon Marché still continues under the original plan and system of its founder. There are three thousand six hundred employees, and all the unmarried employees of the establishment board on the premises. For the proper conduct of such a business the system of course must be perfect, near as may be. Rules and regulations are set forth and strictly adhered to. It is expressly provided that the food shall be wholesome and abundant. A doctor is attached to the establishment who may be consulted by the employees free of charge. Any employee called for military service can, at its expiration, resume his situation. No fines are inflicted under any circumstances.

The Bon Marché forwards to any part of the globe all goods bought at the establishment, and to nearly all the countries of Europe, including Great Britain, it will forward free of charge for carriage any purchase to the amount of twenty-five francs (five dollars). A pretty souvenir volume is issued by the Bon Marché. It contains a useful indicator map of Paris, and a deal of interesting information about the great metropolis. It may be obtained free upon application by postal card. Address simply, Au Bon Marché, Paris.

THE DE SOTO.

SAVANNAH, GEORGIA.

The city of Savannah, with its balmy air, its far famed Bonaventure Cemetery, its pretty parks, broad streets and many natural attractions (acknowledged to be one of the most attractive Southern cities), was long avoided by many pleasure tourists, because it had no hotel worthy of a city claiming fifty thousand inhabitants and doing a business of over one hundred and thirty millions of dollars annually.

Savannah is the greatest cotton port in the world—New Orleans excepted. Savannah has deep water and good docks. Sometimes as many as thirty English ships are in this port at the same time. They take cotton direct to foreign ports. Savannah is easily approached from North and South: presently it is to have communication with the west—direct from Kansas City. When these and other contemplated improvements are made, Savannah expects to experience an era of great prosperity. It is predicted that the city will double its population in the next ten years.

Anyone who doubts that Savannah is steadily moving forward in prosperity has only to take a glimpse at the tax returns made to the city treasurer for 1891, to have the doubt quickly dispelled. In 1890, the returns of personal property footed up $9,948,048, and in 1891 they were considerably over $10,000,000, the increase being about $500,000. The banks alone in '91 made returns of $506,000 in excess of 1890. This shows that there is a great demand for banking institutions. Real estate has increased $1,300,000.

Such being the present condition and future prospects of Savannah, it was time that some movement were made for the better entertainment of visitors, so at last the citizens put their heads together and concluded that no matter how rich a city is in natural attractions, the climax of success is only capped by railway facilities and first class hotels.

Mr. H. B. Plant, head of the Plant System, furnished the railway facilities, and now the citizens of Savannah have supplied the hotel. They formed a stock company, subscribed a million of dollars and opened the De Soto, two years ago, which proved to be exteriorly one of the handsomest houses in this country, if not in the world, and interiorly one of the best appointed—in keeping with the American idea.

Savannah never had a habit of going across the seas for hotel names. It boasts of no Victoria, no Buckingham, no Imperial, but it has a Screven, named after a prominent Georgia family; a Pulaski, named for a military hero, and now a De Soto, in honor of the discoverer of the Mississippi river. Savannah is nothing if not patriotic. It has a Monterey square, a Forsyth park, and among its monuments are the noble columns erected to perpetuate the memory of three revolutionary heroes —Jasper, Green and Pulaski.

The De Soto cost a round million of dollars. It occupies, but does not literally "cover, an entire block of ground," as the writer of the little descriptive pamphlet has it. The house is built in the form of a hollow square, with entrances on three sides. This plan of construction was adopted to leave a large open court in the centre, thus securing an ample supply of light and air; and the plan has succeeded to perfection.

The dining-room, which seats nearly four hundred guests, has air and light its full length, on both sides. Some of the bedroom doors, instead of wooden panels, have panels of ground glass to let light into the halls. The bedroom in which these lines are written is fifteen feet square, not counting a deep recess for the windows, of which there are two, each measuring seven feet six by four feet six. There is also a transom over the door. To such an extent has this love of light been carried that even the elevator, instead of being built with solid sides, has sides of strong, open wire work, through which light and air stream freely.

The interior, while being on a broad, liberal, yes, a luxurious scale, has no striking novelties. It is modelled after the style of the large modern American hotels of the first-class. There is a large and splendid "office" with reading-room, smoking-room, writing-room, and small parlors branching off; there are open fires and all the etceteras of convenience and luxury; the whole ground floor is marble-tiled, the corridors are ten feet wide and richly carpeted; they lead on each side to an inviting veranda; there is pure water from an artesian well and the sanitary arrangements are said to be scientifically correct.

The parlor, with its onyx tables, its gold-framed chairs, delicate carpets, its richly-embossed furniture covering, its mirrors, electric lights and the light-colored walls minus anything that suggests a work of art, is, to my mind, rather cold and stiff. I prefer the home-like drawing-room of the Imperial Hotel in Aberdeen, Scotland, with its profusion of fresh flowers, its cabinets and pretty things, or say, the drawing-room of the Langham Hotel, London, rich and pleasing in subdued, dark colors; but the De Soto is an American hotel, it is kept after the American methods, and without doubt the parlor suits to perfection those for whom it is furnished—then why should anybody criticise its decorations?

But the exterior with its novel and beautiful construction, a combination of architectural styles forming a very pleasing whole, commands instant admiration. There are towers, turrets, arched entrances, Queen Anne windows, fountains and a number of overhanging red-tiled roofs through which waterspouts project in picturesque fashion. The walls are of brick in two different colors with terra cotta trimmings, railings and ornaments of black iron. All of these materials and colors are used with skill and the very best taste, making an artistic combination which is remarkably pleasing. Then the graceful palm trees here and there give the surroundings a tropical appearance and serve to add to the beautiful picture.

The site of the De Soto was well chosen. All of the four streets on which it is built being wide, ample opportunity is afforded to admire from a distance its lines of beauty. Its main front is on a very wide street, Liberty street, probably not quite so broad as Unter den Linden in Berlin, nor has it the grand palaces of that renowned German street; but Liberty street is neat, clean and kept in good order, which is more than can be said of Unter den Linden. The sidewalks are of smooth-faced red brick; between them and the roadway on either side there is a row of trees. There is another row of trees, also a car track, in the middle of the street, and on either side of the track again there is an asphalt drive for carriages. There is abundant space, and although it lacks the solid buildings of larger cities, the street itself is not lacking in attractions.

Within five minutes' walk of the house is Forsyth park, with its acres of forest trees, and plenty of japonicas and roses in full bloom at this writing, January 26. In the centre of this park there is a handsome fountain, modeled after the grand fountain in the Place de la Concorde, Paris. It is a mistake and a pity to half hide it behind japonica trees and rose bushes, from six to eight feet high.

It is very enjoyable to sit in any of Savannah's pretty parks these days, say between noon and four o'clock. There is no danger of taking nor of feeling cold. At night and in the early morn the air is cool (36 to 42 degrees), but in the afternoon it is soft and balmy—anywhere from 56 to 76 degrees. It is an old habit of mine to carry a thermometer in my satchel, so I am not dependent on the hotel instrument nor on hearsay for my facts and figures concerning the temperature. Frost is rarely seen in Savannah, and they never get a sight of snow unless some of the "beautiful" article should remain on the car roofs of trains coming from the North.

The De Soto can accommodate four hundred guests, and besides, the dining-room and the smaller "early breakfast-room" on the main floor, there is a banqueting hall on the first floor in which two hundred guests can sit down comfortably. A novel feature for a hotel is a gymnasium, on the sixth floor, and above this, at the very summit, there is a large "Solarium," fitted up with chairs, tables and lounges. Here you can sit, bask in the sun, and, as Walt Whitman says, "loaf and invite your soul." In this elevated position you get a magnificent view of Savannah and the surrounding country—as far east as the Tybee coast, twenty miles distant.

There are in all three hundred and thirty-eight bedrooms, forty parlors and sixty bath-rooms in the house, affording many choice suites for families. There are no dark rooms nor inner rooms; all have a street view, a park view, or look out upon the court-yard. Every room has a wardrobe built in the wall, and this is covered by a tasteful portière. All the carpets and draperies, by the way, came from W. & J. Sloane, and the electroliers and gasoliers were supplied by Archer, Pancoast & Co., both leading New York houses in their respective branches.

A band of twelve pieces (Cobb's Savannah Band) performs excellent music in an alcove near the dining-room during the luncheon and dinner hours.

The house has been leased for fifteen years by Watson & Powers, who have had long experience in Charleston and other hotels. They kept the Pulaski House here, as a colored driver told me in answer to a question, "a right smart time," which still leaves the number of years rather indefinite. The same gentleman and brother, who drive carriages for the house, and who drove me through Bonaventure Cemetery, said that the fire of two years ago, which burned for two days, destroyed the "'Sonic Hall." He also volunteered this piece of intelligence : " Der Pulaski House is makin' a very big condition," which I translated to mean addition. My esteemed friend, Mr. Marcus Wight and his charming wife, of Lowell, Mass., were our travelling companions for that day, and their delightful company enhanced the interest and the enjoyment of the drive.

If you desire to see a hotel which contains all the latest and best American ideas, and, unlike the hotels of Europe, combines them into a perfect system, telegraph for rooms to the De Soto. It is advisable to take it in, as a resting place, between New York and Florida, or vice versa.

P. S.—This is called a cold winter in Savannah, yet at six A.M., Thursday, January 29, the thermometer marked sixty degrees.

THOMASVILLE, GEORGIA.

Time, eleven A. M., February 1.—Your correspondent is seated at his bedroom window; there are two large windows in the room, and both are wide open. The apartment is twenty feet square with a twelve-foot ceiling; it is not heated artificially and yet the temperature in it is seventy-two degrees. This is not said from hearsay, nor is the record taken from a hotel thermometer, which may be unreliable, but from a portable thermometer of my own.

WHEN THE PLACE WAS SETTLED.—People ask, "How old is Thomasville: when was it first settled?" The writer can answer this question because he had the good fortune to be presented to no less a personage than Mrs. M. A. Bower, a most charming woman to look at and to converse with, who is proud of her fifty-six years, but whom you would judge to be at least ten years younger. Mrs. Bower was the first white child born in Thomasville, and in the first real house erected in the place. It stood on the present site of the Mitchell House. Mrs. Bower is the daughter of Colonel and Mrs. Edward Remington who came here from Pawtuxet, R. I., in the year 1828. Set it down for a fact then that Thomasville is three score years old.

LOCATION. — Thomasville, the capital of Thomas county (this is not from a gazetteer, please believe), stands three hundred and thirty feet above sea level, being on the highest ground between Macon and the Gulf of Mexico, in the Uplands of Georgia. It is two hundred miles from the Atlantic, sixty miles from the Gulf of Mexico as the bird flies, twelve miles from the

Florida State line, a thirty-three-mile drive from Tallahassee, and is reached from Jacksonville at the South or from Savannah coming from the North in a few hours by way of Waycross or Jesup, two places not particularly attractive to the tourist but quite useful as way stations, affording junctions for several lines of railroad.

HEALTH AND PLEASURE.—Thomasville was at one time simply a health resort : people with consumption or other lung or throat diseases came here for relief and they found it. They, the sickly people, still come to get well ; but beside being a health resort it is now also a place for pleasure. Fashion has set its seal on Thomasville. New York and Boston are well represented among the visitors, but the West especially favors Thomasville, and St. Paul, for its size, sends more people probably than any other city. A number of St. Paul citizens have cottages here and have set up fine establishments. Ladies dress for the morning ride or drive ; they dress for the mid-day dinner and again for the evening dance: Ladies at the hotels exchange visits with the cottagers, also with the townspeople, the permanent residents giving strangers a warm, Southern welcome.

FEATURES OF THE TOWN.—To-day Thomasville has churches of all denominations (including a Jewish place of worship), two hotels far superior to any between Baltimore and Jacksonville, unless exception be made of the new Oglethrope at Brunswick ; a number of smaller hotels, numerous boarding houses, two daily newspapers, several good private schools, a flourishing college for girls and one for the other sex, a railway direct to the town—and five thousand inhabitants. The boys' college is a branch of the State University and has at present two hundred and fifty pupils. The other institution, called "Young's Female College," was endowed by a Georgian, and the charge for tuition is so low as to be nominal, ten dollars per year to each pupil. So the religiously inclined have ample opportunity to worship at their particular shrine, and the educational advantages of Thomasville are good.

NATURE'S GIFTS.—The reputation of this place was gained by its dry and balmy atmosphere, its even temperature, its health-giving pine forests and by its freedom from cold or sudden changes. The United States Signal Service report shows that the average winter temperature is about fifty-five degrees, and the average temperature last July, the hottest month here, was eighty-two degrees. While the winter days are warm the mornings and nights are pleasantly cool, and it never snows here. Once during the past fourteen years they did have a flurry of snow. It happened on a Sunday and the churches remained empty; so interested were the inhabitants in the uncommon sight that they neglected the church and all took to snowballing. You need no overcoats nor wraps for outdoor wear, except, perhaps, for an evening drive, or for rainy days; but an umbrella or parasol to protect you from the heat of the sun is indispensable. I am speaking of needing such an article at the present time, February 1.

THE PINEY WOODS OAK.—To those coming from the North the sight of the trees in full leaf is as agreeable as it is strange. The pine, live-oak, hemlock and holly all have their branches thickly covered. There is a gorgeous live-oak on the grounds of the Piney Woods Hotel whose spreading branches measure sixty feet across. There is still a larger one in the town, which people travel miles to see. It spreads ninety feet across. But beauty does not always consist in bigness. The Piney Woods oak is both beautiful and big, but its symmetrical beauty is its main attraction. Is it too warm on the hotel porch? Are the sun's rays too fierce? Cross over the road, fifty yards distant, and seek a comfortable bench or rustic seat in the grateful shade of the pines, in what is popularly termed "Yankee Paradise," but known more correctly as Paradise Park. It includes thirty acres laid out in walks and drives. There is no ice to make your step unsteady, but the needles of the pines render the paths rather slippery.

WHEN TO COME.—You can pick violets in the open air and pluck in the fields a small bouquet of daisies at this writing, but to see Thomasville at its best, I am told that you most come a little later than this, when the grass is all green. You can then pluck wild roses to your heart's content. Then the pear orchards will be in full bloom, and the dogwood blossoms are a sight to behold. I have been here only three days and have seen no rain, but the soil is sandy and one can readily believe what enthusiasts say, that an hour or two after a long and heavy rain walking is again pleasant, the rain having percolated through the ground, leaving the surface perfectly dry, if not hard. And there is seemingly no end of lovely walks. You get out of the town in five minutes, and if you are bent on pedestrian exercise, and have an eye for beautiful scenes, turn your steps in any direction and you will make no mistake.

WHAT TO BRING. — If the ladies of your party are equestriennes, by all means let them bring their riding habits with them: everybody rides. Driving, too, is largely indulged in, the roads being hard, smooth and unusually wide. They extend for miles and miles through the pine woods, and their picturesque beauty you will please imagine; it is not easy to describe it without using more adjectives than I have at my command en route. To sportsmen let me say, do not come without your dog and gun or you will never forget nor forgive the error. Wild turkeys abound, there are snipe in plenty and quail can be bagged by a novice. You see them on the road while driving, and the crack of the rifle is heard almost constantly. Quail on toast is a regular dish at the hotels at least once a day.

THE NEGRO AND HIS WORKS.—Without desiring to attack political problems, to raise dead issues or to discuss questions that have long since been answered, one cannot resist the temptation to obtain information on the result of the emancipation proclamation, for although it is over a quarter of a century old the subject yet has great interest for this country, and for other countries also, for that matter. Here is a statement of facts and figures in condensed, nutshell form upon which chapters and books might be written—the colored population of Georgia pay taxes on real estate amounting to twelve millions of dollars, the realty being estimated at about one half its actual value, and their personal property is estimated at about six millions of dollars. There are instances of marked faithfulness and attachment of slaves to their former owners, some of the blacks still serving their white masters. Among the servants of Mrs. M. A. Bower, proprietor of the Piney Woods Hotel, are two who formerly served this same "master," one of them being the skilful pastry-cook of the hotel. Negroes say that the whites and work do not agree. Possibly not; they are unaccustomed to labor hard in this section, and on the other hand whites claim that the colored are by nature more fitted for work in such a climate. Be that as it may, it is certain that the colored people of the South are not over fond of work, either: you cannot depend upon their working regularly. So soon as they can put enough by to keep them in cracked wheat or hominy and a little tobacco the colored laborers are likely to throw up a job, and are not over particular if they occasionally leave an employer in the lurch. If you are a new settler and are building a house, for instance, they will have no compunction about leaving you some fine morning, or some wet afternoon, before your house is roofed in. Of clothing for warmth they need little, and the weather never being severe their log cabins or pine huts need not be very tight: if they shed the rain that is all that is necessary for them.

THE CHAIN GANG.—The jail at Thomasville was not near large enough until a new plan of punishment was adopted. The colored roughs committed small offences for the very purpose of getting into prison ; in that way obtaining food and shelter, and at the same time "doin' nuffin." Not so now : the town council met and adopted the resolution that prisoners should be made to work, and that is how the "chain gang" came into existence. You will see gangs of colored men repairing the roads and engaged in other public works on the highway. They wear a striped uniform after the prevailing fashion at our State prisons. The two legs of each man are held close enough together by iron chains to prevent the action of running, but yet the chains afford him sufficient freedom to move about and make himself useful with pick and shovel. It is a novel sight for a stranger to meet one of these gangs on the road, and the clank of the locked iron links has a strange and weird sound. To their credit be it said, the men are ashamed of their public disgrace, and the Thomasville prison is now large enough to hold all the applicants for admission. Making the negro work and making him a public show have had good effect. Such a plan is of course not feasible for cities, but it might be adopted with a degree of success in thinly populated districts of Northern States. Tramps give Thomasville a wide berth. If one of the genus unwittingly wanders that way he is given his choice : he must leave at once or join the chain gang and work for thirty days.

UPLAND PRODUCTS.—Cotton is still king in the South, and Georgia produces its full share, but Thomas county is also noted for oats. More oats are produced in Thomas county than in any other county in the United States. This I have from one of the prominent citizens of the town, whose information is as extensive as the manner of imparting his knowledge is agreeable. If you come to Thomasville try to meet Dr. Bower. He practices his profession no longer, being interested in many large enterprises. He can give you more interesting information concerning these parts than probably any other person hereabouts. But you must allow a little for Dr. Bower's enthusiasm. He is apt to look at Thomasville and Thomas county through a rose-colored glass. From Dr. Bower your correspondent learned, among other things, that the Le Conte pear, which grows in such profusion here and in Florida, was brought to this country from China about fifty years ago, and propagated by Commodore Le Conte, a Georgian of French descent. It does not equal the Bartlett in flavor, but its skin is tougher, and it bears transportation better. You may see orchards containing thousands of trees, and the trees average a production of twelve to fifteen bushels. Some trees are said to yield as many as thirty-five bushels. They boast here of the largest pear orchard in the world—two hundred and twenty-five acres. Last year twenty-five thousand crates of pears were shipped from Thomasville to cities in the North and West. Some found their way to the New England summer resorts, and were received with favor. Still, from all I can learn, while the North has its Bartlett, it need not envy the South its Le Conte.

THE POOR KINE.—It is conceded that they raise here in abundance cotton, oats and pears, and that pine trees, roses, magnolias, quail, figs, and other good things grow in profusion, but, on the other hand, the live stock is very poor indeed and meats must come all the way from New York if people demand meat that is good and nutritious. That is where all the meat comes from which is consumed at the hotels. It almost makes your heart ache to see the poor, weak oxen that are forced to work, and the thin, bony cows that must yield their milk. It may be different in summer time, when the grass is rich, but the cattle seem to be very poorly fed now, or not fed at all. They are allowed to roam freely about the streets and byways of the town, and pick up, by day or night, what they can find.

THE WINN FARM.—An exception to this rule must be made in favor of Winn Farm, a tract of eighteen hundred acres, owned by F. J. Winn, several hundred acres of which are under cultivation. The stock there looks better than the animals you see in Thomasville proper, and for which you have nothing but sympathy. They make good wine, too, at Winn Farm, and it is offered in hospitable quantities from the hand of an attractive, cultivated woman, the presiding genius of the place, Mrs. F. J. Winn. The luscious, juicy oranges which are put on the tables of the Piney Woods Hotel in such liberal measure, come from the grove on Indian River, Florida, owned and cultivated by Dr. Bower. The grove contains four or five thousand orange trees in bearing.

THE HOTELS.—There is a standing joke about certain Southern cities where there are only two hotels, that, whichever one you select, you will wish that you had chosen the other. Although the hotels south of the line have greatly improved of late years, the old joke will still apply in certain towns and cities. Not so, however, at Thomasville. There are only two hotels here known to fame, and you will make no mistake if you select either. It is a matter of surprise to find two such hotels in such a comparatively small town. The Mitchell House and the Piney Woods Hotel (I take them alphabetically) are both large, new, handsomely furnished and perfectly appointed houses, containing all the modern improvements, and erected with strict regard for the laws of sanitation. The Mitchell House is an imposing solid brick structure, four stories high, two hundred feet square, with a cultivated park of two acres sweeping before its front piazza. This little park is reserved for the hotel guests and their friends.

The Piney Woods Hotel is within gun-shot distance of the Mitchell House, on the same street, with a front measuring three hundred and fifty feet, the other side overlooking Paradise Park, of which I have already spoken. The Piney Woods stands, as it were, and as its name might indicate, on the very edge of the pine forests, and yet it is only a five minutes' walk from the post-office and a ten minutes' drive from the depot. The pamphlet issued by the proprietor tells you that "the Piney Woods is modelled similar to the Grand Union Hotel, at Saratoga Springs," but this is a mistake of the compiler of the work, and is no compliment at all to the house under consideration—which is far more pleasing to the eye, exteriorly, than the Grand Union at Saratoga. The Piney Woods is built after plans of J. A. Woods, a New York architect, who planned the new Grand Hotel *in the Catskill Mountains*, and with its wide and lofty verandas, its projecting towers, its pretty corners here and there, is a facsimile on a somewhat smaller scale of that favorite and beautiful house. Any one who has seen the hotel on the line of the Ulster and Delaware Railway, can picture to himself the Piney Woods Hotel at Thomasville. The late Captain Gillette, who kept the Mountain Hotel, kept this one also for years. William E. Davies is now the manager of the Piney Woods.

Each hotel, the Mitchell House and the Piney Woods, will accommodate nearly three hundred guests,

THE BEST ROUTE.—The Atlantic Coast Line, called "the short route to Florida," is by all odds the best way to reach Thomasville from the Eastern States and from New York. The vestibule train, "the Florida special" of the Pennsylvania Railroad, which traverses this route, is the quickest and most luxurious train, with its dining-room car, library car, etc., but this only leaves New York on certain days of the week, and you must apply for seats a long time ahead, and then you may not get them. The ordinary trains, with Pullman sleepers, are good enough for the majority of travellers, and they afford people opportunity to stop over and see the cities en route—Washington, Richmond, Wilmington, N. C., Charleston and Savannah. Or, if you prefer, you may come direct from New York, in about thirty-two hours, to Waycross, Ga., where there is connection for Thomasville, distant four hours. But if you "stop over," you must be prepared to travel in ordinary coaches between the Southern cities; parlor cars are not attached to local trains. It would help Thomasville materially if the Savannah, Western and Florida Road (everybody in this section calls it "the S. F. & W.") were to run a quick train with a parlor car to meet the Florida special. The return would not be great at first, but it would prove profitable to the road ultimately. Washington, D. C., seems to be especially favored: the Atlantic Coast Line runs a Pullman buffet sleeping car for Washington passengers direct to Thomasville. Strangers and tourists make it a point to go to the stations to see the Pennsylvania vestibule train at different points of the road, and the colored folk stand and stare at the beautiful appointments with eyes and mouth wide open. "Only God's people," remarked one surprised darkey, "can ride in them carriages."

A NEW SOUTHERN RESORT.

If you tell people in New York that you are "going to Brunswick for the winter," they will probably look at you with surprise; some will say, "Do you mean New Brunswick?" having in mind New Brunswick, N. J.; while others will say, "Brunswick; where is Brunswick, in what State? I never heard of it." Well, new as Brunswick may appear to the majority, it is an old place, having been settled and laid out in the year 1763.

WHERE IS BRUNSWICK?—Brunswick is in the Southeastern part of Georgia, not far from the Florida border, sixty miles below Savannah, seventy miles north of Jacksonville. The city covers an area of two miles square, and is handsomely laid out, the whole adorned by some of the most beautiful groves of live oaks and cedars to be found in the South. It is situated on a small peninsula jutting out into the sea, surrounded on three sides by salt water, but protected from the severity of the ocean winds by outlying islands. Brunswick is only eight miles from the sea and there are no fresh water streams or swamps within many miles to breed malaria, the air being constantly renewed and vivified by the health-bearing breezes of the ocean, that render it, as official statistics show, one of the healthiest cities in the Union.

Among its natural advantages are its climate, uniform and mild in winter, its geographical position being but little north of St. Augustine, ice being seldom seen, and snow rarely, if ever; its forests of pine, palm and moss-covered oak, its healthy soil, pure water, semitropical foliage and plants, the magnificent drives, and last, but by no means least, its superior water facilities, having one of the finest harbors in the South Atlantic. As to the trees: I have stood under the far-famed old oaks of England, I have seen the moss-covered trees of Bonaventure, of which all Savannah proudly boasts, and admired the great oak at Thomasville, whose branches measure ninety feet across; but there is an oak here which belittles them all for age, strength and size. Under the "Lovers' Oak" at Brunswick it is said that one hundred teams can find shelter from the sun's rays. It is called Lovers' Oak because a marriage was once performed under it, several hundred witnesses being present at the open air ceremony.

JEKYL AND OTHER ISLANDS.—There are a number of beautiful islands near here which are fertile almost beyond one's imagination. Everybody has heard of Jekyl Island, and all true sportsmen know it. It is famous as the location of one of the finest club-houses in the country, the island being a paradise for the sportsman and fisherman. It is literally full of game; deer, wild turkey and other fowl are so plentiful that visitors are sure of good sport. Being a natural game preserve, upon which the general public have not been permitted to hunt, the increase has been rapid and the supply practically inexhaustible. The club-house, seen from the river, is a noble structure. Then there is St. Simon's Island, which lies off the coast at a distance of seven miles from Brunswick, and is noted for the wonderful fertility of its soil. It excels especially in fruits— oranges, peaches, figs, bananas, olives, lemons, limes and pecans, growing in great profusion. The climate is almost perfection. Ice is seldom seen, and snow has been seen here but once within the present century,

A DOCTOR'S CERTIFICATE.—Brunswick's peninsular location, almost surrounded by salt water, with immense pine forests on the north, extending hundreds of miles into the interior, conduces to a state of healthfulness excelled by no other place of its population in the whole

South. Dr. H. Buford, Health Officer of the City of Brunswick, makes the following official statement: "The result of my observation and experience as a practitioner in this city and in the country adjacent thereto, during a residence of seven years, proves that our mortuary statistics show a minimum death rate—Poughkeepsie, N. Y., not excepted. During an active practice of seven years I cannot record a single case of scarlet fever or diphtheria. Hay fever and asthma are unknown here."

A MISTAKE OF CONGRESS.—Brunswick is a century and a quarter old, but it went along lazily and slowly, like many other Southern towns and villages, and the war somewhat retarded its progress. Nor was it helped by a committee from Congress which, some years after the war, took a cruise along the Atlantic coast to examine the facilities of our seaports. Congress has not earned its peculiar reputation without deserving it. This committee may have included members who were learned in the law, or who knew how to hoe potatoes, but of harbor advantages and the requirements of ships they must have been innocently ignorant. They reported that "the harbor of Brunswick was twelve feet deep." This went abroad and ships went elsewhere. How near to the truth came this report may be judged by one instance. On Friday, February 3, 1888, the English steamer, the Port Augusta, cleared this port drawing twenty feet of water and carrying 6,559 bales of cotton, weighing over three millions of pounds and valued at $300,000. It was the largest cargo ever cleared from a South Atlantic port, and ships drawing *twenty-four feet of water* enter and leave here without the slightest danger of touching bottom. So much for the congressional report. That the shipping facilities of Brunswick are becoming known may be judged also from the following facts and figures: During the whole month of February, 1887, the exports of cotton, naval stores and lumber amounted to $78,000 while for only the *first five days* of Feb., 1888, the exports amounted to over $300,000. These figures are given on official authority from the collector of the port. Are more significant statements needed to show the marvellous advance and improvement of this place? Here they are—the exports in the year 1886 amounted to less than a million dollars; in 1887 they footed up over two and a quarter millions. The imports of 1886 were less than $5,000, the imports of 1887, $48,000.

A CITY BY THE SEA.—How has all this seeming prosperity and increase of business on the water affected the land? Well, in 1884 the population of Brunswick was 3,000, four years later it was 8,000 ; the increase of taxable property was thirty-three per cent. greater in '87 than '86 ; the comptroller of the State says that this county (Glynn) has made for the last twelve months a larger pro rata increase than any other county in the State of Georgia, for eight years ago there was not a brick building in the place ; now there are blocks and blocks of brick stores and fine dwellings ; increase in the value of the land is almost fabulous, and there is a new brick hotel here, "the Oglethrope," which cost with furniture, $160,000, the equal of which for site and style cannot be found between Washington, D. C., and St. Augustine, Fla.

THE OGLETHORPE.—The new hotel is an evidence of and in keeping with the new order of things. The location of the building is choice—on the highest ground in Brunswick, affording fine views and rare sanitary facilities. The house is not merely considered to be, but is fire-proof. So perfect is the protection against fire that the company insuring the property reduced the usual hotel rate one-half in consideration of the character of the building and the excellence of the fire system adopted. The Oglethorpe stands on the principal street, near the railway depot and steamboat wharf, on a plot of ground about three hundred feet square, the main building having three stories and being two hundred and sixty-seven feet long, with wings running back one hundred and forty feet. It is the largest building in the place, and with its graceful round brick towers at each corner, and its turrets and spires jutting through the roof, here and there, it is the most prominent object you see as you approach Brunswick from any direction, either by land or water. The Oglethorpe, being new, is the latest exponent of all that is best and most approved in modern hotel building, and of course has all the "modern improvements." The drawing-room is a grand apartment, reminding you of the parlor of the United States at Saratoga; the dining-room is lighted from three sides, and seats three hundred persons; the main floor, the entrance, office and lower hall are tiled with Georgia marble in beautiful colors, and there is a covered porch for promenading which reaches up to the second story. It is two hundred and forty feet long, and from twenty to twenty-five feet wide.

The bedrooms of the Oglethorpe are larger, as a rule, than those of most hotels. Even the "small rooms" connecting with the suites are twenty feet long by eleven wide, and have two windows, each seven feet high by three feet wide. The "tower" rooms, with their open fire-places, carved wooden mantels, tiled hearths, rich Moquette carpets, portières of velours, and lace curtains on brass poles are as handsome as the bedrooms of any other hotel that the writer has seen, and if the walls and ceilings were artistically decorated and frescoed, the "tower" rooms of the Oglethorpe probably might compare with those palatial bedrooms of the Hotel Métropole in London. A peculiarity of the Oglethorpe is that there are no back rooms; each one faces the street or overlooks the bay, but a few hundred feet distant. Between the bay and the house the grounds of the hotel are attractively laid out. As to the table and general management of the Oglethorpe, it is only necessary to say that the manager is Warren Leland, Jr., a member of the celebrated Leland family—a name long associated with some of the leading hotels in the United States.

EN ROUTE TO AND FROM FLORIDA. — Brunswick is reached by rail from the North by the Atlantic Coast Line and the Savannah, Florida and Western Railroad by way of Savannah and Waycross, Ga., and from Jacksonville, Florida, by railway to Fernandina in one hour, and thence by steamboat in four hours. The water route is very pleasant. The boats, if not splendid specimens of naval architecture, are at least staunch and comfortable. You take an inside route, hug the shore, pass many beautiful islands and get glimpses of most picturesque scenes.

Tourists contemplating a visit to Florida for health or pleasure do well to break the journey at Waycross or Jessup, visit Brunswick and see the charming country thereabouts. The run is made from Waycross to Brunswick in three hours and ten minutes.

The route Southward is from New York to Quantico, Va., over the Pennsylvania tracks; from Richmond to Charleston via Atlantic Coast Line; from Waycross to Brunswick by the Plant system. Leave New York (Desbrosses or Cortlandt streets) at 9 P.M. or midnight —through car to Waycross.

A CUBAN CITY IN THE UNITED STATES.

KEY WEST, February, 1891.

Key West, in Spanish Cayo Hueso (Bone Island), derived its name, so says history, from the fact that the island was strewn with human bones. The conquerors didn't take time to bury the bones of the conquered. The change, corruption Spaniards call it, from Cayo Hueso to Key West was easy.

The United States bought the island from Spain in 1816. The formation is coral and it contains about two thousand acres. The Hon. C. B. Pendleton, editor and proprietor of the *Equator-Democrat*, and a man of culture who has served in the State Senate, showed me an island, or key, as they call it in these parts, distant from Key West five miles, and which he believed to be the most southerly point in the United States. Another authority informed me that Cape Sable, distant from Key West about sixty miles, is the most southerly point.

To quote Editor Pendleton, Key West is distant from the tropical line only thirteen miles. Doctors will differ; another authority gives it as sixty miles. I am inclined to think that on the tropical question my editorial brother is correct in his estimate, because Key West is only distant from Cuba eighty or ninety miles.

The climate is about the same as that of Havana. In the Cuban capital the mercury never goes below sixty degrees; in Key West the lowest point recorded is fifty-one.

Key West is the ninth port of entry in the United States, collecting more import duty than all the other ports in the States of Florida and Georgia and one-half of Alabama combined.

In 1860 the population was about two thousand, one-quarter of whom were colored; but in 1869, after the rebellion in Cuba, the population of the island began to increase and now it numbers twenty-two thousand, and they claim that it is the largest city in Florida.

The inhabitants are mixed, very much mixed—Cubans, negroes, Americans, Chinese, etc. The negroes come from Nassau, Cuba and other places.

Key West was bought of Spain, as before remarked; the island is nearer Cuba than any other land, it is not in any sense American except that it flies the American flag, and it seems to be now, to all intents and purposes, a foreign place—a Spanish colony, as it once was. Spanish is the prevailing language, and Cubans predominate. All the public notices and handbills are printed in two languages, several newspapers are printed in Spanish, and only one, the *Equator-Democrat*, in English. It is difficult to make a purchase or to transact any business unless you speak Spanish, and there are few drivers or conductors of street cars who can understand you if addressed in English. The car drivers swear at their patient, sadly abused mules in hard Spanish. All the American residents and business men speak the prevailing tongue, or are learning it as fast as they can, for without it they cannot so readily conduct business.

Speaking of the street cars, they are all open, of course, winter and summer. In fact, there is never anything resembling northern winter weather in Key West; light summer clothes and Panama hats are worn the year round.

But you are not obliged to patronize street cars. Riding in private conveyances is at a cheaper rate of fare than even in London, or in a country town on the Continent. In London the smallest cab fare is one shilling (twenty-five cents); in Key West you can ride a short distance for a dime, and a longer distance for fifteen cents. The conveyance is a very light and very dirty wagonette on four wheels. The driver is as dirty as his vehicle, and his horse resembles those poor skeletons which are blindfolded and pushed into the arena at a Cuban bull fight.

Such tropical fruits as the sugar apple, the guava, mango, the soft and sweet sapadillo, thrive in Key West. The climate and salt atmosphere combine to make it the home of the palm. There are many tall, slender and beautiful cocoanut trees, some with their graceful leaves waving as high as eighty feet in the air, making an interesting and pretty picture against a cloudless sky.

But the cultivation of the cocoanut in Key West might be made very profitable as well as picturesque. At present there are comparatively few of such trees; their cultivation ought to be encouraged. The tree has no tap root, and will thrive on a thin soil. It comes into bearing eight or ten years from the nut; and after that the fruit grows and increases every month in the year. Like the orange tree, the older it gets the more it bears. A bearing cocoanut grove costs less to care for than an orange grove, and the revenue therefrom is greater. It requires no cultivation, and is as hardy in its section as the cabbage palmetto, that grows everywhere in Florida. Besides, cocoanuts can be shipped in any month of the year; they require no packing, no care in handling, and they will bear transportation for thousands of miles. There is a good market for green cocoanuts in these parts as well as for matured ones. When the nut is fully grown, but green, it contains about two glasses of clear juice, milk we call it in the North. It is considered a healthful beverage in the tropics and sells per glass in the streets of Havana for the equivalent of five cents.

Nature has favored Key West with a perfect climate. It is surrounded by the Gulf of Mexico, as blue and as beautiful as the famous Danube. Nature in fact has done everything she could to make the place desirable as a residence for man, but man has done little or nothing for himself, thus far, and if the truth must be told, notwithstanding its favorable natural conditions and its lovely surroundings, Key West is not yet a desirable place to live in. It has no sanitary laws, for nothing whatever has been done with a view to sanitation, and yet with the salt ocean all around the little island, how easy it would be to make it healthy and clean, for it is neither one nor the other. There is no such thing as system, no sewerage whatever in the town excepting one iron pipe which leads from one hotel, the Russell House, to the sea, and even that one pipe is allowed to clog occasionally.

A liberally illustrated and large edition of the *Equator-Democrat* was issued in 1889, which presents a very rose-colored view of Key West. In that paper I find that "the pleasant streets running at right angles are as smooth and hard as adamant." I am not certain that I am very well acquainted with adamant, but I know that the streets of Key West are unpaved and that they are the roughest and the dirtiest streets I ever saw. As I have lived in Baltimore, in New York and in New Orleans, my testimony ought to be accepted on such a theme. I speak of Key West in fine weather; what it must be in wet weather I don't like to imagine. If nothing but very deep ruts, holes and great gullies in the roadway resemble adamant then is Key West adamantine beyond doubt.

There is not a boot-black in the town ; none is needed. Nobody thinks of blacking his shoes ; it would be absurd. I spoke on this point with a young New Yorker who hails from the fashionable precincts of Madison avenue. He is a business man who is liberal in the matter of money, usually dressy, and extremely neat in his person. He has been in Key West six months, and in all that time not a brush has passed over his shoes.

I regret to differ with my learned and courteous friend, the editor of the *Democrat*, on the subject of hotels. Let him speak for himself. He says that "The Russell House, the leading hotel in the city, is second to none in the State in accommodations." Now I had an idea that St. Augustine and Jacksonville and Tampa were in Florida, and that there were such hotels "in the State" as the Ponce de Leon and The Cordova at St. Augustine, and the new Tampa Bay Hotel at Tampa Bay, not to mention a number of other first-class houses "in the State."

Directly opposite the Russell is the Duval House. You may never have heard of it; it is not one-third the size of the Russell House. I know nothing of the apartments of the Duval, for I investigated no further than the dining-room, but that was enough to establish its good reputation. It will be a long time before I forget how beautifully garnished a dish they made at the Duval of a red snapper, and the delicious flavor of their *omelette soufflée* remains with me still. The Duval is presided over by a Cuban lady, Mrs. Bolio, who kept for years one of the leading hotels in Havana. She is evidently a woman who knows what good living is.

Cigar-making is a very large and important industry in Key West. The place was selected for cigar-making because the climate is suited to the "curing" of tobacco in the leaf, and because it is near Havana. There is something also in the name. Everybody does not know that this (Spanish) island is United States territory, and some smokers if they see a "Key West" label on a box of cigars believe, without stopping to think, that they are smoking a foreign-made cigar. Now a Key West cigar if made from Havana tobacco of fine quality has just as good a flavor as if it were made in Cuba, but the Key West cigar can be sold at a lower price because the import duty on cigars is much higher than the duty on the raw material.

Having the same climate as Havana, the best climate in the world for tobacco curing, and the cigars being made by Cubans, who are the best cigar-makers in the world, Key West turns out just as good cigars as can be produced anywhere—provided always that tobacco of the first quality is used. And the cigar need not consist entirely of Havana tobacco. A cigar of choice flavor is made of a mixture of tobaccos—Havana "filler" and "binder," with, say, a "Connecticut seed" or Sumatra wrapper.

The manufacture of cigars has without doubt aided largely in building up the business of Key West. One authority says that there are two hundred factories, employing five thousand operatives, and transacting a business amounting to seven millions of dollars annually. But this report may be exaggerated. However, here are some more figures, and if the reader is mathematically inclined he can draw his own conclusions: Key West during 1890 turned out one hundred and forty millions of cigars.

There are very few Spanish or American cigarmakers in Key West; the majority are Cubans, with a very small sprinkling of negroes. There are so many factories and so many operatives that, although it is a cigar-producing place, very few cigars indeed are sold at retail. Everybody smokes, every one invites you to smoke; cigars are almost as free as the air. It would be a paradise for a young dude who has a slender purse and who is addicted to the weed.

Upon the courteous invitation of P. Pohalski & Co., who have a branch in Havana, with headquarters in Warren street, New York, I paid a visit to their factory, which is one of the largest in Key West, and I was much interested in what I saw. Pohalski & Co. erected their own factory, upon their own ground, and it is one of the most imposing edifices in Key West. They also built upon their own land a number of small houses which they rent to their workmen at a moderate figure; for its size it is quite a respectable colony.

Although very large, employing several hundred hands, the factory is orderly, exceedingly clean and neat, showing good government. Perfect system reigns throughout the entire establishment. The first floor is used for the business offices, for cases of tobacco and for the "strippers;" the whole of the second floor is occupied by cigar makers, and the third floor is used by the "packers," also for curing leaf tobacco and for storing cigars in boxes.

A "stripper" is one who, with the dexter finger and thumb of the right hand pulls the stem from the leaf while the leaf is damp, the leaf being held in the left hand. It is done by a dexterous and quick movement, not a vestige of the leaf remaining on the stem. The most costly leaves, for wrappers, are only entrusted to experienced operators. The strippers in this factory are numbered by scores. They are all females, all Cubans, and range in age from ten years old to women of fifty.

It is not a pleasing sight to one who associates woman with habits of refinement, to see the older women, while at their work of stripping, smoke long, thick cigars. They hold the cigar between their teeth and seldom remove it, not even to talk. They are rough-looking cigars, rolled into shape by the women themselves from the leaves they are stripping.

A more pleasing picture is presented on the cigar-making floor, above. You will be surprised upon entering to see a man standing erect in the centre of the room, book in hand, reading aloud. You cannot help but notice, although Spanish may be Greek to you, that the reader's voice is powerful and well trained, reaching to the extreme corners and to the most distant ears on the vast floor. He is a professional reader. The several hundred men club together, each paying a nominal sum for the reader's services. In this way, while engaged in their work, they hear the news of the day and are regaled with the latest Spanish novel.

"Packing" cigars is a technical term. It is not simply to tie them up with pretty silk ribbons and place them neatly in a box. A packer is one who assorts the colors also. It is a very nice and delicate piece of work. It demands a good eye for color and long experience, and then it can only be done in a certain light, of course not by artificial light, nor unless the day is bright.

An overcast, murky and heavy sky is not good for packing—assorting, it might be called. In a few hundred loose cigars placed on a table ready for "packing," the casual observer will probably see only three or four colors. They are first assorted roughly to bring together those of decided colors—light brown, medium, dark brown, etc. Then a pile of dark or light shades is gone over again and again until the different piles of cigars are alike, as if they were all made from one leaf and turned out by machinery. The packer also discards a cigar that is not perfectly made, or one not uniform with the rest. A special few, exact as to form and hue, are selected for the top row, to catch and please the eye of the smoker when the lid of the box is raised. A good packer is paid better than any other operative in the business. Men and women are employed in it, some of them earning as high as twenty-five or thirty-five dollars per week.

The sponge trade is also a very large and important industry here. The sponges are found in this part of the Gulf of Mexico, and the trade gives employment to a great many people. I visited the largest sponge house, that of Arapian & Co., and saw there in different stages, sponges valued at a quarter of a million dollars.

Such a stock of sponges, as you can easily imagine, occupies much space. My only surprise was to find such valuable merchandise housed in a light frame building. A fire would spread easily, and the whole would be rapidly consumed.

I have spoken of the dirty, unpaved streets of Key West; it would be unfair not to mention a lovely drive which you can take for a few miles on the edge of the Gulf. You go around the old forts, you see lighthouses and other interesting objects en route, the bracing air from the Gulf fans your cheeks, the ocean is spread out before you, and if you return in the early evening, and near dinner time, you will most likely be favored with a grand sunset, and you will surely have a keen appetite.

Key West is reached from New York by steamers of the Mallory line, and from New Orleans by New Orleans and Havana steamers, but decidedly the best and most luxurious way of going to the island is by the Plant line of steamers which leave Tampa, Florida and Havana, Cuba, three times a week. The "Mascotte" and "Olivette" were built for this route. They are both staunch, swift, beautifully appointed ships, whose commanders were in the Atlantic service for years, the "Olivette" being the fastest boat of her size in the world—a model vessel.

If you are going to Key West for pleasure—it is possible for people to go there with that end in view—you will go from New York to Jacksonville via the Pennsylvania and Atlantic coast lines and there take the Jacksonville, Tampa and Key West Railroad, although part of this "railway" journey consists of a sail on the Gulf of Mexico, from Tampa.

The island, with all its objectionable features, has churches of different denominations, it has convents, good schools, and has one large substantial and beautiful brick and stone building for a custom house, for which the government appropriated one hundred thousand dollars.

Key West has a police force numbering fourteen officers, including men of all colors and several nationalities.

ST. AUGUSTINE.

AN ANCIENT CITY MODERNIZED.

ST. AUGUSTINE, FLA., Feb. 8, 1891.

What a contrast, to leave the dust and dirt of Key West, its unpaved roadways, full of deep ruts, large holes and great gullies: Key West, with its mixed population of twenty thousand negroes, Cubans, Chinamen and white folks: Key West, minus sidewalks, and minus many evidences of a high state of civilization: what a contrast is it to arrive in this beautiful city of the South, with its smooth-paved streets, its cleanly and aristocratic air, and its three wondrously beautiful Spanish hotels, all within speaking distance of each other. It is like leaping, if I may use such an expression, from hades to heaven.

The changes here within the past three years are great. Most important to the tourist is the erection of a railway bridge which crosses the St. John's River. Three years ago you were obliged to stop at Jacksonville if you approached from the north; if from the south, you steamed across on a ferry-boat from Palatka. Now you take your seat in a drawing-room car at Jersey City, in the North, or at Tampa, if you approach from the South, and you need not leave the car until the conductor calls out "St. Augustine"—thirty-one hours by vestibuled train from New York, twelve hours by the West India Fast Mail from the Gulf, at Tampa.

As to other changes, much land has been reclaimed from the river, miles of roadway have been asphalted and paved with wooden blocks; the old fort is being restored, for which work the government has appropriated

ST. AUGUSTINE. 181

$15,000; many new houses have been built, all of coquina and in the Moorish style; to the oldest house in the town has been added a new stone tower; there has been erected a new City Hall, which includes a fine market; and to crown it all, as it were, there is a new church, a Memorial Presbyterian Church, built in memory of the beautiful daughter Mr. Flagler lost two years ago. The structure is so attractive, so pleasing to the eye, that in driving away from it you find yourself constantly turning around to keep its graceful architectural lines in view as long as possible.

It is probably not possible to enhance the splendor of the Ponce de Leon Hotel, the drawing-room of which, with its magnificent proportions, its onyx fire-place, its ceiling decorations, its rich carpets and furniture, and its rare paintings by Bridgman, Koppay, and other artists, is not rivalled by any other hotel in the world. To call it palatial is no compliment to "the Ponce" parlor, for I have seen no apartments in royal palaces that are more pleasing, and I have been favored with a view of many palaces in many countries. But the approaches to the great hotel and its own grounds have been improved and are now finished.

The same remarks will apply to the exterior of the Alcazar Hotel, the smooth and pleasant walk around the outside of which measures just half a mile. The colored boys know: they use it semi-occasionally for a foot or bicycle race: "twice around the Alcazar is one mile" they will tell you.

One of the novel features of this establishment is a swimming pool, into which the sulphur water rushes up from the artesian well with great force. There is room in the pool (40 by 120 feet) for scores of swimmers, and there is always a number of visitors looking from the galleries above on the lively scene below. With the mercury ranging between 70 and 80 the sulphur water is indeed refreshing; and they say it is quite invigorating. Temperature of the water, 75 degrees.

In the Hotel Cordova you will notice some changes, for the indefatigable manager, E. N. Wilson, is never content with his efforts. There is a new dining-room for instance. The best seems not good enough for Mr. Wilson, and his critical eye is always finding some way to improve the house and to add to its comfort. He has redecorated the parlor. The walls are now richly papered but the tints are not satisfactory—to Mr. Wilson. The furniture and carpets are in dark colors, so Mr. Wilson later on contemplates covering the walls with white and gold for an artistic contrast. Expensive? Yes, I should say so, but who cares for the expense? Mr. Flagler has a very long purse and Mr. Wilson has *carte blanche*. If the owner in planning these hotels had thought only of pecuniary profit probably they would never have come into existence in their present form. It is an idea with him to beautify the ancient city, and a half million dollars more or less make little or no difference to Mr. Flagler. Yet his hotels are conducted with a careful regard of business-like methods, although this is not apparent to the casual observer.

By the way, I have the very best of reasons for knowing that Mr. Flagler's private acts of charity are many and munificent. After making full and proper inquiry into a case presented to him he always responds, but he never wants his generous acts to be made public. He will not thank me for this "mention," I feel sure, but it is his due and possibly no harm can come from printing it.

Mr. Flagler has bought all the land around and about his three hotels, so that nobody can erect anything anywhere near him. He is not the man to do anything by halves.

The sitting-room in which this is penned is one of a suite I occupy in the castellated tower on a corner of the

Hotel Cordova. The walls of the building are of gray
coquina. Outside each window is a small and separate
"kneeling balcony," protected by ornamental iron railings, painted a reddish brown—such balconies as you
see in some buildings in Madrid. The windows have
white lace curtains and the shades are alternate blue
and crimson—contrasting pleasantly with the neutral
tint of the outer walls. To the east, within stone's
throw, is Cordova Park ; to the west, the same distance,
is the one-acre park of the Alcazar, with its tropical
foliage, pretty walks and handsome fountain; while
diagonally opposite, same distance again (about one
hundred feet), loom up the terra-cotta turrets, towers,
arches and gabled roofs of the Ponce de Leon Hotel,
with its grand park of four and a half acres. This may
convey some idea of the situation; to describe the scene
requires the pen if not the pencil of an artist.

The Cordova drawing-room has its tables and chairs,
and it contains some books also ; not odd volumes
picked up haphazard, but books bought and selected
by an artist, book-worm and connoisseur. In the Cordova library you will find "Burke's Peerage," "Almanach
de Gotha," "Webster's Royal Red Book," "Kelly's
Handbook to the Titled, Landed and Offical Classes,"
"The County Families of the United Kingdom," De-
brett's "House of Commons and the Judicial Bench,"
"Castles and Abbeys of England" and "Stately Homes
of England." I have enumerated only a few of the ordinary volumes relating to Great Britain, but there are
also rare and valuable tomes richly and beautifully illustrated, descriptive of life and scenes in different countries. For instance, one set in three volumes is "Mas-
terpieces of Industrial Art and Sculpture at the Interna-
tional Exhibition," by J. B. Waring, published in 1862.
This mammoth work is richly illuminated, bound in red
morocco, picked out with gold, and measures one foot
by a foot and a half. It probably cost in London twen-

ty-five pounds, and gives one some idea of the money and good taste expended in selecting the Cordova library. If one is fond of instructive books his taste can be gratified at the Cordova.

At the majority of hotels you eat ordinary oranges, brought to the table direct from the store-room : at the Cordova only Indian River oranges are used, selected " Indian Rivers," and instead of coming direct from the store-room they come from a refrigerator. After this process they become Grateful and Comforting, to quote the names which Epps, the famous cocoa man, gave his two daughters. Perfect quiet reigns in the dining-room. The waiters are governed, well governed, by a head waiter whose head is level. He would even satisfy that "cranky critic," as he has been called, Max O'Rell. The men, when serving dinner, wear dress coats, black trousers and white cravats. Instead of a loose waistcoat they wear a broad black sash around the waist, and instead of noisy boots they wear shoes having cloth uppers and rubber soles—black tennis shoes. Not a word is heard from the servants, except in polite response to an order, and they glide about like dark angels.

ABOUT TAMPA.

THE INN, PORT TAMPA, FLA.,
January 31, 1891.

Tampa is of interest historically, being the place where Ferdinand De Soto landed May 25, 1539. From here he started on his search for the mines of wealth supposed to exist in the new world, which resulted in the discovery of the Mississippi river. It is here also that Narvaez, having obtained a grant of Florida from Charles V. of Spain, landed with a large force April 16, 1528.

Tampa is on the Gulf coast of Florida, two hundred and forty miles from Jacksonville. There are two trains daily with Pullman cars from Jacksonville and St. Augustine to Tampa, passing through Palatka, Sanford and Winter Park, both having direct connection with all Eastern and Western cities and one being a through train from New York.

Its rapid growth during the past seven years from about eight hundred inhabitants to as many thousands, has been brought about by the Plant system, which completed the South Florida railroad to Tampa for the purpose of developing Tampa commercially.

Dr. Long, a United States army surgeon, wrote of Fort Brooks, at Tampa, "This post has always been considered a delightful station." Dr. Long's reports and other reports to the surgeon-general at Washington show it to be one of the most healthful stations in the country.

Peninsulas have always been thought desirable because of their climate, which gives them advantages over other localities, and among peninsulas Florida is unrivalled because of its latitude and particularly as it is affected by the warm waters of the Gulf of Mexico.

The investment of large capital in constructing a new hotel in Florida with the expectation of drawing to it the requisite patronage, demanded a knowledge of the requirements of winter tourists who visit the place for health or pleasure. Those requirements have been carefully studied by Mr. H. B. Plant, president of the Plant Investment Company, acting under the advice of eminent scientists, in the selection of Tampa. The new hotel is situated on the west side of the Hillsborough river where it empties into Tampa bay, opposite to and facing the city, which is within easy walking distance. From the river to the front of the hotel there are extensive lawns and flower beds, with orange, palm and other tropical trees, the hotel grounds and property including twenty-two acres. At the rear of the house there is a long stretch of pine lands.

As you view the house at a distance, from the deck of a steamer, or from a car window, with its long stretch of brick front, its iron and stone trimmings, its many towers with great and gorgeous silver-bronzed, balloon-shaped domes, each surmounted by a shining gold crescent, it impresses you at once as being a great oriental palace. And this idea is aided by the palms and other tropical trees and shrubs by which it is surrounded.

The oriental idea also strikes you as you enter. There is a grand "office," the ceilings are supported by stout marble columns, and the music-room, the drawing-room, and all the minor rooms on the main floor are furnished in the very best taste, the matter of expense never seeming to be a question with those who selected the furniture and decorations in different parts of the world. It is safe to say that very few winter or summer resort hotels in this country are as richly furnished.

The hotel has been most thoroughly constructed and is practically fireproof, the outer and inner walls being of brick, with steel beams and concrete floors. There has been the most approved scientific work in drainage and plumbing, and there is an abundant supply of good water. On each floor the wide hall extends the entire length of the main building—512 feet. There are no inside rooms. Every room has the sun during some portion of the day, and a large number of suites have private baths. The house is heated by steam, in addition to which there are open fire-places in the rooms. The latest improvements have been introduced in lighting.

The other day I was in the Savannah depot of the Savannah, Florida and Western railroad waiting for the Florida special vestibuled train, when I heard a colored "depot hand" say that he wished the Tampa Bay Hotel had been built elsewhere. "Why, may I ask?" "Well," answered my civil and sable informant, "I am tired of handlin' de stuff for dat hotel; we'se been a doin' it in dis yer depot for de whole year. But it's comin' putty near de end now, I guess. Las' Saturday der went thro' de depot three whole cyars filled with nutting else but cyarpets, all for dat house." These remarks give one some faint idea of the size of the new hotel.

Mr. Plant did a great deal for Tampa when he ran his railroad down there, his lines of steamers from Tampa to Havana and Mobile have greatly helped the prosperity of the place, and now he has crowned his good work by putting up a magnificent hotel utterly regardless of the cost. If there was not already a Plant City in Florida, I should suggest to change the name of Tampa to Plant City. The house will accommodate four hundred guests; the rates are five dollars per day.

It is only open during the winter, from Christmas until the first of April. But do not go to Tampa without your summer clothes.

All the above relates to the big new hotel at Tampa Bay, but all of it is written at the Inn, in Port Tampa, distant from Tampa Bay proper nine miles. The Inn is "little," it accommodates only seventy-five guests, but it is a gem of a hotel. It is built on, or rather over, the water on piles, and is like an island, being actually surrounded by water. There is always a pleasant breeze on one side of the house, and a breeze is very grateful in this latitude. As I write, the mercury in a thermometer hanging outside my bedroom window marks 75 degrees ; this is at 5 P.M., Saturday, January 31. We sleep with open windows, and nothing more than your pajama or a sheet is necessary for a covering.

Two sides of the dining-room are composed entirely of sliding-windows through which you can see wild ducks and fish in great quantities. I have seen wild ducks hauled in by the waiters through the open windows of this dining-room. You can throw a line into the water as you sit at dinner and if it be properly baited you will probably find a mullet at the end of the cord before you reach your *café noir*.

It goes without saying that there are good sailing and fishing at Port Tampa : Spanish mackerel and the pompano abound, the latter conceded by epicures to be one of the most exquisitely flavored fish in the world. Here also is the famous tarpon—Silver King he has been christened. In fact Port Tampa is a very paradise for sportsmen. It is easy to supply the table with oysters, fish and game in profusion. The table by the way is liberally provided, and the service by Swiss and French waiters is good.

The dining-room of the Tampa Inn reminds you of

the dining-room of the Hygeia Hotel at Old Point Comfort, not for its size, but for its water surroundings, and the scene outside brings up recollections of the Surf Hotel at Fire Island. Picnic Island, across the Gulf one mile, might be a bit of Long Island. But there the similarity ends because the Inn, unlike the Surf Hotel, is a new house and is luxuriously furnished.

Steamers leave here weekly (every Tuesday) for Mobile, and tri-weekly (Monday, Thursday and Saturday), for Key West and Havana.

The railway depot conveying you to Tampa Bay (frequent daily trains), is at the door of the hotel, and from this same depot you can get a through car to Jacksonville or to New York.

The rates at the Inn are four and five dollars a day. It is proposed to keep it open all the year.

MONTEREY, CALIFORNIA.

MONTEREY, CAL., March 25, 1891.

The name Monterey means Mountain King and was bestowed on the place in 1602 by Don Sebastian Vizcaino in honor of Jaspar de Zuniga, Conte de Monte de Rey, at that time Viceroy of Mexico. It was he who suggested and projected the expedition undertaken by Vizcaino.

When the members of this expedition returned to Spain the place returned to its primitive condition and nothing was heard of it till a band of Franciscan missionaries arrived on this coast in 1768, one hundred and sixty-eight years after the first discovery. This expedition came under the direction and guidance of the president of the band, Father Junipero Serra.

At the risk of being charged with sacrilege, I will interpolate right amid this ancient history a bit of fresh news imparted to me yesterday by a carriage driver. He showed me from the road a high plateau overlooking the sea, where plainly to the naked eye were to be seen preparations for receiving a statue, which is to be in place and to be dedicated before long. It will be in honor of Father Junipero before mentioned; it will cost ten thousand dollars, and the wife of Senator Leland Stanford will foot the bill. The site for the statue is a magnificent one, and if the work of art be worthy of its position, the city of Monterey will have something it may be proud of.

There's a "History of Monterey County" by E. S. Harrison. I didn't know before I came here and looked into it that Monterey was the first place settled in the State of California; that the first custom house in the

HOTEL DEL MONTE.

State (now an old rookery) was established here; that Monterey was once not only a bustling city, but the capital of the State. It is not a wholly deserted village now, but its commercial glory, like that of Newport, R. I., which was once a greater port of entry than New York, has departed, never to return. But Monterey will always be dear to the hearts of Californians, from its historic associations and connections.

"The first European lady to come to California," says Harrison, "was the wife of Governor Fages, who arrived in Monterey in 1783. Their child, born about 1784, was probably the first child born in California of European parents."

Monterey is one hundred and twenty-six miles from San Francisco, and is reached in four hours by the Coast Division of the Southern Pacific Railroad Company. On the way, in San Mateo county (*en passant*, what musical names all these counties and mountains have), within ten to forty miles from the starting point, Fourth and Townsend streets, you pass the rural homes of San Francisco's millionaires. Some are set in great forests of oak surrounded by acres of flowers in perennial bloom. Next, the beautiful city of San José comes in view, and a flourishing city it appears to be from the car windows. As the train rolls along you keep in sight for many miles the dome of the Lick Observatory, which glistens in the sunlight on the summit of Mount Hamilton.

And then you haven't eyes enough to take in and enjoy the beautiful views of ocean, river, valley and mountain as the train dashes along—the Coast Range mountains on your left, on the right the Santa Cruz mountains, with the sun setting behind them—a glorious moving panorama.

After passing what is called the most fertile valley in the State Monterey is reached, if that be your destination, but there is a more important station one mile this side of Monterey. When the conductor calls out "Hotel del Monte" very few passengers in the cars remain seated, and the train speeds on to the sleepy old town of Monterey, almost empty.

The first action which the Pacific Improvement Company took when they concluded to make of this place a summer and winter resort was to purchase some land for the purpose, so they purchased *seven thousand acres*. Part of this domain was a forest, and of this they selected for their hotel "garden" a simple matter of *one hundred and twenty-six acres*. Forty acres of this they cultivated in flower-beds, lawns, vegetables and fruit; the rest they allowed to remain as nature left it, after hiring the services of a landscape gardener to lay out within their gates a few miles for drives and paths.

Then it occurred to them that it would be well to have a grand outside drive as an additional attraction, so they made one, cutting away mountain, forest and bluff; going through the woods, four or five miles; skirting the ocean for the same distance; altogether a nice little post-prandial drive of *seventeen miles*. But this is not much—for California. The drive being private property it is used only for the guests of the Hotel del Monte, the owners of which keep it in the best order, and in summer time have it watered. It is macadamized and in as good condition as the drives in Central Park, New York.

The road winds toward the bay through a forest of oaks and pines. For two or three miles it will be cool, dark, shaded and sweet smelling, and presently you get a view of the ocean. If the wind is high, as it was on the twenty-second of March, you will see foaming white-caps in the distance, and the spray dashing wildly on the bare brown rocks in the foreground, making a picture which, on the day we saw it, was awfully grand. I don't mean this in the sense that girls do when they

say a thing is "awfully nice ;" I mean that the boisterous waves were almost frightful with their impetuous rush and their terrible roar.

To quote dear old Fitz-Greene Halleck, whose statue in Central Park few recognize :

> The winds of March were humming
> Their parting song, their parting song.

It was a habit of my predecessor on the *Home Journal*, General George P. Morris, to publish annually this sweet song of Halleck's in the *Home Journal* during the first week of March. It was a singular fancy of Morris's and it pleased his brother poet.

But I am getting away from my story—and the surf. The seals didn't seem to mind the roaring surf or howling wind. Their unearthly bark formed part of the grand chorus. They tossed their heads and rolled their ungainly bodies about with all the grace at their command, which is not saying much for their sylph-like movements. No; water is their element.

If you expect to see the seals of the same color as the sealskin sacques worn by women, you may not see the seals at all, for they match in color with the brownish gray rocks on which they romp. They have not gone through the process of "London dyeing." I didn't take the trouble to get out of the carriage and go down to the shore, so in this instance I accepted the driver's word that there were five hundred seals on the rocks.

The cultivated grounds of the Hotel del Monte astonish you with their size and beauty and with the neatness and order in which they are kept. Probably not elsewhere is there such variety in horticulture. Everything from everywhere seems to thrive here. Nor do I know of any section of country where there are such noble oaks and pines, but probably the company claim too much when they say that "the garden is the finest, the most gorgeous, the richest and most varied in all the world." A few years have elapsed since I examined Kensington and Kew closely, but it seems to me that the Tuileries gardens, which I saw one year ago, are richer, and I know that the gardens in Hyde Park, through which I strolled last August, are more pleasing to the eye and to the sense of smell. I speak of the floral display only; it must be remembered, however, that the Del Monte gardens are not at their best in March.

The trees are wonderful. I carry with me not only a thermometer but a tiny tape measure, the latter in my pocket. I asked the driver to stop as we were driving through the grounds, while I measured a pine and I found that it was four and a half yards in circumference near the ground. The driver told me how tall it was, but I will not quote him as I'm not giving you "California stories." This pine was not pointed out nor did I select it for its size. There were others within a few feet of where this giant stood just as large, and for all I know there are hundreds on the ground much larger.

Of course the palm abounds, all trees of tropical growth are here; there are calla lilies for borders, violets, heliotrope, nasturtium, honeysuckle in wild profusion, and this in March, mind you. Is there ivy? "Well, rather," as an Englishman might answer such a question. A leaf now lies on my table which measures five inches across. The grounds are in charge of a skilled landscape gardner with a force of thirty-five men —English, American and Chinese.

Foreigners from other lands may rail against the Chinese as much as they please, and our legislators may be right in excluding them lest they overrun the country, but it must be said in their favor that they are a peaceful, industrious set, and there are no better servants for indoor or outdoor work. Under certain conditions, however, they are as obstinate as mules. When you engage them you must be exceedingly careful in giving them instructions, for they will always continue to do what they are at first told to do; you cannot change their ways.

Mr. George Schönewald, manager of Hotel del Monte, while we were chatting in his office, illustrated it to me in this way: "Observe that Chinaman wiping carefully the casing of that white door. He was told when he first came here that he was to do that sort of work at this time of day, and if the heavens fall he'll do it. If I were to ask him this minute to leave that door and polish this plate glass window he might obey, but it would upset him for the day, if not for all time. If you change your mind and want the work done in a different way you had better change your Chinaman, you can't change their ways. But seven Chinamen will do the work of fourteen white men."

And this brings me to the fact that nearly all the walls and all the interior woodwork of these great buildings are painted white. The lack of color becomes a little tiresome to the eye, but one thing comforts you, it is kept white—not a mark, not a spot to mar its perfection. Chinamen are always washing either doors, windows, surbase, or whatever part of the floor is not carpeted; all is pure white except the floor of the beautiful dining-room, which is of dark English oak kept highly polished.

The series of buildings is in the modern Gothic style, the main building three hundred and fifty feet front, with a central tower eighty feet high and wings or annexes two hundred and eighty feet long, showing an entire floor area of sixteen acres. An acre or two, more or less, is nothing—in California. The bed-room in which this is written is an ordinary room here, eighteen by sixteen feet. Even the marble wash-basin is worth measuring—three feet three in circumference. Running water, gas, fireplaces; and closets built with partition walls in every room. There are five hundred and ten rooms, and seven hundred people can be accommodated comfortably.

I am surprised here, as I have been elsewhere in California, at the low rates which obtain at hotels. A placard on the door of this well-furnished room, with beautiful walls and ceiling and a luxurious bed, reads: "Rate for this room, with board, for one person $3.50; for two $6.50. With bath-room $4 and $7 per day." And in the bath-room there appears to be an inexhaustible supply of boiling water. There is no charge made in the ladies' billiard room, which adjoins the parlor; no charge for use of boats on the twenty-acre lake.

If the plumbing is right, and so it appears to be, there is no trouble with the question of drainage, the ocean being at the door. The drinking water is brought from Carmel river, eighteen miles distant, in the mountains. A ton of ice per day is made on the premises. Some of the vegetables are raised near the hotel, and there is a dairy farm connected with the property measuring untold acres.

Native wines are sold at Hotel del Monte lower than I've seen them either here or abroad. It's easy to be a "swell" at Del Monte. A half bottle of Zinfandel is opened and served at table for fifteen cents, and a very good wine it is, too, so far as pleasing my palate goes. But I don't profess to be so well versed in wines as the late Sam Ward or the present Ward McAllister. There is a secret, however, in the low charge for California wine at Hotel del Monte—the company have their own vineyards. What haven't they got? They have nothing less than a Steinway concert grand in the parlor and another in the ball-room.

There's a feature that almost escaped being put down, and yet it is worthy of special mention. To the first floors in the two annexes you neither ascend nor descend any stairs; nor do you to the second floor. To the first floor you descend an inclined hall or arcade; to the second you ascend an inclined arcade. If you have a room even on the third floor you only walk up one flight of stairs, unless you prefer the elevator.

This is not a new idea, however. I remember being shown through an old, unused palace in Berlin which was constructed in the same way. A member of the royal house was weak in the knees from rheumatism and so was rolled on a sedan chair up and down in this way. The porter at this hotel, wheeling his truck "upstairs" loaded with trunks, reminded me of the rheumatic royalty.

In all hotels recently constructed there is an electric bell as well as an electric button in every room. If you leave word to be called in the morning, there's no rapping outside your door—rapping loud enough to awaken every sleeper near your apartment. There is an electric button in the office which connects with a bell in your room, and to this call you will respond. There is no escape from it; you must get out of bed to stop the ringing.

The first Hotel del Monte, opened in 1880, was destroyed by fire: the new house was erected four years ago. The present manager, Mr. George Schönewald, opened the first house and superintended the construction of the second. As his name indicates, he is not to the manor born. He arrived in this country twenty-five years ago without a penny in his pocket, but with a determination to make a position for himself. There is no secret in his success. Anybody can gain success who will follow the Schönewald method. It was not "blind luck" with him, but industry, unceasing industry, directed with unusual intelligence.

Schönewald fitted himself thoroughly for his position. On his arrival in this country he decided to be a practical confectioner, and not long after he received the highest salary ever paid in the State to a confectioner. Then he took to cooking and earned the highest salary ever paid to a cook in the State. Step by step has he moved from the very bottom round of the ladder to the management of one of the largest and finest hotels in the country.

Schönewald is a worker. He is supposed to take three meals a day, but sometimes his breakfast is not touched till late in the afternoon. From my window I have seen him driving about rapidly in a buggy before my toilet was completed; and your humble servant, as a general rule, is out of bed before seven A.M. The interests of the company first, his own comfort last, seems to be this manager's motto,

Yes, your Germans are workers. Mrs. Schönewald is her husband's helpmeet: she fills the position of housekeeper at Hotel del Monte, and that probably accounts for the bed-rooms being so comfortably furnished —a rocker here, an easy, arm-chair there, with a neat white "tidy" on the upholstered back. There's nothing like a woman's eye, a woman's thoughtfulness in providing all the tasteful etceteras which make a home comfortable and complete.

I will close with a clipping from the tourist book, "To the Golden Gate," issued by the Pennsylvania Railroad:—"The Eastern traveler coming to California's coast and failing to see 'Del Monte' has indeed missed not everything, but a goodly part."

Profile of Front. Hotel Del Monte.

Old Oaks. Del Monte.

HOTEL DEL CORONADO, CORONADO BEACH, CALIFORNIA.

SAN DIEGO AND CORONADO.

CORONADO BEACH, CAL.,
March 5, 1891.

I was induced to think about coming to Southern California by the tempting descriptions in Henry T. Finck's book, "Scenic Tour of the Pacific Coast," and by interesting articles in the Century Magazine. Toward San Diego and Coronado Beach my steps were turned by Charles Dudley Warner's glowing accounts in Harper's Magazine.

I had always accepted with a grain of salt the flattering reports so widely published, and now that I have seen for myself these wondrous things, my friends will scarcely credit my story, so enthusiastic have I become.

However, I do not intend that you shall rely on my mere "say so." I've been looking up official and other authorities—men of wide reputation, who have a name to lose.

First, as to climate. This is the fifth of March; I have been here one week to-day, and every day of the seven has been about alike—dry, sunshiny, only on one or two days cloudy. On some days of the seven I have seen men bathing in the ocean, and the bathers said that the temperature was enjoyable—this in February. I am told that you can bathe in the surf the year round, but never mind what "I am told."

And in temperature, I believe it to be the most equable climate in the world—but away with "beliefs," I have a thermometer of my own, and the hotel has one also, but I have watched closely a government, self-recording instrument which is so placed that no ray of the sun nor no reflection can approach it, and the figures, signed by an official of the signal service in the United States army, record something like this for the current week: five A. M., 55 degrees; noon, 68 degrees; five P. M., 64 degrees. The figures quoted, to be exact, are those recorded on February 28; some days since then have been a trifle cooler.

You may suggest: "If there is almost continual sunshine during daylight, and the ground is always covered with grass and wild flowers, it must be very hot and trying in summer."

Must it? Remember there is a bay on three sides of Coronado, and the Pacific ocean is on the other. But I will ask you to remember nothing. From the compiled records of the United States signal station here, I have "boiled down" a lot of facts and figures into this condensed form, to wit:—in ten years, from 1876 to 1885, both years inclusive, there were only one hundred and twenty days on which the mercury rose higher than 80 degrees. And the summer nights are far more pleasant than those you experience in New York.

What about the winter then? Here is the answer,

gathered in the same way from the same official source. There were only ninety-three days in those same ten years upon which the mercury reached as low as 40, and on no day did it remain at 40 for more than two hours.

By comparing, as I did, the United States record of the mean temperature at Coronado for one year with a computation—made in the same year by Dr. Bennett of the mean temperature of the Mediterranean records, I find that the winter temperature of Coronado is 8 degrees *higher* than the winter temperature of the most favored foreign winter resorts, and the summer temperature 10 degrees *lower*, thus making an average of 9 degrees in favor of Coronado as an all-year-round resort.

I haven't the honor of Mr. Douglas Gunn's acquaintance, but in his interesting pamphlet concerning this region he says: "With scarcely a perceptible difference between summer and winter you wear the same clothing and sleep under the same covering the year round. The average annual rainfall is about ten inches, with an average of thirty-four rainy days in the whole year. And here most of the rain falls at night; there are very few of what Eastern people would call "'rainy days.'"

My week's experience agrees with Mr. Gunn's observations. He says: "Almost every morning, about two hours after sunrise, a gentle sea breeze commences, attaining its maximum velocity between one and three P.M., then decreasing, and changing to a gentle land breeze during the night. The sea breeze increasing as the sun gains its height, modifies the power of its rays, and keeps the skin just comfortably warm. The gentle land breeze at night cools off the heat absorbed during the day, and makes every night refreshing."

I could go on and quote to the same effect from no less distinguished an authority than the scientist Agassiz, who was in this locality nineteen years ago; also from Dr. Chamberlain in the New York Medical Record, who says "it is the sanitarium of the Military Division for the Pacific," and from one known to me personally, Dr. Titus Munson Coan, a New York littérateur of reputation, who calls this "the most charming spot on earth;" but I fear that you might make some such remark as a very young clubman did (fifty years ago) on seeing "Hamlet" for the first time. Asked for his opinion, he said: "It's a very good play, Fred, but too d——d full of quotations."

THE LOCATION.—Coronado Beach proper occupies about one-half of the peninsula that forms the bay of San Diego. It is situated in the extreme southwestern corner of the State, in latitude 32 degrees 42 minutes 37 seconds north, longitude 117 degrees 9 minutes west, and is four hundred and eighty miles southeast from San Francisco. The peculiar shape of this unique peninsula makes it difficult to describe. Beginning as it does, very near the boundary line of Lower California, in Mexico, it reaches away to the westward for miles, until, at a point opposite the present city of San Diego, it forms a conjunction with what seems to have been an island, which, if squared, would measure about a mile and a half on each side. On the northeast and southeast are the slopes and peaks of the Coast Range and Lower California chain of mountains; southward lies the Pacific ocean; on the west is Point Loma, which forms the western boundary of the entrance to the bay, and breaks the force of the winter winds from the Pacific.

But how do you get to the hotel? Well, Coronado is one and a half miles from San Diego, San Diego is one hundred and twenty-five miles from Los Angeles, and Los Angeles is a station of the Southern Pacific Railroad, also a station of the Atchison, Topeka and Santa Fé road. San Diego is also reached by steamer from

San Pedro and from San Francisco, eight hours from the former, two days from the latter.

· The Pacific Coast Steamship Company runs a fine line of boats. I made the trip on one, the Corona, a well-appointed vessel of 1500 tons, built on the plan of the Olivette and Mascotte, which run between Tampa and Havana. The Corona makes about thirteen knots ; not so swift as the Olivette ; no boat of her size is as swift as the Olivette.

Some of the conditions of land and water are similar to those at Fire Island—ocean on one side, bay on the other. But while Fire Island lacks vegetation, every inch of ground here which is allowed to remain so is green, or is carpeted with flowers—literally carpeted. No ; Fire Island will not quite answer for comparison. There is no use for a horse, nor is there a horse on the land or the sand of Sammis, while here there are fast trotters, lovely drives and a race course. The two places are alike, in that surf and still water bathing can both be had, as well as sailing and rowing. But there is other sport here—shooting, for instance. I saw two men go out this morning after breakfast, empty-handed (one of them was E. S. Babcock), and I saw them return this evening with a bag which they said contained "about one hundred quail." I saw the birds counted and they numbered one hundred—lacking eight.

Is the ocean too cool for you or the surf boisterous, there is a plunge bath off shore with water heated to 80 degrees. The tank measures 40 x 60 feet, so you can flounder about like a veritable fish.

But you neither shoot, fish, swim, ride nor drive? Then there are charming and varied walks—on the edge of the rough ocean, on the edge of the smooth bay, on the high bluff at the side of the former, or through pretty country lanes and lovely gardens.

There is a charming walk of about one mile from the hotel to the ferry, and planks are laid about half the distance. You pass by or pass through pretty parks. On each "sidewalk" there is a row of young fan palms six to eight feet high, these alternate with daisy bushes six feet in circumference, the palm trees and bushes being about eight feet apart; here and there rows of young pines ten or twelve feet high.

A MAGNIFICENT VALLEY VIEW.—To my mind one of the most delightful morning or afternoon excursions hereabouts is made at an expense of forty cents, without walking a block. Steam railway from hotel to ferry, boat across the bay to San Diego, next a horse car to cable road, then five miles by cable road through a country rich with gorgeous mountain, valley and ocean views, to "The Pavilion." The Pavilion, erected on the summit of a mountain, is an amusement building surrounded by well-kept paths and terraces from which a view is had of Mission Valley, a valley and a view not unlike that which you get from the old Catskill Mountain House and which many people prefer to that, because this view is not so extensive and can all be taken in and enjoyed at a glance, with the naked eye. You can see cattle and dogs in Mission Valley from your elevated position, and you see men ploughing and engaged in other farm labor. It is a spectacle that is worth going a hundred miles to see, and if you can afford it you would not begrudge as many dollars as it costs cents to make the trip. You are at a loss for words to describe your feelings of pleasure when the grand Mission Valley view bursts upon you. You remain silent in awe and admiration.

Are these walks and excursions not of your choice, or should the weather be inclement, there are verandas about the hotel measuring a mile or more.

Neither have interior amusement and exercise been forgotten. There is a dancing hall (to which reference will be made further on), there are bowling alleys and there are some billiard tables—as many as thirty—some for men on the lower floor, some for the other sex on the main floor, and some for both sexes on the floor above. Just think of thirty billiard tables in one house.

The tables for women are well patronized. It is remarked that women favor billiard playing in the evening and in evening dress, and it is also noticed that the figure of a beautiful woman with her shapely arm in short sleeves of lace is seen to excellent advantage when leaning over the table, the white arm forming a pleasing contrast in color to the dark green baize of the table.

CORONADO'S RAPID GROWTH.—The Coronado Beach Company was organized a few years ago with a capital of three millions of dollars. The directors are E. S. Babcock, Charles T. Hinde, John D. Spreckels, H. W. Mallett and Giles Kellogg. The president is E. S. Babcock. The company some years ago laid out that part of the peninsula known as Coronado Beach into streets and avenues; but up to January 1, 1887, not a house was built. Now the streets are lined with beautiful villa residences—some of them substantial, imposing brick buildings—handsome cottages and many business blocks. There are three or four hotels, several nurseries, lumber yards, planing mills, foundries, factories, fruit packing establishments and shipbuilding yards. There is a handsome Methodist Episcopal church; the Presbyterian, Episcopal and Catholic denominations also have places of worship. A commodious school-house has a large number of pupils and Coronado has a weekly newspaper. With the growth of young Coronado came the growth of old San Diego—in fact, the latter reflects and shares the popularity of the former. San Diego's population, which in 1884 was twenty-four hundred, now numbers over twenty thousand. Imagine the population of a town increasing eight fold in seven years.

Neither crooked like those of London, nor narrow like those of Boston, are the streets of Coronado. Like the streets in Philadelphia and San Diego, they are named after trees: Orange avenue is one hundred and forty feet wide, Palm and Olive avenues one hundred feet wide. A boulevard one hundred and thirty feet wide extends around the entire property. What about the sewer system? Unlike Key West, in Florida, Coronado with its unequalled water facilities has taken advantage of its excellent natural position. With the bay and ocean at its doors, the sewer question was quickly and easily solved—every street is already sewered. Investors were not taking any chances when they placed their funds in Coronado's keeping.

A GOOD PURCHASE.—The whole of what is now the flourishing city of San Diego was bought twenty years ago by a Mr. Horton for twenty-six cents an acre. He built the Horton House, and for him the Horton Block was named. San Diego's neighbor, Coronado Beach, was bought half a dozen years ago for one hundred and eighty thousand dollars by a company which has since parted with a parcel of the land for a million or two. They kept some choice pieces for themselves. Among the parcels of land is that upon which Hotel del Coronado stands, and upon which was expended a million and a half dollars. San Diego and Coronado Beach both experienced "booms" about three years ago, when many men became suddenly rich, some of them since becoming poor. Not a few now are what is known as "real estate poor," their money is "locked up" in land for which purchasers cannot be found at present—at least not at the price which "raged" three years ago.

Choice pieces on the main street of Coronado Beach sold as high as $500 per front foot, which is about the price of lots in certain parts of New York—say in Harlem—with this difference, that "lots" here are one hundred and sixty feet deep. Had there not been real value in the land when the bubble burst, the bottom would have dropped out entirely when "hard pan" was reached. As it is, land and lots are again finding ready purchasers, and houses are being built in goodly numbers. That there is a steady growth, a healthy increase, and a great future for San Diego and Coronado Beach is a matter of certainty.

WATER, ICE AND SANITATION.—In my travels about the world I advise my daughters to be cautious of the water in new places and to drink as little as possible; here, on the contrary, I urge them to drink freely. The water is not only pure and most agreeable to the taste, but it contains medical properties which are beneficial to the system. Of this we are assured by testimonials from leading physicians in different States; among them Dr. W. H. Mason, late professor of physiology in the University of Buffalo, N. Y., who, referring to the analysis, says: "The water may be regarded as a regular elixir of life." Its ingredients are almost identical with the famous Bethesda waters of Wisconsin.

At all events, a company with a capital of half a million dollars has been formed that has secured possession of the springs, fourteen miles distant. It has been "piped" to Coronado Heights and Coronado Beach and the yield is now five million gallons per day, which can be easily doubled by development. The water is used as drinking water at the hotel and with carbonic gas it is bottled for shipment to all parts of the country. If widely and liberally advertised, there is a fortune in Coronado Springs. All the ice used on the premises is made from this spring water, distilled, so that it is absolutely pure, which is more than can be said of Rockland Lake or Maine ice. The machinery at the hotel has a capacity of twelve tons per day.

THE HOTEL.—The structure, which with the furniture cost one and a half millions of dollars, is built around a quadrangular court 250 x 150 feet, the court being another name for a beautiful and well-kept tropical garden. This feature reminds you of the open garden about which the United States Hotel at Saratoga is built (which house has earned the name of "the model hotel of the world"), only the Coronado garden is filled with tropical plants and trees, and beautiful flowers bloom the year round. It never looks as do the gardens in Saratoga at the end of September. There are orange trees, lemons, figs, loquats, olives, limes, pomegranates, the banana, etc.

Mention of limes calls to mind that by invitation of the courteous and intellectual gentleman in charge of the Coronado nurseries, I cut a large cluster of limes and sent it to a friend in New York as a souvenir. Such a profusion of flowers you never saw, unless you have seen Coronado. For instance, a short time ago, in this nursery, thirty thousand roses were cut in one day from less than a quarter acre of rose bushes, and the flowers were merely cut to save the bushes. Everybody in the neighborhood carried away great baskets of roses to fill bags and pillow-cases.

We were loaded with flowers, cut from the trees and bushes, in the open, as we walked through the paths of the nursery—actually "loaded," for the ladies of the party not only carried hands and arms flowing over with flowers—but their necks and shoulders were thickly entwined with smilax. The flowers included the delicate heliotrope, the sweet honeysuckle and the sturdy camelia, and they also embraced many flowers new and strange to us, for everything seems to grow here, side by side—everything that grows in the temperate, semi-tropical and tropical zones,

The hotel is situated on the southeastern portion of a beautiful mesa (the name here for a slight elevation) which slopes gradually, in terraces, from its centre toward the Pacific ocean on one side and the bay of San Diego on the other. No one style of architecture has been followed, as the reader will see from the accompanying illustration. It partakes of the Queen Anne style, also of the classic Norman era, bringing up recollections of a grand old Norman castle : but the architect has availed himself of different schools, producing a complete and uncommonly beautiful whole. It is a striking object and the series of buildings form a noble picture against the sky line when viewed four or five miles distant—from San Diego or from the ocean.

The projectors seem to have had a fancy for the biblical number seven. The building covers seven acres; counting guest chambers, sixty parlors, large and small, the private dining rooms and other public rooms, there are in all seven hundred rooms, and there is accommodation for seven hundred boarders.

Why one side of the house is enclosed in glass I cannot understand, when you can sit out doors every day in the year and bask in the sun. This is a good arrangement for Atlantic City, but not necessary, it seems to me, for Coronado Beach.

THE DRAWING-ROOM.—This is not a cold, bare and barn-like apartment such as you find the parlors in so many American hotels. It is cozy and home-like, with an air of marked refinement. The dark walls are relieved with some choice engravings, and here and there you'll meet with a living plant, and there is always a vase or two filled with fresh flowers, such as greet the eye and please the sense of smell (in summer time) in an English country hotel, say in the Lake district. The Coronado parlor is cheerful, and with its low ceiling and pillars of unpainted wood, calls to mind the beautiful parlor of the (Spanish) Hotel Cordova in St. Augustine. In fact Mr. Babcock tells me that some of the features of the house are reminiscent of the grand hotels in Havana, where he lived for some time.

OTHER PUBLIC ROOMS.—But beside the drawing-room there are a number of other large and beautiful apartments near by—the ladies' billiard-room, the reception-room, writing-room, chess-room, etc.—something like the elegant public rooms (which are not so very public) in the Hotel Victoria, London. There are a dozen or more suites of rooms with private parlor for each suite, opening on the garden.

THE DINING-ROOM.—This is unique. At first glance, especially if you are in the middle of the room, which is oval, it strikes you as rather bare, monotonous and inartistic ; very practical, with room for six hundred people, but not entirely pleasing. But the longer you stay the more you admire, particularly if you are lucky enough to get a table near an end of the room, either that end which overlooks the garden or the end from which you can see the ocean, the bay and the mountains beyond. It measures 176 x 66 feet, and the ceiling is distant from the floor 33 feet. The whole immense apartment, floor, walls and ceiling, is of light colored wood— white Oregon pine and solid oak worked into panels of all sizes and shapes conceivable. The materials and light colors, or color rather, are suitable to this climate and in time you get to like them.

The breakfast room is no miniature apartment either, 47 x 56 feet, with ceiling as high as the dining-room ceiling. It is far more attractive to my eye, its floor being carpeted, and having a high dado of California redwood, which serves to relieve the lighter woods. But Americans demand size for their beauty, and they have it in the dining-room with its floor area of 10,000 feet. To quote the writer of a pamphlet, "it fills the beholder with an astounding admiration." Better than that, to my taste, they have a skilful *chef*, and he fills your platter with most appetizing dishes—if you get a good waiter.

WHERE THEY DANCE.—In the extreme southwest corner of the building is the ball-rcom, with an extended view of the beach and the ocean; indeed, you cannot get away from the ocean unless you get away from Coronado. The designer of this room has also "gone in" for size. It is a circular room, no less than 60 feet high and 120 feet in diameter, giving a floor area of 11,000 square feet. Too much room for a small "dance," but splendid for a ball or grand concert.

A feature of the ball-room is a stage for amateur theatricals, which, for size and appointments in the matter of lights, would not discredit a regular theatre.

A RICH AND ROYAL SUITE.—Taken as a whole, there are more prettily furnished bedrooms in Long's Hotel, London, than in any other hotel I have ever seen. The tower rooms in the Oglethorpe, at Brunswick, Georgia, are large and remarkably beautiful, and the bridal suite in the Ponce de Leon is supposed to be very choice, but the Ponce de Leon "show" apartments will not compare in beauty nor in completeness of detail with the bridal suite in Hotel del Coronado. These rooms in the Coronado are not so palatial in size nor in the matter of costly frescoes as the rooms in the London Métropole, in which I found Mr. and Mrs. Augustin Daly last October, but they certainly are among the most tastefully furnished hotel bedrooms I have ever seen, and it is not surprising that the photographic views of these apartments find many purchasers.

The window has an eastern view that is extremely pleasing. To the right are seen the ocean's rough breakers, to the left is the smooth bay of San Diego, while to the immediate front, as you lie in bed, if the curtains are parted and you are awake at 6.20 A. M., you can see the sun creeping up behind a range of great mountains, miles and miles away. The soft cloud of black smoke curling from the tall, round, red brick chimneys of the electric light engine house between you and the golden sky beyond, does not mar the picture in the least.

Across the centre of the principal room of the suite are three arches, supported by the side walls and by two wooden fluted columns, and under the arches are heavy portières of double silk, salmon pink on one side, old gold on the other. The windows are draped elaborately and beautifully—light blue silk shades, lace curtains next to the windows, with inner curtains of heavy pale blue silk, lined with silk of a rose tint. The furniture is of mahogany, upholstered with blue silk plush, the carpet is a rich moquette in delicate colors, and the toilet set is in Haviland Limoges decorated in deep blue, white and gold. The ceiling is daintily frescoed. From its centre depends a three-light electrolier; from the wall, over the bureau mirror, juts out a bracket with two electric lamps. The mantel is ornamented with two side pieces of Limoges and a bronze cathedral clock—a miniature representation of the clock in the Houses of Parliament, in Westminster. If you do not get from these notes the idea of a luxurious and tasteful apartment, the fault is not with those who furnished it, but with the pen which has failed to describe it.

SANTA CRUZ, CALIFORNIA.

Santa Cruz, Cal.,
March 27, 1891.

In area, Santa Cruz county is one of the smallest in California, but in resources, productiveness of soil and natural attractions it might be called the largest in the State. In its equable climate is grown almost everything indigenous to the north temperate zone.

The county is in central California, eighty miles south of San Francisco; it has a coast line of forty miles, and includes, according to the United States Government survey, 280,000 acres. So rich is it that there are not more than five thousand acres of waste land in the entire county. South of this is the Pajaro Valley, the most fertile spot of California, called "the wonder of the Pacific."

There is not much stock-raising in Santa Cruz county. The mountains, being heavily timbered, are not adapted to grazing. Nor are citrus fruits cultivated to any great extent; but the apples of Santa Cruz county are superior to any grown in the State, the quality of the wine is unsurpassed in the State, and the remarkable richness of the soil renders the cultivation of potatoes, beans, hops, sugar beets, etc., profitable to a degree unknown in less fertile sections. The vegetable products of the county form one of its most extensive industries. E. S. Harrison, a trustworthy authority in California history, calls Santa Cruz "a vegetable wonderland."

Let me illustrate the natural advantages of this region by a comparison. While riding on the Southern Pacific railway over the Texas plains, a month ago, the travelling auditor of the company, who was on our train, surprised me by stating that the company is glad to lease its lands at four cents an acre annually. Land within a couple of miles of where this is written is leased to Chinamen for farming at fifty dollars an acre annually, and they realize from it a profit per acre of two or three hundred dollars.

The City of Santa Cruz, the principal city and county seat of the county, lies between the Pacific ocean and the northern side of Monterey bay, about eighty miles south of San Francisco. It nestles among the foot-hills of the Santa Cruz mountains, and its outskirts are bathed by the sea. The city proper has a population of six thousand five hundred, and if East Santa Cruz is included, the population is about nine thousand. The city is growing rapidly. New business houses are constantly going up, capital is coming from the East, and everywhere are evidences of a steady, healthy increase.

Santa Cruz has good railroad facilities. Two branches of the Southern Pacific run here direct. They are called the broad gauge and the narrow gauge roads. The broad gauge is an important line running through Santa Clara and Pajaro valleys, passing San José and the larger towns between San Francisco and Monterey. The narrow guage runs from San Francisco no farther south than Santa Cruz. It is more of a local line and stops at the smaller places—places, however, of such great interest to tourists as Big Trees. The steamers of the Pacific Steamship Company plying between San Pedro (near Los Angeles), and San Francisco stop here, regularly, on their way north and south.

In writing from Hotel del Monte in Monterey, I mentioned some large oaks and pines ; there are as big and still bigger trees here, or very near here, at a place appropriately named Big Trees. It is a ten minute ride on the narrow guage road of the Southern Pacific, or an hour's drive by carriage from Santa Cruz. You need not go to Yosemite, Calaveras or Mariposa to see giants of the forest; here they are, a grove of 320 acres, some of the trees 300 feet high and 46 feet in circumference. These figures are quoted, but I measured a few specimens myself. One about four feet from the ground was 52 feet in circumference. The interior of another, "General Fremont," had been burned out. Four persons beside myself stood inside of it, and thirty-five more, we calculated, could have found room in comfort. This measured six feet in diameter about five feet from the ground—inside measurement—the "shell" of the tree being probably a foot thick. There are dozens and scores and groups of trees in this wonderful grove, nearly as large.

The trees are of the famous California Redwood species, the wood hard as flint and very heavy. The largest specimens are named and bear tablets, "Daniel Webster," "General Grant," "General Sherman," "Ingersoll's Cathedral," etc. Under the shadow of the last named, the honorable gentleman held forth one day to an admiring audience. "Big Trees" is owned by a wealthy widow of San Francisco, Mrs. Walsh.

Powerful and proud as are these giants of the forest, some of them have been uprooted by nature's convulsions and lie humbly and horizontally on the ground. I noticed that a few of these were charred. The keeper of the grounds explained that year after year fire had been tried, but the hardy giants would not yield to flame. They are so thick and hard they won't burn as they lie. "Then why not cut them up," I suggested. "Oh!" was the answer, "lumber is worth nothing here; it is so plentiful."

They have done a little "cutting," however. In exchange for a dime you will get a piece of red wood quite heavy enough for your satchel, or a piece of the bark much too clumsy for your coat pocket. The bark is three or four inches thick.

This is a famous wine country. We visited the tunnels of the "Santa Cruz Mountain Wine Company," whose vineyards are visible nine miles away on the hills. The tunnels are dug out of the soft, sand-stone rock and are dark and rather cool. That is to say, the air seemed cool when compared with the atmosphere outside, but as a matter of truth, which is often stranger than fiction, the thermometer showed the temperature in the tunnels to be 52 degrees, and it remains at about that figure all the year round. There are three such tunnels, each 380 feet long, 24 feet wide, and 18 feet high. The vineyards of the company include two hundred acres.

In these deep, cool tunnels the company has stored in great vats no less than two hundred thousand gallons of wine. Bottle after bottle was opened for our party and so cheaply was it held that the glasses were freely washed with the wine as the different kinds were tasted —port, sherries, clarets and white wines.

The claret has good body, and if you add a little water to it, as the French treat *vin ordinaire*, it makes a very good drink for a thirsty soul at the dinner table.

California Angelica has been a popular wine for twenty odd years: the Angelica produced in Santa Cruz is sweet, smooth, oily and delicious.

A brand of Sauterne so pleased my palate that I ordered twenty gallons to be shipped to New York. But I'll let you into the secret of this seemingly extravagant order; the price is only one dollar per gallon—and not Jones, but I, paid the freight. In ordering this wine I was guided first, by my own taste—it has delicious flavor; secondly, I felt assured that it was absolutely pure. The grapes are here, on the spot, ship loads of them, in the season, and there's no incentive for adulteration.

The well-kept roads and fine drives about Santa Cruz

are not its least attractive feature. One of them you can take from the shore, driving over a bridge of the San Lorenzo river, passing Phelan Park and the twin lakes, on the borders of which are the summer home and settlement of the Christian Church. You keep the mountains in view all the way, and a turn here or there shows you the city, the bay, or the ocean.

The three-mile cliff drive takes you immediately above the rock-bound shore of the Pacific, where you see giant crags upon which the everlasting waves have had their effect. Some of the rocks stand off from the shore twenty and fifty feet, and through these the powerful waves have worked great holes, through which the waters rush with a tumultuous roar, dashing their spray far above. These "natural bridges" would be considered a rare sight if they were the only feature of this scene, and would attract people from a distance, but where there is so much to admire and astonish, they are only one among the many marvels that here make an embarrassment of pictorial riches.

The city has two banks, good public schools and water-works; it is sewered to the ocean, it has horse-cars, fine public buildings, and two flourishing newspapers, the *Sentinal* and the *Surf*. Good society is not lacking, and beautiful homes abound. Duncan McPherson has a fine Gothic villa; the residence of Mayor Bowman commands beautiful views of the bay and the town; the home of William Kerr, two miles out of the city, is a handsome structure in the Queen Anne style, having two wide entrances and bay windows, affording extensive views of the valley and bay. Colonel A. J. Hinds, a pioneer of Santa Cruz, has built himself a charming home, and Mrs. P. B. Fagen's house on Mission street, one of the principal residential streets, attracts the attention of all passers-by. Other pretty homes are those of D. K. Abeel, R. Bernheim, Mr. Glover and Mrs. E. J. Green.

Mr. J. Philip Smith, a New York capitalist, who has travelled far and wide and who passes much of his time in Europe and New York, came here with his family four years ago, bought a two-acre site upon which a fine house stood and this he enlarged and reconstructed, laying out the grounds in a tasteful way, making it one of the handsomest residences in Santa Cruz. It has a high and enviable position near the Sea Beach Hotel.

It reminds you at once upon entering it of a Parisian interior and on closer examination you are not surprised to learn that many of the things of beauty which adorn the rooms had a French origin. The Smiths are great travellers and in their journeyings about the world have "picked up" any number of art works and curios which now find an appropriate resting place.

One of the finest views here, one of the most beautiful of its kind in the State probably, is to be had from Logan Heights, the estate of Judge J. H. Logan. Judge Logan is president of the Santa Cruz bank and one of the most esteemed citizens of this section. The house, not imposing architecturally, stands on a mesa or plateau of about twenty acres, in which beautiful roses and other choice flowers bloom the year round. From this elevated position a series of bird's-eye views are spread out before you, the extent, beauty and variety of which are not easily described.

At this point you are two hundred feet above the Pacific ocean. Immediately below, in the foreground, is the whole city of Santa Cruz, with its high school, its gardens, reservoirs, depots, hotels, and its church spires. To your left, eastward, are the villages Soquel and Aptos, famous lumber centres. A few miles further off in the same direction, glistens Monterey bay, backed by the Santa Cruz mountains.

Southward, beyond the city at your feet, winds the bay of Monterey. Look twenty miles further south, and, in this clear atmosphere, you see the sleepy old town of Monterey with the mountains as a background for the picture.

To your right, westward, is the ocean again—altogether, forming a number of diversified and beautiful pictures.

There are a number of good hotels at Santa Cruz—the Pacific Ocean House, the Wilkins House and Ocean Villa. The last named looks cozy and comfortable as it stands in its own pretty garden, with a commanding view. The leading house is that owned by D. K. Abeel, the Sea Beach House, which he has recently enlarged and reconstructed, putting in all the modern improvements, and putting in as landlord John T. Sullivan, who, after securing a long lease, furnished it in good style. It was designed by G. W. Page, a prominent architect of San José, and presents a most pleasing appearance, viewed either from the heights or from the shore, above which it stands nearly one hundred feet, and to which its grounds, beautifully terraced and ornamented with flowers, gracefully slope. "Modern improvements," of course—every room in the Sea Beach Hotel has running water, but the improvements include hot water also.

The parlor is on the main floor, in the corner round tower of the building, and, with its many windows, is uncommonly pleasing. Through or from these windows you get the best features of the scenery hereabouts, from the tasteful flower gardens of the hotel grounds to Loma Prieta and the mountains in the distance, or to Monterey, beyond the bay in the foreground.

The lessee, Mr. Sullivan, is not unknown to New York. He was a tried friend of Horace Greeley's and a trusted officer under Hon. Thomas L. James in the New York Post-office, in which place he rose after faithful service of fifteen years to be superintendent of the newspaper department. Mr. Sullivan has been in Santa Cruz only five or six years. I saw a modest little two-story building in which he started here, "keeping boarders," and he now finds himself in the leading hotel of the town, owning his own furniture, a fine stable, and with the prospect of making his fortune. With success Mr. Sullivan has made many staunch friends, among them the mayor of the town, judges, bank presidents and other leading citizens.

The steamship landing is nearer the Sea Beach Hotel than it is to any other house; the broad guage station is at the door, so to speak, and the narrow guage station is two minutes walk around the corner. The house is open all the year. Santa Cruz is attractive in winter, but in summer it must be delightful.

NATURAL BRIDGE, SANTA CRUZ.

REDONDO BEACH.

REDONDO BEACH, CAL.,
March 13, 1891.

New Orleans obtained its sub-title from the crescent shape of its banks on the Mississippi river. The trend of the Pacific shore here suggested the pretty name, "Redondo," in Spanish, signifying round.

It is midway between Capistrano, south, and Point Duma, north, and is sixteen miles in a southwest direction from Los Angeles, from which city there are several trains daily over two roads—the Santa Fé and the new Redondo Beach railroad. All passenger steamers to and from San Francisco and way points stop at Redondo.

Three years ago Redondo was a waste, or at best it was a cattle ranch. There was not a house nor a hut here, now it is a garden spot of Southern California. It came into existence as if by magic, as do many flourishing towns on the Pacific slope.

Beautifully situated on grounds rising gradually from the ocean, backed by rich, tillable lands and ranges of green hills, with seaport facilities not surpassed in California south of San Francisco, its rapid growth is not surprising.

The creation of Redondo, according to plans which promise such a satisfactory result, is due to Californians —men of irrepressible energy and wide experience in large affairs—Captain J. C. Ainsworth, Captain R. R. Thompson and Captain George J. Ainsworth, not captains by courtesy, either. They planned and have established successfully railroad and steamship lines in Oregon and the northwest.

That they have ample capital at their command may be judged by a few figures given at random. Their first step was to buy one thousand acres of land; second, to build a railroad and wharf; third, to secure an ocean front of *one mile*, then to erect a hotel four hundred and fifty feet long to accommodate three hundred people. It was first opened May 1, 1890.

In the hotel they built a music room, 48 x 80 feet, spending two thousand dollars simply on an inlaid floor; there is a tennis court which cost seven thousand dollars; they laid a Portland cement walk from the station to hotel, sixteen feet wide and a quarter of a mile long, expending another ten thousand in that way—altogether it is easy to believe that checks for more than a million have been drawn in the enterprise. These Californians, with their big trees and their forty-thousand-acre ranches, do nothing in a small way.

Do you ask what are the natural attractions of the place? "First, last and all the time," there is the almost wonderful climate—genial, balmy and equable, such as you will find nowhere but in Southern California. The hotel proprietor tells me that the average winter temperature is 61 degrees. In case you should not care for figures at second hand, here is a record from my own thermometer. Yesterday, March 12, noon, 68, this morning at seven it registered 53; at this writing, eight P.M., 60, the instrument hanging outside my window.

The summer here, I am assured, and I firmly believe, is more delightful than the winter, and the hotel will be kept open the year round. Like the Hygeia at Old Point Comfort, Redondo attracts people from a distance in winter; in summer it is largely patronized by residents of San Francisco, Los Angeles and other cities of the State.

I do not agree entirely with Mrs. Malaprop that "comparisons are odorous." They often serve a very useful purpose in illustration. At any rate I am given to the habit of comparing, be it a good or a bad habit. What is large or small, fine or coarse, hot or cold, wet or dry, good or bad, except by comparison?

For once, however, I am put to my wits' ends for comparison. Redondo is like no place on the Atlantic coast, because, although directly on the seashore, every foot of ground, almost up to the edge of the ocean, is covered with fine grass; and the most tender flowers grow and flourish in profusion everywhere, almost within a few feet of the surf. This in winter, mind you —a Southern California winter, though. It is not so, even in summer, on the Atlantic coast, in the United States, nor in England. Yes, I have it: I can indulge in the old habit; the climate of Redondo is like that in the South of France: in fact it is in the same latitude: there!

In the hotel nurseries, which are distant from the surf but a few hundred feet, you may revel in roses, heliotrope, tulips, mignonette, daisies, etc. There are tall calla lilies in plenty and the pleasing sight of acres and acres of pinks of various colors is one that is very fascinating. The hotel farm of two hundred acres, where choice stock is kept, supplies the house with more than all the milk, cream, butter, fruit and vegetables it requires.

The hotel is only four stories high, yet there is an elevator; of course electric lights and all modern improvements. Neither is the building deep, but it has great length, to give views of ocean in front and of green hills in the rear. It stands north and south thus affording ocean views from three sides. Of the 225 rooms, every one has a sunny exposure at some hour of the day; every one is well ventilated and lighted; every one is an "outside room," and every guest feels that his is the best suite in the house.

The porch is not one straight, unbroken line like the porches of so many summer hotels in the east. It has a few graceful curves in it and from it you may watch the craft sailing by—coast steamers to and from San Francisco and other ports. The golden sunsets you may see from this porch are such as no artist could represent. It is not within the possibilities of paint and canvas to reproduce such gorgeous scenes. On a clear day without the aid of a glass Catalina island is visible thirty miles away.

The dining-room of the hotel juts out in a northerly direction and has windows on three sides. From a distance it looks as if it might have been an after-thought in construction, but the architect planned it this way, to give what was most desired — light, ventilation and pleasing views, and he succeeded.

Two hundred and sixty can sit down to dinner at one time.

There are no loose wardrobes nor clothes presses; all the bedrooms have closets built in the walls. Every room is supplied with hot and cold water running into marble basins. Every room has a tiled fireplace in color and design to match the carpet, and what is also worthy of mention, the furniture in the bedrooms is not duplicated, nor are the carpets.

The drinking water is from an Artesian well. It has been analyzed and pronounced pure. The plumbing seems to have been done in a careful manner, and the question of sewerage need give nobody concern. The hotel stands on a *mesa*. The refuse goes through an iron pipe and empties into the sea half a mile from the house.

There are no better fishing grounds on the coast, so they say. If you are lucky with the line you may catch bonita, Spanish mackerel, baracouta, smelt and yellow tails, whatever they are.

The circular of the Redondo Hotel as to rates merely says, "same as any first-class hotel." This is hardly in accordance with the facts, as I see them. The terms at the Redondo are from three to four dollars per day, while hotels in the east, of the same class, charge from four to five dollars. Why such low rates obtain in California hotels is something I intend to find out before I leave the State. For illustrated circulars address Redondo Hotel Co., Redondo Beach, Cal.

PASADENA.

PASADENA, March 10.

People who care more for comfort than for great "style," who prefer a quiet, home-like, family house to one of noise and bustle, those who are seeking health, pure air and out-door life with grand views rather than the music, dancing and entertainments of a fashionable hotel may jot down as a memorandum "The Painter Hotel, at Pasadena, Cal," thirty-five minutes by train from Los Angeles and fifteen minutes by "free 'bus" from passenger station.

It is a new house, was built in '88; it accommodates seventy-five boarders, and is owned and kept by J. H. Painter's Sons. The house is airy, the bedrooms are comfortably (not luxuriously) furnished, the parlor is pleasant, the class of guests select, the table is well provided, and at once, let me say, ere the important fact escapes me, the rates are remarkably low for the nice appointments and good fare supplied—only $2.50 per day for transient guests, and from $12.50 to $17.50 per week to season boarders, for people come to stay for a month or so—some spend the whole winter here. The house is open the year round, it being pleasant in summer as well as in winter. It is a mountainous district, and the ocean, from which come soft winds in summer, is only thirty minutes' distant in a south and south-westerly direction.

Yes, and here are two more facts—Pasadena is one thousand feet above the sea, and the Painter Hotel, which is one and a half miles from the centre of the town, stands on the highest point hereabouts.

The grounds comprised in the property include ten acres, upon which the owners grow their own fruits for the table—peaches, apricots, raisins, prunes, etc.

Do you want to visit the town? Street cars pass the door of the Painter. And if you want a view it will "pay" you to climb up to the roof of the hotel, where there is an observatory. Three miles off is the Raymond Hotel, plain to your view in this clear atmosphere. On one side is the San Bernardino range of mountains, on the other the Sierra Madre range. You may see San Jacinto, ninety miles away, also Wilson's Peak, upon which the new observatory, with its powerful lens, is to be placed; and beautiful San Gabriel valley is spread out immediately beneath you, a feature of which, at this writing, are acres of large, orange-hued poppies, so bright that you could almost imagine them aflame, especially if the wind is blowing, thus giving vibration to the thin, delicate leaves.

The drives are a most delightful feature:—to the city proper, with its wide avenues of beautiful residences, to San Gabriel mission, and to "Lucky" Baldwin's ranch, a pleasant afternoon drive.

Those who are planning a winter or spring tour will thank me for suggesting a visit to the Painter House, but if people demand "style," if they would dance to orchestral music; if they demand great size in a dining-room and grandeur in the drawing-room, and they are willing to pay for it, all these are also obtainable here, or rather at East Pasadena, which is only three miles distant; eight miles from Los Angeles. And the price, $4.50 per day, $21 to $28 per week, is reasonable considering what you get for the money.

Reference is made to the great Raymond Hotel, which was built in 1886, where they have a bar, as well as billiards and bowling; elevator, electric lights, a reception-room, music-room, grand parlor, and a dining-room which accommodates three hundred persons.

From your seat at table you see "Old Baldy" looming above the clouds eleven thousand feet and snow-covered ten months out of the twelve, looking like a great sugar-loaf and recalling the Jungfrau, near Interlaken, Switzerland.

Like the dining-room of its modest neighbor, the Painter Hotel, every table in the Raymond is decorated daily with fresh flowers plucked from the hotel grounds —this is "winter," mind you. The grounds of the Raymond cover a space of fifty-four acres, so there is no lack of fruit (oranges, lemons, etc.), to say nothing of the roses, blue bells, honeysuckle, dandelions, heliotropes and violets which may be picked *ad libitum*—if you don't regard the painted signs.

A view from one of the Raymond's verandas is not much unlike that from the front steps of the Grand Hotel in the Catskills, only the former is far more extensive.

The proprietor of the Raymond is W. Raymond, of Raymond's Vacation Excursions, Boston, and the manager is C. H. Merrill, of the Crawford House, in the White Mountains. The post-office address is East Pasadena, Cal.

Orange Grove avenue and Marengo avenue and the paths in the grounds leading to the houses are lined with luxurious fan palm trees, interspersed with great cacti and not a few century plants, which it is proven here bloom much oftener than once in a hundred years. The calla lily, that delicate plant which is so tenderly cared for in the East that the flower is wrapped in cotton wool, here grows in such profusion that it is used for hedges. You will see fields of "callas" at Pasadena, raised for shipment to large cities. The whole of Pasadena is like one immense garden, a garden city indeed.

PASADENA COTTAGES.—You would scarcely credit it, so I won't tell you, that some of the "cottages" in this new place are as large and elaborate as those on the New Jersey coast, between Seabright and Elberon, and some of them would not look out of place alongside the the grand Newport "cottages."

Mr. Kernaghan, editor of the *Pasadena Star*, has a fine home here. One of the prettiest places belongs to and is occupied by Mrs. Kimball, the widowed daughter of Rufus Hatch of New York.

Charles Frederick Holder, formerly of New York, came out here six years ago for his health, and having obtained it has made this his home. He has a cozy cottage on Orange Grove avenue in which is his study, where you may find him at his ease, wearing a short black velvet coat or smoking jacket.

Mr. Holder is a journalist and littérateur, a frequent contributor to current magazines and leading newspapers. He has published two or three brochures on Pasadena. One of his contributions concerning this section was an illustrated article which appeared in *Harper's Weekly*. It was entitled "The Rose Tournament," and described a beautiful ceremony which takes place here annually, on New Year's day. Mr. Holder's style is finished and scholarly and his language choice, with no waste of words. Being a man of cultivated taste, with a rare poetic fancy, he is at home here, when treating of this lovely country with its wealth of fruits and flowers.

Among others who have built houses and who occupy country seats at Pasadena is Governor Markham, of California. A Mr. Nelmes has a lovely ten-acre place, and with it a generous heart. A sign placed conspicuously outside his gates reads as follows: "All are welcome to drive through these private grounds and groves. Eastern tourists are each invited to pluck one orange."

Near the Painter Hotel are many beautiful homes owned by "Eastern people." One is owned by Dr. Green, of Woodbury, N. J., another luxurious place is that of Mr. McNally, of the publishing house in Chicago of Rand, McNally & Co.

Professor Low, of Norristown, Pa; J. W. Scoville, a Chicago banker, and E. T. Hurlburt, a capitalist of Chicago, are owners of fine estates, and of less notable places there are owners in Pasedena by the hundred.

It strikes you as rather odd to find winter and summer together, hand in hand as it were. At your feet flowers; raise your head and snow on the mountain peaks is visible to the naked eye.

The one-horse cars which ply between Pasadena and East Pasadena, California, like some of the one-horse cars of some other cities, have a driver who acts as conductor also, but the driver in the Pasadena cars serves as collector as well. There is no automatical nor mechanical contrivance to receive the fares, nor is there any way of recording them. When a passenger gets on the driver leaves the front platform, and, letting the horse take care of himself, or handing the reins to a front-platform passenger, he runs back and collects the new fare. There are not many cars on the line—one starts only every half hour—and as most of the passengers are through passengers, and few get on or off between the two points named, the animal being very docile, there is no difficulty in one man doing the whole work. The driver getting on and off his car reminds me of the elevator in Philp's Hotel, Glasgow, which will not budge upward if there are as many as four or five people in the car. The man who runs it gives the rope a pull, on the ground floor, then leaves the car, walks up the stairs, getting up to the second or third flight in ample time to give the rope another pull and to let the passengers out.

Some people talk of the winter months in California as "the rainy season." This may be an old story, told of what was the case years ago. It certainly is not true to-day. Examining the records, I find that from

January 5 to February 1 of this year there was no rain at all in Pasadena, and in all of that time there were but two cloudy days—January 23 and January 28.

I have been in Southern California now for about three weeks and have seen it rain only on two days and one night—two days in Los Angeles and one night, for one hour, at Coronado Beach.

I don't advise you to throw away your umbrella, as did a tourist from Colorado when coming here, but my experience would show that there is very little use for such an article in Southern California, even in what used to be called " the rainy season."

LOS ANGELES.

Los Angeles, March 17.

If you are going from Los Angeles to San Diego, or vice versa, don't go by boat unless you have a great affection for the sea. First, you must change at San Pedro, from cars to boat; second, the waterway occupies much more time; but what is most important, if you go by rail, over the Sante Fé route, you get magnificent and diversified views of the ocean, close views of foot hills and distant views of snow-capped mountains. You pass through a fertile country, see picturesque cottages, large sheep and cattle ranches, and great rifts in the mountains that make you smile when you think of "gaps" in the east, which are so widely advertised. The train skirts the edge of the sea for scores of miles and recalls similar scenic features of land and water which you admire in travelling from Aberdeen to Ballater over the "Great North of Scotland Railway," a pretty little road with a big sounding name. If you should have to stop on a switch, or for a "heated journal," for five or ten minutes, you can step off the car platform and in a few minutes you can gather a large bouquet of sweet, wild flowers, among them fragrant "mignonette" as they call it here. Southern California might well be named the land of flowers, and this branch of the Sante Fé is entitled to be called by that much abused term, picturesque.

FLORIDA ORANGES "BEATEN."—I wrote last season about some Florida oranges which Mr. Orvis showed me at the Windsor Hotel, Jacksonville. The largest of them, if I remember aright, measured thirteen inches in circumference and weighed twenty-three ounces. I asked, "who can beat these?" They are "beaten." This morning I weighed an orange in Los Angeles which turned the beam at thirty-three ounces and which measured nineteen and one-quarter inches. This particular orange was light for its size, because it was not quite ripe nor "full" when picked. It came from George Bunce's grove (pray do not print this "grave") at Rivera, a small town nine miles from Los Angeles. The grove was only set out in 1888. All the oranges on the tree from which this one was picked were as large and as heavy as the one described, but there were only three of them.

All the ticket brokers' offices, all the fruit stores, segar shops and all the shops of small traders and of places patronized by men have their doors and windows thrown open during business hours. No "protection" from the weather is needed. It is never cold enough for closed doors or windows in the daytime. Nor are some of these places of business closed even at night except by strong iron-wire netting covering the fronts of the stores. This open feature strikes a visitor as very strange at first, but one soon becomes accustomed to it. All through the winter open street cars are used.

Three years ago, when the Los Angeles boom was at its height, the foundation was laid near Main street for what was intended to be the largest hotel in the United States. There it stood and there it stands to-day (the foundation), the bricks appearing just one foot above the ground level. These bricks enclose a space of two acres. Pullman, of sleeping-car fame, was one of those interested, and he says that the idea has not been entirely abandoned. The idea may yet exist but the open lots and the brick foundation look very lonesome. Meanwhile Mr. O. T. Johnson erected a very handsome hotel, The Westminster, on the corner of Main and Fourth streets, which will accommodate two hundred and fifty guests. The site of the Westminster is choice;

the house contains all the modern improvements; it is well furnished and well patronized.

As I write, in my bedroom of the Westminster Hotel, looking north I can see, without rising from my seat, great high mountains covered with snow. They present a most beautiful picture in this clear atmosphere, with the sun shining upon them.

That "cranky critic," as the New York *Hotel Gazette* calls Max O'Rell, would be suited at the Westminster Hotel. O'Rell complains because in American hotels guests have regular seats; that each person upon entering the dining-room is not allowed to sit just where he pleases. The contrary is the rule in the hotel mentioned. A notice is prominently posted near the elevator which reads: "Positively no seats reserved in the dining-room." The waiters are young, intelligent American girls of a good class, some from New York and some from Nebraska, all uniformed in white. They look neat and clean, are alert to take an order and quick in serving it.

Strawberry short-cake was part of the dessert at to-day's luncheon in the Hotel Westminster. Fresh-picked strawberries are served every morning for breakfast. Not a dozen or two small, hard berries, such as I have seen served for a "portion" at hotel tables in Florida during February, but a saucerful for each guest of large, ripe berries that have a delicious flavor. Strawberry ice-cream was on the dinner menu—the cream made, not from "strawberry flavoring," but of the honest fruit. Fresh peas and Lima beans figure on the bill, also oranges in profusion, picked from the groves hard by.

All the way between New Orleans, La., and Los Angeles, Cal., on the Southern Pacific railroad, you pay five to ten cents each for oranges; as soon as you reach Los Angeles, boys with baskets of the golden fruit swarm about the cars crying out, "Oranges, three for a nickel, six for a dime." If you have a little patience you will hear, "Oranges, eight for a dime," and if you wait till the train is about to start you can get ten for a dime. Possibly after you are out of hearing they are sold at ten cents a dozen.

In the cars of the Southern Pacific railroad that run between Los Angeles and the seaport town of San Pedro appears this printed notice : "WARNING :—Passengers are hereby warned against playing games of chance with strangers, of betting on three card monte, strap, or other games. You will surely be robbed if you do."

THE CALIFORNIA.

SAN FRANCISCO, April 1, 1891.

California being one of the largest of these United States, the Californians thought that their chief city should have large hotels, so they built in San Francisco the Baldwin House, the Lick House, the Occidental and larger than any of these, the Palace Hotel, "larger than any hotel in existence," it is claimed. Whether this claim is well founded or not, the Palace is large enough to suit the most extravagant American ideas. It occupies three acres of ground. It has seven hundred and fifty-five bedrooms; number of rooms all told, ten hundred and fifteen.

But with the growth of the State and the growth of culture and good taste, Californians and tourists from other States demanded something above and beyond mere size; and so a few months ago was erected "The California." There are several "California Hotels" in San Francisco, in fact, an old house directly opposite the California now calls itself "The New California," probably because the name is new. So many houses with names near alike give trouble to the Post-office people, but the title of the house of which I write is simply "The California."

It is in a central and accessible part of the city—in Bush street, just off Kearney street, which runs nearly parallel with Market, being not far from the *Chronicle* building, which with its great clock tower running up hundreds of feet in the air, serves as a finger or sign-post from many parts of the city.

The front is of cedar-colored sandstone, and with its modern, low-arched entrances and high, round towers, is uncommonly pleasing to the eye. There are one hundred and forty rooms in the house, and it is nine stories high, the higher floors being most desirable. The light is better as you ascend, and the views from the windows across the bay and the Golden Gate are a constant delight. From my bedroom window I can plainly see the graceful movements of the white squàdron, which, with the green hills in the far distance make a magnificent picture. The California was erected by "an estate," and the estate considered not the expense. They started out with the idea to build a hotel as near perfection as possible, and they succeeded.

Every known precaution is taken against fire. It was the intention from the first to build a house as proof against fire as men, money and materials could make it. Scientists were consulted as to sanitation and plumbing, and to these points special thought and attention were given, Such luxurious fittings in marble and silver plate I have never seen surpassed, if equalled; not even in my recent ten-thousand-mile tour through the South and West, and I have visited hotels that cost all the way from one to three millions of dollars.

Instead of marble and brass, which are used so freely in large American hotels, rare and beautiful woods prevail in decorating the interior of the new house. The ground floor is finished in quartered oak, the second in bird's-eye maple, the third and fourth in sycamore, the fifth and sixth in red birch, and the seventh, eighth and ninth in oak. The wood was cut, carved and polished especially for the building, and is of the most exquisitely beautiful grain.

Max O'Rell would be pleased. Printed rules are not posted on all the bedroom doors: it would be an act of vandalism to thrust a nail into hard wood of such high polish and beautiful grain. The furniture and carpets harmonize in colors and are very rich: there seems to have been no thought of economy. The bedrooms are furnished as you would furnish your own apartment, provided you had a large bank account. They only lack pictures, mantel ornaments and such dainty etceteras, as you find, for instance, in the bedrooms of Long's Hotel in London, to give them a finished, homelike and elegant air.

Some idea as to the extent to which this wood decoration is carried, may be gained when it is told that the wood used to decorate the parlor and music-room cost six thousand dollars, and yet they are small apartments when compared, say, with those of the Windsor Hotel, New York.

The music-room adjoins the parlor, and is only separated from it by a pair of portières. It is circular, with a frescoed dome. It is only twenty-four feet in diameter; but a veritable bijou is this music-room. It has tables and a cabinet of onyx, pieces of statuary and bronze, two piano lamps and a pedestal upon which stands a vase decorated with scenes painted by a French artist. The vase itself is three feet high. There are two semi-circular upholstered recesses in this room curtained in front. Occasionally these recesses are put to a very good use. I have seen young couples, a modern Claude and Pauline, engaged in very close conversation behind the curtains, whispering "soft nothings" to each other. "Soft" without doubt were the words spoken, and, so far as I heard, they amounted to nothing.

In the central front wall of this room there is a window, and pendant in this window is a colored lamp in which electric light is continually burning. There are similar lamps hanging in each of the cozy recesses—the scene, with its Moorish surroundings, reminding you of an Oriental synagogue, in which there is a similar lamp, and in which, according to Jewish custom in public places of worship, the light is never allowed to go out. Of electric lamps, there are twenty-five hundred in the house.

There is a ladies' waiting-room which is strictly reserved for ladies ; there is a ladies' billiard-room, as well as one for gentlemen ; there is a banqueting-room for public dinners at the top of the house, and at the bottom of the house there are cellars which contain a stock of choice wines valued at twenty thousand dollars.

The European plan is gaining in popularity in this country. When you proceed to write your name on the register at the Palace Hotel the clerk asks, "European or American plan?" At the California no such question is propounded; it is kept entirely on the European plan.

But they have a restaurant which is a feature, if not the feature of the house. It measures 120 x 30 feet, it has tiled floor, mirrored walls, beautifully decorated ceilings and countless electric lamps. During the dinner hour a band, stationed in a half-hidden gallery at the end of the restaurant, performs music that is properly called pleasing—light selections which suggest good cheer, and which no doubt aid digestion. The restaurant is entered from the street as well as from the interior, and such is its popularity that it is patronized by many people who are not otherwise guests of the house.

It is equal in style of service to any café I know of—to the Café Savarin or the Brunswick in New York ; in fact, the manager, A. F. Kinzler, is a son of Francis Kinzler of the Brunswick.

The question of moustached waiters was easily settled at the California. They are skilled and experienced French and Swiss waiters, and there was no demur to the order, shave the upper lip.

SALT LAKE CITY.

Salt Lake City, Utah,
April 6, 1891.

On the last Sunday of last September I was one among the five thousand people who enjoyed the masterly eloquence of Spurgeon at his Tabernacle in London; to-day, Monday, I was in the Mormon Tabernacle, where a conference was being held, and in which were gathered as many people as the great building would hold,—seated and standing, twelve thousand.

Several Mormon elders held forth, but what they said did not particularly interest me. It was, for the most part, a defense of their form of "religion," and they claimed they had a right, in this free country, to teach and practice their peculiar doctrine.

The acoustic properties of this great edifice are excellent; I tested them in different parts of the house, and heard almost every word that was said by the several speakers. Each spoke but for a short time, ten or fifteen minutes.

The most interesting part of Monday's "session" to my mind was the musical part, a chorus of two hundred and fifty male and female voices singing to the rich and powerful tones of what is claimed to be the largest organ but one in the world.

A strange feature of the assemblage was the great number of young children and babes in arms; the crowd of baby carriages in the halls and entrances being very noticeable.

The exterior of the Tabernacle, from its oval shape, is often likened to half an egg bisected lengthwise;

to me it looks like a tortoise, with its low curved roof and its remarkably short pillars, only a few feet apart.

But it is a mammoth tortoise, 250 x 150 feet, with not a column nor a pillar to obstruct the view—the largest span of unsupported wooden roof in the world.

The Temple in Salt Lake City, the corner-stone of which was laid on the twelfth of April, 1853, is, like the municipal buildings in Philadelphia, the City Hall in San Francisco and the Cathedral in Cologne, still unfinished, although $3,500,000 has been expended in its construction so far. The Temple's dimensions are 200 x 100 feet.

It is built entirely of granite. The towers are beautiful. When completed they will be 200 feet high. A marble slab 12 x 3 feet is inserted in the centre tower. Upon that slab appears this inscription in gold letters:

"Holiness to the Lord, the house of the Lord. Built by the Church of Jesus Christ, of latter-day saints. Commenced April 6, 1853. Completed"—space is left under the word "completed" in which to insert the date, but that space may not be filled during the next quarter of a century.

The first blocks of granite for the building were hauled from the quarries, a distance of twenty miles, by oxen, but for many years past the granite has been brought to the city by a railroad planned originally by Mormons.

Salt Lake, on account of its unpaved streets, must be miserable as a place of residence. In wet weather the mud in the streets is from six inches to two feet deep, and in dry weather the dust is intolerable. It is probably not quite so bad in these respects as Key West, Florida, but it is always disagreeable enough. Yet the city is well laid out; all the streets are over one hundred feet wide; there is a good system of electric street-cars, and there are many fine granite and brick business blocks. Salt Lake has an evident air of prosperity. Its population has more than doubled in the past ten years. In 1880 it was 20,000; in 1890 45,000.

Brigham street, the Fifth avenue of Salt Lake, contains not a few private residences of which any city might be proud.

The leading hotel is "The Templeton," owned by a company of which D. C. Young is president. The manager of the hotel is Alonzo Young. The president and the manager are both sons of Brigham Young, but are half brothers only. Brigham sleeps with a couple of his wives in a cemetery a few hundred feet from the hotel.

The Templeton is new and substantial, but it was not erected for a hotel, and it lacks some conveniences which you expect to find. It is better adapted for an office building, which was its original purpose.

The dining-room is on the top floor, as is the dining-room of the Auditorium in Chicago, and the Vendome in New York, and as is the kitchen of the Windsor Hotel in London.

From this room in the Templeton, if you secure a choice seat, you get most magnificent views. You are surrounded by snow-covered mountains, and to the west you see the principal buildings of the city—the Mormon Tabernacle, the Temple and the Assembly Hall, all enclosed and fenced within a ten-acre lot.

We were unfortunate in the time of our visit to Salt Lake. The city was crowded on account of the Mormon conference and all the hotels were full. At the Templeton they had an insufficient number of waiters and they served saucers of ice cream on warm plates.

But perhaps we are hypercritical in our notes on the shortcomings of hotels in Salt Lake; some allowance must be made for the fact that we had just come from a week at "The California"—that new and beautiful hotel in San Francisco which is kept by A. F. Kinzler, the comforts and elegancies of which, fresh in our memory and with their flavor, so to speak, still lingering on our palate, had for the time spoiled us for less perfect accommodations and an inferior style of living.

I had occasion to look at the city directory of Salt Lake and in turning over the leaves I noticed that there are living no less than nine widows of the lamented apostle of Mormonism, Brigham Young.

THE AUDITORIUM HOTEL.

CHICAGO, May 16, 1891.

During his engagement here I met Mr. Willard, the English actor, walking on Michigan avenue, with Mr. Hatton, the English dramatist, for companion.

"Mr. Willard, where are you staying," I happened to ask. "At the Richelieu," said the handsome and intellectual-looking Englishman. "I looked at the Auditorium," he went on to say, "but it appeared to me too large, and such a stronghold that it almost reminded me of a prison."

I am not surprised that its great size was an objection in his eyes, because Englishmen prefer smaller, quieter and more home-like houses; those great palaces in Northumberland avenue, London, were built rather for American patronage. But that the Auditorium looks as solid and strong as the rock of Gibraltar should not be regarded as an objection. In the eyes of most people this is a great advantage, especially when we remember the flimsy character of many of our hotels—those at the seaside, for instance, or those in small towns, to say nothing of many make-shift hotels in New York.

Among other excellent features of the Auditorium building there is this to commend it: it is called and is believed to be absolutely fireproof. The first and second story outside walls are of dark granite, the upper walls are of dark Bedford stone. The materials used interiorly are iron, brick, terra cotta, Italian marble and hard wood.

The whole structure covers one and a half acres. It stands on three streets, Michigan avenue, Wabash avenue and Congress street, with a frontage measuring seven hundred and ten feet. The height of the main building is ten stories; there are eight floors in the tower—two above the main tower—twenty stories in all; the entire height from street level to top of tower two hundred and seventy feet. Some authorities estimate the cost as high as four millions; the lowest estimate I have seen printed or heard mentioned is three million two hundred thousand dollars. It is possibly safe to say that about three millions were invested in the enterprise, and I am told that it has yielded a profit from the start—the hotel certainly has.

The structure includes a theatre called "the largest and most magnificent in the world"—the "Auditorium"—used for conventions and meetings, having a stage and what is called "the most costly organ in the world." Of course, being Western, everything must be the biggest and costliest. There is also a Recital Hall, which seats five hundred persons. The business portion of the building includes stores on the ground floor and one hundred and thirty-six offices above, some of which are in the tower. The United States Signal Service occupies part of the seventeenth, eighteenth and nineteenth floors of the tower. From this tower you may get an extended view of the city when the fog from the lake is not dense, and when the chimneys of the town are not emitting black smoke. The best time to get a view is on a clear Sunday, when many of the factory fires are extinguished.

The Auditorium building is owned by "The Chicago Auditorium Association," and is managed by them; the hotel proper, which forms only a part of the great structure, is managed by "The Auditorium Hotel Company," and is a separate business concern.

It is kept on both the European and American plans. For those who choose the former there is a grand café on the ground floor; for those who prefer the latter there is a dining-room on the top floor, on which floor the kitchen is also situated. To the dining-room two elevators are constantly running. In the whole building there are thirteen elevators: in the hotel proper there are eight elevators, five for the use of guests, three for servants.

Besides the café below, and the public dining-room above, there are a number of private dining-rooms, and on the sixth floor there is a banqueting hall which will seat five hundred people and which may be called magnificent. It is built of steel, on trusses, and spans one hundred and twenty feet over "The Auditorium." On the panelled walls are painted beautiful scenes in oil by skilled artists.

It does not lack for light, this banqueting hall; it contains four hundred electric lamps. In fact, the electric plant of the building is the largest private plant in the world—it is Western, you know. Its first cost was $100,000 and it costs to operate $175 per day. No electric department in any place, either public or private, that I have visited is cleaner, neater or more methodical in system. The tools are hung on the walls, behind glass doors. No workman may remove a tool without giving a receipt for the same and the tool must be returned to its place immediately after it has served the purpose for which it was removed or the man pays a fine.

"The office" is not a small, unimportant looking apartment like the "counting house" of an English hotel. It is after the American style, large and showy, but there is not a waste nor a wilderness of space as there is in some Chicago hotels, the "offices" in some of the Chicago houses being used not only for a public rendezvous but also for a public thoroughfare—people pass through them in going from one street to another to save themselves the trouble of walking around the block.

The floor of the office of the Auditorium Hotel is of Italian marble—mosaic work in artistic designs. To go into figures again, there are of mosaic floors in the house fifty thousand square feet, containing fifty million separate pieces of marble, each piece put in by hand. The ceiling, which is richly decorated, and from which depend numberless electric lights, is supported in the centre by five marble columns nine feet in circumference. The chairs and sofas, here and there, are of oak, plush-covered, and the walls are of nothing less luxurious than Mexican onyx, than which for the purpose probably no material is richer. Leading from the office to the parlor floor there is a white marble staircase twelve feet wide. This combination of rich materials and artistic work, with ample space, gives the Auditorium office a gorgeous, yes, a palace-like appearance.

The dining-room on the tenth floor, measuring 175 by 48 feet, affords extended views of the lake and a stretch of Chicago's grand boulevard, Michigan avenue, as far as the eye can reach. The lower part of its walls is of mahogany panels; the six massive pillars which support the ceiling are of mahogany, the tables and chairs and Venetian blinds of the same costly wood. As well as six pillars, there are six arches in this room, which also has an arched ceiling. The walls above the mahogany dado up to the ceiling are in yellow and gold, the ceiling delicately and beautifully frescoed.

On one of the semi circular arched walls above the mahogany pillars which support it, is painted a lake fishing scene, on the other a duck-shooting scene. The latter is taken from the estate of Ferd. W. Peck at Lake Oconomowoc, Wisconsin. It represents two or three men in sporting costume in a canoe, which is half hidden by tall grass and cat tails. The man in the bow stands ready to take aim at a flock of ducks which are preparing for flight. Mr. Peck is one of the originators of the Auditorium enterprise and the present president of the company.

THE AUDITORIUM HOTEL. 247

There are five hundred electric lights in the dining-room; the floor is of marble mosaic. For the American plan two dinners are served. You can take your choice or eat both if your appetite serves; first dinner, from twelve till two; evening dinner from six to eight.

The bedrooms are heated by steam and also have fireplaces. Of course, they are lighted by electricity. The bedroom in which this is penned measures twenty-one by thirteen feet. As there is no step-ladder at hand I must guess at the height of the ceiling—about fourteen feet. The dimensions given do not include a very large clothes closet built in the wall and a very small wash-room, too small, indeed, but supplied with hot and cold water. On either side of this bedroom are similar rooms each having two heavy, double doors of oak, so that while the rooms are "communicating" the sound is not "communicated" from one room to the other.

The walls are painted and frescoed in tints to match the wood-work, which is of light varnished oak. Part of the furniture is of dark, highly polished oak, the rest of cherry, covered with olive or old gold plush. These hues in turn match the Wilton carpet which is bordered, and upon which, here and there, is a handsome rug.

The curtains are of reddish-brown plush, lined with old-gold silk; inside these are lace curtains, and against the windows are Venetian blinds of oak. The windows are of plate glass, large and massive—much too heavy, in fact, or else the sashes are not put in by a master hand. They are raised or lowered with great difficulty, notwithstanding a pair of brass handles is attached to each lower sash. For such large, weighty windows they have a better plan in the Windsor Hotel, London. Long, loose ropes with light, wooden handles attached are fastened to the upper and lower parts of the upper sash, and by this method the heavy windows are raised or lowered with perfect ease.

But I have wandered away in thought from my apartment in the Auditorium, which is lighted by a handsome, seven-lamp electrolier pendant from the ceiling, with a convenient tap just inside the door to turn on or off as you enter or leave the room.

There is an electric dial in each room, the invention of the New Haven Clock Company. Upon this dial the inventor and hotel-keeper combined have anticipated as many as twenty-four wants of the guest, from a chambermaid to a doctor; from a telegraph blank to a hansom cab. Max O'Rell may poke fun at this anticipation of so many wants in American hotels, but if they had such an arrangement in Continental hotels, their system would be greatly improved.

You need not trouble yourself about good air or bad air at the Auditorium: the house is ventilated automatically, by machinery. Among other modern improvements is a letter chute which extends to the top of the house. Your letters from any floor drop into a locked United States post-office box, opened at intervals by the official carrier.

There are four hundred and fifty rooms. As hotel men usually reckon "about one and a half guests to a room" there is accommodation for six hundred people. Charge for rooms: European plan, $2 to $5 per day; American plan, $4 to $6 per day.

The house is managed by James H. Breslin and R. H. Southgate. It is not necessary to explain who these men are, and to commend them, at this late day, would be no compliment.

MAX O'RELL ON AMERICAN HOTELS.

M. Paul Blouet (Max O'Rell) is a brilliant writer and a clever, entertaining talker, but in his article in the *North American Review* for January, 1891, entitled "Reminiscences of American Hotels," he shows that he lacks fairness as a critic, and that he writes without the necessary knowledge of his subject. His remarks concerning the American methods of conducting hotels may be amusing, but when he makes comparisons between English and American hotels and their systems, it is evident that as a critic he is open to criticism. In his opening page he says:

"When you enter a hotel not a salute, not a word, not a smile of welcome. The negro takes your bag and makes a sign that your case is settled. You follow him. For the time being you lose your personality and become No. 375, as you would in jail."

The facts are just the contrary. The clerks, porters and waiters in American hotels are only too glad if they can learn your name. They will pronounce it and announce you on the smallest possible provocation. Max O'Rell's remarks on this point would exactly fit if he were writing about some large hotels in London patronized by Americans. At those houses, the Langham excepted, you do not enter your name in a register, and you are known only by the number of the room you occupy. If a friend calls, his card will be carried about on a silver salver by a little page whose duty it is, in going through the halls and public rooms in search of you, to bawl out at the top of his voice not your name, but the number of the apartment you occupy; and to this you are expected to respond.

But people are not so apt to know the hotel customs which obtain in cities where they live, and that may account for M. Blouet's ignorance.

This French-English humorist tries to make it appear that in every American hotel the fire-escape consists of "twenty yards of coiled rope." I believe that the New York State Legislature expects all hotels in that State to make such provision, but if it is done in New York it is certainly not the case in other States, as I know, for I have lived at hotels in many States of the Union during the past few months, westward as far as California, and as far south as New Orleans.

Mr. O'Rell feels very much injured because order and method reign in the dining-room. He says:

"When you enter the dining-room you must not believe you can go and sit where you like. The chief waiter assigns you a seat and you must take it. I have constantly seen Americans stop on the threshold of the dining-room and wait until the chief waiter had returned from placing a guest to come and fetch them in their turn. I never saw them venture alone and take an empty seat without the sanction of the waiter."

Chaos would reign indeed if the regular guests of a hotel had no regular seats, and if every newcomer were allowed to sit where he pleased. Of course the head waiter assigns seats. This good custom obtains in England and France as it does elsewhere; without it there would be confusion for all concerned.

It would be strange if such a close and keen observer, as Max O'Rell certainly is, did not make some good points in such a labored article. He makes one when he objects to the solemn, almost funereal air which pervades an American dining-room. People can be well mannered and yet be and appear to be, in good spirits, whereas we seem to make a business, a sad business of eating—it cannot be called "dining." You seldom or never hear such a thing as a laugh in our hotel dining-rooms, and yet everybody knows that laughter is the best aid to digestion. There is a time for everything, and when should there be good cheer if not at dinner time?

O'Rell shows that he is unfair and uninformed when he is discussing some of the important features of our hotels, but he scores another good point when he talks of the shameful waste of food in American hotels. I quote in full his remarks on that head. They cannot be too often repeated:

"The thing which, perhaps, strikes me most disagreeably in the American hotel dining-room is the sight of the tremendous waste of food that goes on at every meal. No European, I suppose, can fail to be struck with this; but to a Frenchman it would naturally be most remarkable. In France where, I venture to say, people live as well as anywhere else, if not better, there is a perfect horror of anything like waste of good food. It is to me, therefore, a repulsive thing to see the wanton manner in which some Americans will waste at one meal enough to feed several fellow creatures."

ANNOUNCEMENTS.

THE HOME JOURNAL,

A WEEKLY NEWSPAPER OF

LITERATURE, ART AND SOCIETY,

FOUNDED IN 1846 BY THE WELL-KNOWN POETS,

GEO. P. MORRIS AND N. P. WILLIS,

retains its prestige as the exponent of that literary and art culture which gives grace and refinement to social intercourse.

Readers at a distance will find the best life of the metropolis reflected in its pages. It is also in an especial sense an

INTERNATIONAL JOURNAL,

and by its correspondence and essays brings its readers into touch with the social life of the

GREAT EUROPEAN CENTRES OF CULTURE.

THE HOME JOURNAL contains more advertisements of SUMMER AND WINTER RESORT HOTELS, and devotes more editorial space to them than any other newspaper.

It has particular value as an advertising medium for EUROPEAN HOTELS, being the organ of cultivated and fashionable Americans—those who pass their summers in Europe.

PUBLISHED EVERY WEDNESDAY.
SUBSCRIPTION, $2.00 PER YEAR.   FIVE CENTS A COPY.

MORRIS PHILLIPS & CO., Publishers,
240 Broadway, New York.

DEMPSEY & CARROLL,

THE ART STATIONERS AND ENGRAVERS,

UNION SQUARE, 36 EAST 14TH STREET, NEW YORK CITY.

CORRECT STYLES.

**WEDDING INVITATIONS & ANNOUNCEMENTS
RECEPTION & VISITING CARDS.**

HIGH GRADE STATIONERY,
MONOGRAM, ADDRESS AND HERALDIC DIES.

HAND PAINTED
MENUS AND DINNER CARDS.

RICH LEATHER GOODS,
PLAIN AND SILVER MOUNTED.

IMPORTED STATIONERY NOVELTIES.

THE "WORLD'S GREATEST PASSENGER TRAIN."

* * *

This proud title has been bestowed by an appreciative public on the

PENNSYLVANIA LIMITED.

* * *

IT is well deserved because the train affords more conveniences, more comforts and more luxuries than any other train in the world. One may eat, sleep, work or transact business as if in hotel or club. To this end there are luxurious sleeping cars, dining cars, ladies' maids, bath rooms for both sexes, a barber shop, financial news and stock reports, stenographers and type writers, United States Mail boxes and a library.

* * *

IT is the favorite train between New York and Chicago, and a trip on it is a long-remembered leasure tour.

* * *

THE Pennsylvania Limited leaves New York from the Pennsylvania Railroad Station, foot of Desbrosses and Cortlandt Streets, every morning at 10 o'clock for Chicago and Cincinnati.

J. R. WOOD,
General Passenger Agent.

CHAS. E. PUGH,
General Manager.

ANNOUNCEMENTS.

ATLANTIC COAST LINE
Via WASHINGTON.

SHORT ✠ LINE

BETWEEN

BOSTON, PHILADELPHIA,
NEW YORK, BALTIMORE,
WASHINGTON,

AND

RICHMOND, SAVANNAH,
WILMINGTON, BRUNSWICK,
CHARLESTON, ALBANY,
THOMASVILLE, PALATKA,
JACKSONVILLE, SANFORD,
ST. AUGUSTINE, TAMPA,
PUNTA GORDA,

ALL FLORIDA POINTS, AND HAVANA, CUBA.

EASTERN OFFICES:

229 Broadway, New York. 33 South 3d St., Philadelphia.
228 Washington St., Boston. 106 East German St., Baltimore.
511 Pennsylvania Avenue, Washington.

ANNOUNCEMENTS.

TO ALL
WINTER RESORTS
—IN—

South Georgia, Florida, Cuba, the West Indies and Mexico,

Via HAVANA, CUBA,

REACHED BY THE

Plant System
—OF—

RAILWAY AND STEAMSHIP LINES,

In connection with Pennsylvania R. R., via New York, Washington and Atlantic Coast Railways, and with the principal railway lines between all cities of the West and South-west, forming through train and sleeping-car service, and

JACKSONVILLE, ST. AUGUSTINE, TAMPA AND PORT TAMPA, FLORIDA.

FAST AND COMMODIOUS STEAMSHIPS BETWEEN

Port Tampa, Key West and Havana; Port Tampa and Mobile; Port Tampa and St. James City (Pine Island), Punta Rassa, Fort Myers, Naples, and resorts of the Gulf Coast; Port Tampa and Manatee River.

The magnificent Tampa Bay Hotel, at Tampa, and the Seminole, at Winter Park, on the South Florida R. R., are open during the season of Winter Tourist travel, and are maintained at a high standard of excellence.

The Inn at Port Tampa is open the entire year, and is in an attractive, healthful and convenient place for passengers to await the arrival and departure of steamers and trains.

For further information apply to any Railroad Ticket Agent, or to

J. D. HASHAGEN, Eastern Agent,
261 BROADWAY, NEW YORK.

FRED. ROBLIN, Traveling Pass. Agent,
261 BROADWAY, NEW YORK.

H. B. PLANT, President,
12 WEST 23d STREET, NEW YORK.

ANNOUNCEMENTS.

THE DE SOTO,

SAVANNAH, GA.

ONE of the most elegantly appointed hotels in the world. Accommodations for 500 guests. Special rates for families and parties remaining a week or longer. Tourists will find Savannah one of the most interesting and beautiful cities in the entire South. No place more healthy or desirable as a winter resort.

Send for Descriptive Illustrated Booklet.

WATSON & POWERS.

ANNOUNCEMENTS.

PARIS. HOTEL PARIS.

ANGLO-FRANCAIS,

6 RUE CASTIGLIONE. 6

THIS first-class Hotel, situated in the best part of the metropolis, opposite the Hotel Continental and the Tuileries Gardens, is highly recommended for comfort, cuisine, moderate charges and sanitary arrangements; Otis American elevator.

VARGUES, Proprietor.

ANNOUNCEMENTS.

HOTEL BINDA,

11 rue de L'Echelle,

AVENUE DE L'OPERA,   PARIS.

LARGE and small apartments; lift to each floor; smoking and drawing-room; bathroom on each floor; table d'hote, 6 francs, from 6 to 8 o'clock, at separate tables; restaurant a la carte.

ADVANTAGEOUS ARRANGEMENTS MADE WITH FAMILIES WINTERING IN PARIS.

Electric Light all over the House.

CHARLES BINDA, PROPRIETOR,
Late with Delmonico, New York.

ANNOUNCEMENTS.

London, Chatham and Dover RAILWAY.

A. THORNE,

Formerly at H. B. Claflin & Co.'s, New York,

AMERICAN REPRESENTATIVE IN ENGLAND,

London, Chatham and Dover Railway,

VICTORIA STATION, LONDON, S. W.,

ATTENDS the arrival of the principal steamships at Liverpool and Southampton, and arranges for Special Saloon Carriages upon either the North Western and Midland Railways from Liverpool, or by the South Western Railway from Southampton to London, and thence to Dover from Victoria Station by the **London, Chatham and Dover Railway.** From Dover to Calais (the shortest sea passage to France) by the magnificent S.S. "Calais-Douvres," "Empress," "Victoria," and "Invicta," owned and controlled solely by the London, Chatham and Dover Railway Company.

A. THORNE secures Private Deck Saloons, and from Calais to Paris and other prominent points Special Saloons and Sleeping Cars as required.

TELEGRAPHIC ADDRESS: "CALDOVER," LONDON.

The London, Chatham and Dover Company's trains run from Victoria, St. Paul's and Holborn Stations through the prettiest and most picturesque parts of Kent, and passengers have the privilege of stopping over at Rochester to visit the Cathedral and the Castle, and at Canterbury to view the Cathedral (containing the tomb of the martyr Thomas à Becket), and other places of interest.

ANNOUNCEMENTS.

Are You Going to Europe?
EDWIN H. LOW,
Low's Exchange and General Steamship Office,
947 BROADWAY, MADISON SQUARE, - NEW YORK.
57 CHARING CROSS, TRAFALGAR SQUARE, LONDON.

Choice Berths secured on **ALL LINES** without **extra charge.**

Cabin plans of all European and Coastwise Steamers on file, and complete list of sailings of all Lines to any part of the world. Full and reliable information given.

WHILE IN EUROPE have all your Letters and Cables sent care of Low's Exchange, 57 Charing Cross, Trafalgar Sq., London; they will be registered and numbered by **Mr. Low's own system,** whereby it is practically impossible for one to go astray or be lost. They are promptly forwarded to any part of Europe, according to instructions.

NELSON MONUMENT.—VIEW FROM LOW'S EXCHANGE.

POSTAL RATES: 1 year, $10.00; 6 mos., $5.00; 3 mos., $2.50; 1 mo., $1.00.

Low's Exchange in London is established for the general convenience of travelers. Railway and Steamship Tickets—to all parts—issued. Baggage stored and checked, passports, steamer chairs, foreign moneys, letters of credit cashed, American news and newspapers, &c.

LOW'S POCKET CABLE CODE

is a handy little volume published by Mr. Low for cipher cabling. The cost of cabling is twenty-five cents per word. By purchasing two copies of this code you have 10,000 cipher words and phrases by which you can reduce the expense at least four-fifths. It is alphabetically arranged and so simple that anyone without the least knowledge of codes can understand it. **Price, 50 Cents, bound in Cloth.**

ANNOUNCEMENTS.

THE CALIFORNIA,
BUSH STREET, NEAR KEARNY,
SAN FRANCISCO, CAL.
THE ACME OF PERFECTION ATTAINED IN AMERICAN HOTELS.

It is a recognized fact that San Francisco has made, from time to time, the greatest effort to surpass all other cities in her Hotel accommodations, and it must be conceded that the acme of perfection has now been reached.

The California was opened last December, and there is nothing on the Pacific Coast, so far as artistic taste, elegance of appointments and lavish expenditure go, which can compare with it.

The California is unsurpassed in style of service by the best hotels of the United States. Heretofore there has been no strictly European-plan hotel in San Francisco.

A visit to this city is incomplete without seeing the California, unquestionably the most beautiful and luxuriously furnished hotel in America.

A. F. KINZLER, MANAGER.

ANNOUNCEMENTS.

MONTEREY–CALIFORNIA.

MIDWINTER SCENES

AT THE CELEBRATED

Hotel del Monte,

MONTEREY, CAL.

AMERICA'S FAMOUS SUMMER AND WINTER RESORT.

ONLY 3½ HOURS FROM SAN FRANCISCO

By Express Trains of the Southern Pacific Company.

Rates for Board: By the day, $3.00 and upward. Parlors, from $1.00 to $2.50 per day, extra. Children, in children's dining-room, $2.00 per day.

Particular Attention is called to the *moderate charges* for accommodations at this magnificent establishment. The extra cost of a trip to California is more than counterbalanced by the difference in rates at the various Southern Winter Resorts and the incomparable HOTEL DEL MONTE.

Intending Visitors to **California** and the **Hotel del Monte** have the choice of the **"Sunset," "Central,"** or **"Shasta" Routes.** These three routes, the three main arms of the great railway system of the **Southern Pacific Company,** carry the traveler through the best sections of California, and any one of them will reveal wonders of climate, products and scenery that no other part of the world can duplicate. For illustrated descriptive pamphlet of the hotel, and for information as to routes of travel, rates for through tickets, etc., call upon or address **E. HAWLEY,** Assistant General Traffic Manager, Southern Pacific Company, **343 Broadway, New York.**

For further *information, address*

GEORGE SCHÖNEWALD, Manager Hotel del Monte,

OPEN ALL THE YEAR ROUND. **MONTEREY, CALIFORNIA.**

ANNOUNCEMENTS.

REDONDO HOTEL

THIS new but already popular seaside resort is located on the Pacific Ocean, under the shelter of the prominent headland known as Point Vincent, while to the south and east are the Palos Verdes and other hills.

The Redondo Hotel has been spoken of as the "crowning effort of all hotels on the Pacific Coast," covering over an acre of ground, reposing gracefully upon a slight eminence "where the broad ocean leans against the land," with fine vistas of sea and shore meeting the eye in all directions. Of the 225 rooms, every one has a sunny exposure at some hour of the day, every one is well ventilated and lighted, every one is an "outside room," and every guest feels that his is the best suite in the house.

The building is supplied throughout with modern improvements. It has incandescent electric lights in all the rooms and arc lights on the grounds. There is cold and hot water and grates in every room. The halls and lobby are heated by steam. The latest and most improved hydraulic elevators are in use.

On the hotel grounds is the best tennis-court in the State, well-arranged and complete in every detail, with club-room, baths, etc. There is also a nursery of several acres and a large green-house, where the most beautiful and delicate flowers bloom the year round, and the hotel draws from this source the freshness and fragrance of perpetual spring.

Redondo Beach is cooler than Cape May in summer, it is warmer than San Fernandino in winter. The temperature of the water of the ocean varies less than ten degrees in the course of a year, and surf bathing is always enjoyable. The bathing beach is the finest on the coast, and is provided with a commodious bath-house and every appliance for the convenience and safety of the bathers.

Special rates made for families and permanent guests.

For further information address

REDONDO HOTEL CO.,
Redondo Beach, California.

ANNOUNCEMENTS.

The Sea Beach Hotel has large, light rooms, affording extensive views, wide verandas, surf bathing, fishing. Livery. Electric lights and electric bells. Rates from $2.50 per day. Illustrated Souvenir mailed free. Address

JOHN T. SULLIVAN, PROPRIETOR.

ANNOUNCEMENTS.

WINDSOR HOTEL,

NEW YORK.

HAWK & WETHERBEE.

CONVENIENTLY SITUATED ON FIFTH AVENUE, NEAR THE GRAND CENTRAL RAILWAY STATION, ELEVATED AND SURFACE TRAMWAYS, THEATRES, PLACES OF AMUSEMENT, CHURCHES AND CLUBS.

HAS BEEN RECENTLY FITTED THROUGHOUT WITH THE LATEST MODERN SANITARY PLUMBING.

THE DRINKING WATER USED IS CHEMICALLY PURE AND THE ICE IS MADE FROM DISTILLED WATER.

CUISINE AND SERVICE UNSURPASSED.

COOL AND ATTRACTIVE IN SUMMER.

COMFORTABLE AND HOME-LIKE IN WINTER.

STAGES WHEN DESIRED, WILL MEET ALL STEAMERS AND CONVEY PASSENGERS AND LUGGAGE DIRECT TO THE HOTEL AT MODERATE CHARGES.

RAILWAY TICKETS, SLEEPING CAR AND DRAWING-ROOM CAR ACCOMMODATIONS CAN BE SECURED IN THE HOTEL; CABLE AND TELEGRAPH OFFICE, RUSSIAN AND TURKISH BATHS, AND EVERY COMFORT AND CONVENIENCE FOR TRAVELERS.

WELL-LIGHTED AND VENTILATED SPACIOUS PUBLIC ROOMS, CORRIDORS, DRAWING-ROOMS AND PARLOR SUITES, SINGLE OR DOUBLE ROOMS WITH OR WITHOUT BATHS.

ALL LANGUAGES SPOKEN.

ANNOUNCEMENTS.

YOUR ADVERTISING

IS SOLICITED.

Estimates, containing Selected Lists of Suitable Publications with Rates for Advertising, furnished free on application.

ANNOUNCEMENTS.

AUDITORIUM HOTEL,

Michigan Ave., Congress St., and Wabash Ave.,

CHICAGO.

The most massive hotel structure in the world, built entirely of stone and iron, ten stories high, absolutely fire-proof. Overlooking Lake Michigan, situated within four blocks of the business centre of the city. American and European plans.

BRESLIN & SOUTHGATE.

GILSEY HOUSE,

Corner Broadway and Twenty-Ninth Street,

NEW YORK.

European Plan.

J. H. BRESLIN & CO., - - **PROPRIETORS.**

ANNOUNCEMENTS

VISITORS TO EUROPE!

CIRCULAR CREDITS.   FOREIGN EXCHANGE.

Cheque Bank Cheques are the most convenient of Exchange to carry.

They are issued in books from £10 up to any amount.

They can be cashed at 3,000 Banks and 1,000 Hotels.

They are cashed in the currency of the country visited, free of commission.

They are no good until signed.

Special letters of identification are issued.

Travellers' mail matter promptly attended to without charge.

Send for circulars and testimonials, list of Banks and Hotels, etc., or apply to

E. J. MATHEWS & CO.,
Bankers' Agents,

2 WALL ST., NEW YORK.

ANNOUNCEMENTS

11 and 12 DOVER STREET, PICCADILLY, · LON
277 FIFTH AVENUE,   · - - NEW
1703 MICHIGAN AVENUE, - - - CHI

KATE REILY

HAS always on view at her three well-known lishments, in London, New York and Ch a varied assortment of the newest and most goods in

Costumes, Mantles and Milline

Madame Reily pays six or more annual vis Paris, where she has also a permanent agent. She secures the freshest novelties, as they appear seizing all that is best and most becoming in tl coming fashions adapts it to the especial require of her extensive clientèle.

Madame Reily's excellent taste has obtained f the esteemed patronage of all the most fashion aristocratic and artistic ladies of both hemisphere

PERFECT FIT GUARANTEED BY FIRST-CL FRENCH FITTERS.

H 258 83

www.ingramcontent.com/pod-product-compliance
Lightning Source LLC
Chambersburg PA
CBHW031339230426
43670CB00006B/385